Comprehensive Business Studies

Second Edition

Alan Whitcomb

BA, MEd, PhD

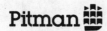

PITMAN PUBLISHING
128 Long Acre, London WC2E 9AN

A Division of Longman Group (UK) Limited

© Alan Whitcomb 1986, 1989

First published in Great Britain 1986
Second edition 1989
Reprinted (with amendments) 1990

British Library Cataloguing in Publication Data
Whitcomb, Alan
  Comprehensive business studies. – 2nd ed
  1. Business studies – For schools
  I. Title
  658

ISBN 0-273-03009-4

Printed and bound in Great Britain

Contents

The Marketing mix · Product life cycle · Product range and
product mix · Make a note of it.

Part 4 COMMUNICATIONS

Part 5 PEOPLE IN BUSINESS

Preface to second edition

This book is intended for use as a basic text by students preparing for GCSE Business Studies and other related examinations. Syllabuses obviously vary and some may contain elements not included in this book. However, the aim has been to present a wide-ranging and comprehensive textbook, produced in a readable and interesting style and which can be used in mixed ability situations. It is hoped that the manner in which the material has been presented will prove attractive to students as well as providing support for the classroom teacher.

The first edition of this text was very much a speculative venture. It was produced at a time when GCSE syllabuses had not been finalised, and before the needs of teachers and students were clear. However, the first edition has been highly successful, drawing favourable responses from teachers and reviewers.

This new edition benefits from reference to the various syllabuses as well as suggestions from many readers. Some elements of the original text have been rationalised and condensed, and the overall length of the book has been considerably extended. This has allowed the incorporation of many new elements including cash flow, financial projections and break even, product life cycles and many others. In addition, greater depth has been given to many aspects of the original text. But the original clear, direct style of writing has been maintained.

Some new features have also been incorporated into the format of the book. At the end of each of the six parts a selection of coursework and assignment suggestions are given. These include scope for student choice and tasks which give opportunity for differentiation. In addition, at the end of each part is included a section of stepped data-response questions.

Teachers will be pleased to learn that a companion text *Assignments for Business Studies* is available. This contains a wide range of exercises to draw on the interest of the student, and encourage individual study and enquiry, as well as helping examination preparation. Some computer software is also available which supports both of the afore-mentioned books.

The result of these varied publications is a truly *comprehensive* package that teachers will undoubtedly continue to find supporting them in the classroom, and which students will find readable and stimulating.

Acknowledgements

The author and publisher would like to thank the following for permission to reproduce copyright material:

The Advertising Standards
  Authority Ltd
Associated Container
  Transportation Services Ltd
Barclays Bank plc
BBC
British Leyland Austin Rover plc
British Telecom
British Trades Alphabet
Burger King (UK) Ltd
Cadbury Ltd
Canada Maritime Ltd
The Commission of the European
  Communities
Dominique De Buys
Employment News
Executive Post
Financial Times
The Hammerson Group
  Developments

D H Letchford
Lloyds Bank plc
McDonald's Hamburgers Ltd
Midland Bank plc
Mitchell Cotts Freight
National Girobank
National Westminster Bank plc
Office of the Data Protection
  Registrar
Pandair International Airfreight
Peterborough Development
  Corporation
The Post Office
J Sainsbury plc
The Stock Exchange
Wimpey Homes Holdings Ltd
Wimpy International Ltd

Part 1

BUSINESS STRUCTURE AND ORGANISATION

1 Background to business

Development of economic activity

DIRECT
PRODUCTION

Early man was engaged in direct production. He produced all his needs directly for his own use, and unaided by others. He would hunt animals and gather plants and berries for his food. This forced man to lead a nomadic way of life, moving from one fertile area to another and following the herds of animals.

Later man began to farm in a very basic way, penning animals and planting seeds. This enabled him to settle in one place, build a permanent home and improve his way of life. One of the improvements was that he found he was producing more goods than he needed (*surplus*). He began to exchange his surplus goods with the surplus of others.

BARTER

The exchange of one thing for another without the use of money is called *barter*, and this was the way that the earliest form of trade took place. But there are drawbacks to the barter system, these are as follows:

1 *A double coincidence of wants* has to occur for barter to take place. The person who has a surplus to exchange not only has to find someone who wants his or her surplus, but the person found must also have what is wanted.
2 *An exchange rate* has to be agreed even if a double coincidence of wants has occurred. Imagine the difficulty in trying to agree how many chickens a pig is worth.

3 *Divisibility of goods* is not always convenient. Some rates of exchange will not allow exchange to take place because some goods cannot be split into smaller parts. For example, if one spear is worth half a chicken it is not possible to trade with only one spear because you cannot have half a chicken and also have it alive.

4 *Storage of wealth* is difficult with the barter system. At times there is a need to store a surplus for use at a future time when a scarcity exists. But many items used in barter (e.g. food) cannot be stored for long periods of time.

MONEY

The use of money solves all of the above problems of barter, but early money was not in the form of coins and notes with which we are familiar today. The difficulties of barter led early man to the use of generally accepted items which everyone was willing to take in exchange for their goods. These items included such things as shells, dogs' teeth, beads, grain, spearheads, hides, arrowheads, fishhooks and animals, and they became substitute money.

Even today many things are used instead of money in some parts of the world, and when a country's economy collapses the people may revert to using goods instead of money. For example, in Germany during the latter part of the Second World War cigarettes, coffee and stockings were used as money.

Qualities of money

For something to be considered as money, or in the place of money, it must be:

- *durable* (hard wearing)
- *divisible* (easily divided into smaller units)
- *portable* (convenient to carry)
- *acceptable* (people must agree to its use).

The use of money allowed early man to sell his surplus of goods in exchange for money and use the money to buy his needs from the surplus of others. Money was now acting as a *medium of exchange*, and the process of trading was much simpler.

In time metal became a popular substance used as money in any part of the world where it was common, and the use of metal eventually led to the development of the coins with which we are so familiar today. Look back at the list of the qualities of money. Can you see how metal money so conveniently meets all those qualities?

Functions of money

Money has three basic functions. It is a medium of exchange, a measure of value and a store of value.

1 *Medium of exchange* – money makes trading relatively simple and makes barter unnecessary. It enables workers to specialise in labour and accept money for wages rather than goods. Workers will accept money because they know it is acceptable to others in exchange for goods.

2 *Measure of value* – money can be used to measure or price the value of goods and services. This is especially important when the items cannot easily be compared. For example, how many hours of work by a farmer is a tractor worth?

3 *Store of values* – money can be stored for use at some later time, whereas to store goods such as food for a long time is inconvenient. This makes it possible to 'save for a rainy day', to have some wealth to draw on when a scarcity occurs. In other words, money can be earned at one time and spent at another.

INDIRECT PRODUCTION

In modern industrial society few people satisfy their needs directly. Instead they co-operate with others to indirectly produce the needs of everyone. This is often referred to as *division of labour* or *specialisation*. Work is divided among several people, allowing them each to specialise in doing what they do best, which is to the benefit of everyone. There are two main ways of looking at specialisation.

Specialisation by product

Instead of everyone trying to produce all they personally need, they each concentrate on contributing to one commodity or service, using the money that they earn to purchase the goods or services of others. In this way the total needs of an individual are met by the contributions of many others.

Specialisation by process

By organising production into several stages or processes workers become more specialised and expert in their work. For example, in a car factory each worker might specialise in a part of the assembly of many vehicles in one day as they pass along the production line. By organising production in this way, workers become more specialised and expert in their work. This enables them to produce more with the same resources.

Advantages and disadvantages of specialisation

Advantages:

- Workers become skilled at doing a particular job.

- Jobs become simpler and easier to learn.

- Time-saving machinery and semi-skilled labour can be used.

- Costs per unit produced are less because of the simple processes and better use of labour and tools.

- Labour is potentially more mobile.

Disadvantages:

- Repeating a single task can become boring.

- Individual crafts and skills are lost by use of machines.

- Greater use of machinery can lead to unemployment of workers.

- All production may be halted by strikes, machinery breakdown or shortage of materials.

- Slow workers may be unable to keep pace with others.

Production of cars

Specialisation by process – *the car factory*
Explain the difference between this and specialisation by product.

(a) *underframes are automatically welded*
(b) *bodies are welded by robots*
(c) *bodies are fixed to underframe*
(d) *windscreens are fitted by robot*
(e) *accessories are fitted*
(f) *finished cars are delivered to garages for customer's viewing*

High-speed machine wrapping. Courtesy of Cadbury Ltd

Scarcity and choice

In a world where specialisation has become highly developed with not only individuals but whole communities specialising, it is vital for exchange to take place if everyone's wants are to be satisfied. The bus driver works for wages but needs food, so the wages are exchanged to obtain his needs. This involves making choices.

Everytime we go shopping we are involved in a basic economic activity, that of making a *choice* because of *scarce* resources. We have only limited money available, but invariably we would like to buy more than we can afford. Consequently, we have not only to make a choice, but also to form a *scale of preference*. In other words, we put what we want into an order of priority.

Scarcity and choice are not problems that are restricted to individuals alone. Businesses and countries face these problems of choice also. Businesses must decide how to profitably use the capital that shareholders have provided. A country has limited resources and the people or their representatives will try to use or allocate them to the best benefit of the community.

The success with which choices are made has a considerable influence on the well-being of individuals, the prosperity of a business and the quality of life of a country's residents. We are fortunate today in that we have many people, organisations and agencies who are available to advise us and to help us to make wise decisions on the best way to use the scarce resources available. However, it has taken thousands of years of experience to reach this stage of human development.

Economic systems

The processes of production, exchange, scarcity and choice looked at so far in this chapter take place within a political framework. In other words, the decision of what to produce or what choices to make with scarce resources available, is influenced by the political situation within which the decision is made. Countries differ in the extent to which they interfere with the economic system. There are three basic approaches adopted by governments: free economy, controlled economy and mixed economy.

FREE ECONOMY

A free economy is based on the private ownership of the factors (means) of production and the means of distributing goods and services. Consumers express their wants through their demand for goods and services, and the private producer seeks to satisfy the demand if the profit motive is sufficient. Therefore, in a free economy the purchaser of goods decides demand and not the state. Sometimes such economies are referred to as market economies, unplanned economies, free enterprise, laissez-faire system, or capitalist system. The USA and Japan are typical examples of a free economy.

Advantages of free economy

- All members of the community are free to participate in business enterprise for the purpose of making a profit.
- Those engaged in business enterprise have to compete with many others for custom. This has the effect of maintaining efficiency, keeping prices down and improving the standard of goods and services.
- The consumers play a major part in deciding what will be produced because it is the consumer who creates the demand and the producers who try to satisfy this demand.

Disadvantages of free economy

- Advertising is a major feature of free enterprise and this can be used to create an artificially high demand for some products. In other words, demand may be created by the producer rather than the consumer.
- In a free enterprise society successful businesses may buy out smaller firms in order to obtain control of a larger share of the market. This reduces competition and increases the danger of monopolies arising.

- In response to the profit motive, companies may restrict supplies of some goods or services in order to keep prices and profits artificially high.

CONTROLLED
ECONOMY

In a controlled economy the state controls the factors of production and the means of exchange and distribution. The state estimates what quantity of goods and services the community will need over a given period, and then directs the factors of production to produce these goods and services. In other words, unlike the free economy, it is the state that decides what the community needs and consequently demand does not originate from the consumers. This type of economy is sometimes called a centralised economy, planned economy, collective economy, or a socialist system. The USSR, China and Cuba are examples of controlled economies.

Advantages of controlled economy

- The state can assess the needs of the whole community and try to provide benefit for all the population. The means of production can then be directed towards this end and wasteful competition can be eliminated.
- It is not possible for a private monopoly to emerge under this system.

Disadvantages of controlled economy

- The state has control over the factors of production and this discourages enterprise and inventiveness.
- A considerable number of non-productive government officials are required to plan and operate the economy. These officials may not necessarily have the skills needed to decide what the community needs, and decisions may be subject to many rules and regulations. This may result in delays in reaching decisions.
- Centralised production may not respond as quickly to changing conditions and trends as private enterprise.
- The absence of competition and profit motive can hinder both creativeness and efficiency.

MIXED ECONOMY

As the term implies, a mixed economy is a combination of elements taken from a free economy and some from a controlled economy. Britain is an example of this type of economic system. Some sections of British industry are owned and operated by the state but large portions of the business world remain in private hands. The contents of this book are largely set in the context of a mixed economy.

Types of production

Earlier in this chapter we examined direct and indirect production. With direct production, which is a characteristic of countries that are economically backward, individuals or small groups satisfy their wants entirely by their own efforts and unaided by others. Indirect production, which is a feature of all developed societies, involves specialisation, working for wages and using the money earned to buy the goods and services produced by other people. Indirect production can be divided into three categories, primary production, secondary production and tertiary production.

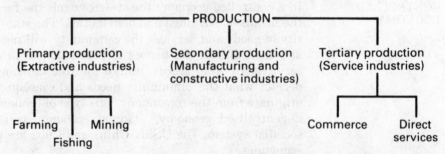

PRIMARY
PRODUCTION

Primary production is concerned with the extraction of basic materials provided by nature, which are either above or below the earth's surface. The extractive industries are farming, fishing and mining. Without these much subsequent production would not take place.

Farming involves production of foods in the form of fowls, animals and plants and also other produce of the land such as trees and flowers.

Fishing has always played a major part in the provision of food for Britain which is not surprising as we are a country surrounded by the sea. Deep-sea fishing is carried out in the open sea and is subject to international rules which try to ensure that each country has its own fair share of the catch. Protected fisheries are a growth industry that exists to farm fish in inland lakes and reservoirs, producing high yields from a small area.

Mining extracts raw materials such as coal, ore, oil, gas, etc. from below the earth's surface.

SECONDARY
PRODUCTION

Secondary production consists of the manufacturing and construction industries. They take the raw materials produced by the extractive industries and change their form into some end product.

Manufacturers may be involved in the production of a complete item, or they may make parts which will be assembled into a finished article.

Construction industries take raw materials and partly finished products and change them into buildings, roads and bridges, etc.

TERTIARY
PRODUCTION

When goods leave the producers they do not usually pass immediately to the consumer. They have to be stored, transported, insured, advertised and sold by traders. These and the many other commercial activities that make up tertiary production further the change of ownership of goods from the producer to the consumers. Tertiary production is sometimes called the service industry, but more often it is referred to as *commerce* and *direct services*.

Commerce

Commerce can be divided into two clear areas, *trade* and *services to trade*.

(a) Which form of production is illustrated here?
Why does this form of production also depend on the others shown overleaf
(copyright: Farmers Weekly – photo by Peter Adams)

- *Trade* is the process of changing ownership. Traders are the businesses directly involved in the buying and selling of goods and services. Trade can either take place within a country (home trade) or between countries (foreign trade). Home trade involves the activities of wholesalers and retailers. Foreign trade involves importers (who buy goods from other countries) and exporters (who sell goods to other countries).
- *Services to trade* are the commercial activities that assist trade in its job of selling goods and services.
  The activities that provide these services are:
1 Banking – providing short-term finance and providing facilities for easy payment transfer.
2 Finance – various institutions (e.g. the Stock Exchange) providing long-term finance for industry, commerce and consumer credit.
3 Insurance – spreads the risks faced by industrial and commercial businesses.

(b) Fishing

(c) Mining
Courtesy of British Coal

4 Transport – engaged in the movement of commodities from one place to another.

5 Communications:

(a) Postal – transfer of written communications through mail services.

(b) Telecommunications – immediate distance transfer of written, verbal or data communications by electronic devices.

(c) Advertising – provides potential customers with information about goods and services available.

All of the elements of both trade and services to trade are the subject of individual chapters in different parts of this book.

Direct services

In addition to commercial services there are groups of people who provide direct services, which are not related to trade but which people use because they provide services which are essential to the well-being of the community. Direct service occupations include the services of doctors, nurses, teachers, actors and actresses, policemen, hairdressers, authors and many others who offer a personal service.

Interdependence of industry

Let us now summarise what we have learnt from this chapter.

- *Direct production* is a characteristic of underdeveloped and primitive economies.
- *Indirect production* is a feature of all advanced economies, and this form of production is most common today.
- *Specialisation* is an essential part of indirect production and it involves people doing what they do best.
- *Commercial activities* are positioned between the producer and the consumer and these provide the means of buying and selling goods and services. They play a vital part in allowing people to specialise, earn wages and then buy their wants. They also play a major role in co-ordinating and promoting the activities of producers. We will now examine some of the ways in which this is done.

Traders support producers by carrying out the distribution of goods and bridging the time gap between production and consumption. For example, retailers and wholesalers order goods from producers and hold them until they are required. Exporters are involved in the distribution of home produced goods overseas. This not only provides work for producers, but also raises foreign capital which is needed to pay for the imports of raw materials that the producer needs. Importers buy from other countries the raw materials and finished goods that we cannot economically produce at home, thus allowing home producers to specialise in manufacturing products for which they are best suited.

The services to trade also play a major part in combining the activities of producers and promoting their enterprise. Finance provides the money for the capital assets needed by business, and also for consumers

and businesses who wish to buy on credit. Banking makes transfer of payments between buyers and sellers of goods possible and also provides a variety of other services that facilitate payment and encourage production and trade to take place. Insurance overcomes some of the risks involved in producing and trading such as the danger of loss or damage to capital assets or goods. Transport makes the physical link between producers, traders and consumers, and gets goods to the right place at the right time and in the right condition. Advertising helps producers and traders to bring their commodities to the attention of

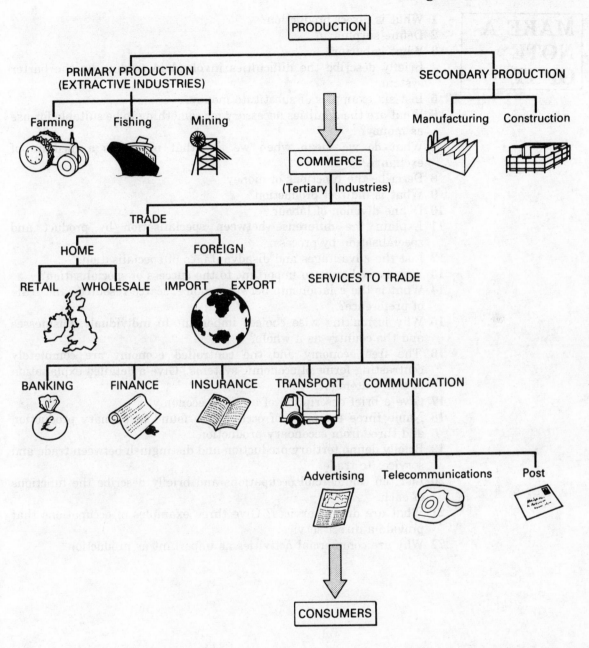

PRODUCTION

PRIMARY PRODUCTION
(EXTRACTIVE INDUSTRIES)

SECONDARY PRODUCTION

Farming   Fishing   Mining

Manufacturing   Construction

COMMERCE

(Tertiary Industries)

TRADE

HOME   FOREIGN

SERVICES TO TRADE

RETAIL   WHOLESALE   IMPORT   EXPORT

BANKING   FINANCE   INSURANCE   TRANSPORT   COMMUNICATION

Advertising   Telecommunications   Post

CONSUMERS

potential customers. Postal communications and telecommunications enable businessmen to communicate with each other and their customers at the various stages of production and distribution.

We can see from this section that commercial activities are essential to production, but many of the commercial activities would not be needed if it were not for producers and specialisation making exchange necessary. In other words, primary, secondary and tertiary production are interdependent.

MAKE A NOTE OF IT

1 What is direct production?
2 Define surplus.
3 What is barter?
4 Briefly describe the difficulties involved in trading by the barter system.
5 List six examples of substitute money.
6 What are the qualities necessary for something to be suitable for use as money?
7 What do we mean when we say that money is a medium of exchange?
8 Describe the functions of money.
9 What is indirect production?
10 Define division of labour.
11 Explain the difference between specialisation by product and specialisation by process.
12 List the advantages and disadvantages of specialisation.
13 Why is exchange so important to the success of specialisation?
14 What is the relationship between choice, scarce resources and scale of preference?
15 Why is making wise choices important to individuals, businesses and the country as a whole?
16 'The free economy and the controlled economy are completely contrasting forms of economic systems.' Give a detailed explanation of this statement.
17 Give a brief description of a mixed economy.
18 Name three examples of occupations found in primary production and three from secondary production.
19 Briefly define tertiary production and distinguish between trade and services to trade.
20 List ten commercial occupations and briefly describe the functions of each.
21 What are direct services? Give three examples of occupations that provide a direct service.
22 Why are commercial activities as important as production?

2 Organisation of production

Factors of production

AIM OF PRODUCTION

The purpose of production is to provide people with the goods which they need or want to consume. *Needs* are things that are essential to human survival. There are three primary human needs. They are:
- food
- clothing
- shelter.

Production also provides the many things that man *wants* to consume but are not necessary for survival. These things help to make the quality of life better, for example, television, cars, books, etc.

In Chapter 1 attention was drawn to the fact that there are only scarce resources to meet our unlimited wants. The scarce resources which are used to produce the commodities people want to consume are collectively described as the *factors of production*. They are:

- land
- labour
- capital.

FACTOR OF LAND

Land as a factor of production includes not only geographical area but all natural resources found in the earth and sea. Land in this sense includes:

- geographical surface area
- rivers, lakes and seas
- minerals and chemicals.

The factor of land is fixed in supply, that is the supply cannot be increased, although the quality of the soil may be improved by the use of fertilisers, drainage, land reclamation, etc.

Production cannot take place without land. Primary, secondary and tertiary production and all economic activity involve the use of land.

FACTOR OF LABOUR

Labour is the factor of production which is man's physical and mental contribution to the creation of goods and services. It is the factor that converts resources into goods and services which others want. This contribution to production is rewarded with wages, profits, or interest.

Look at these photographs and identify the primary human needs and the factors of production (copyright: Farmers Weekly)

All production requires some labour. Even the automated factory requires workers to supervise machinery, program computers to operate equipment and process paperwork, etc. Therefore, it is important that there should be an adequate supply of labour, containing the appropriate skills required.

DETERMINANTS OF LABOUR SUPPLY AND QUALITY

Determinants of labour supply

- *The size and structure of the population* – a large population will give a larger supply of labour. But a high proportion of very young or very old people will tend to reduce the supply of labour.
- *The number of women at work* — this is influenced by many factors such as economic conditions in the country, wages and attitudes towards working mothers, etc.
- *Hours of work* – in Britain and many developed countries there has been a general trend towards a decrease in the working week. This has the effect of reducing the supply of labour.

- *Quality of labour force* – it is not enough to have sufficient numbers of people available for work. They must also have the appropriate skills that are needed. If the required skills are not available the effect is to limit the supply of labour.

Determinants of labour quality

- *Quality of education* – education plays an important part not only in producing a knowledgeable workforce, but also contributes towards making people more mobile and adaptable to change.

- *Training resources* – a shortage of workers with particular skills can be overcome by training more of these specialists through the education system or in-service occupational training.
- *Natural talent* – some skills are important but are natural talents and cannot be taught, although they may be increased by training; for example, acting, drawing or playing a musical instrument.

FACTOR OF CAPITAL

Capital has a number of meanings many of which are financial and these are examined later in Chapter 8. Here we need to look at capital as a factor of production, and in this respect capital can be defined as wealth employed in the production of further wealth. In other words, it is the buildings, machinery, equipment, stocks and many other things (producers' goods) used in making the items we consume (consumer goods).

Capital in this sense takes two basic forms, fixed capital and working capital. Both of these are examined in more detail in Chapter 8, but basic definitions are given here.

Fixed capital – buildings, machinery and other equipment with a long life which can be used several times in the production of goods and the creation of further wealth.

Working capital – stocks of raw materials, cash, bank balance and other items required for the day-to-day operation of the business and which are continually being used up.

The entrepreneur

It is quite valid to argue that entrepreneurship can be considered as a fourth factor of production. Entrepreneurs play an important part in the economic system. They are those who organise and co-ordinate the other factors of production. They are the owners or managers of business enterprises who, by taking risks and making decisions, enable production to be carried out in anticipation of demand. This book is very much concerned with entrepreneurship.

If entrepreneurs successfully predict future demand for commodities, they are rewarded by a special form of income called profit. If, however, their judgment is incorrect, they may get no reward or may make a loss. For example, wholesalers may buy large stocks of a new chocolate bar but they have no guarantee that they will be able to sell them. If people were not willing to take these risks far fewer businesses would exist.

Location of industry

One of the most important decisions a firm must make is where to site its factories. The decision taken will be influenced by many factors. The following are typical of the factors influencing location of industry, but most choices of site are a compromise between several advantages and disadvantages.

INDUSTRIAL
INERTIA

Industrial inertia refers to a situation where a firm continues to stay at a particular site even though the original reason for establishing in that area no longer applies. For example, in the past industries may have located near canals or coalfields, but they do not move to another area even though these facilities are no longer being used.

SITE FACILITIES

A production unit may be sited in a particular place because the site gives easy access to required resources such as local sources of power or fuel, raw materials, mineral deposits, etc. Today, improved transport facilities have reduced the importance of locating for these reasons, but in some cases it is still a major economic factor. For example, some industries require large quantities of water for cooling purposes and may locate near the sea or a reservoir.

TRANSPORT
INFLUENCES

Siting near to good road, railway, sea, or air links can save in distribution costs or in the movement of raw materials. Efficient transport facilities allow producers to distribute their products effectively over a wider geographical area, and also make it possible to site production units further from their market, where sites may be cheaper.

MARKET PULL

Whilst efficient transport facilities give production units more freedom in choice of site, they are still drawn considerably by the pull of markets. The tendency in Britain has been for industry to be drawn towards the south and south-east, but market forces can also be seen to influence location of production units near other major markets and high population centres.

LABOUR SUPPLY

No matter where a factory is sited it will need supplies of labour. These must be adequate not only in total quantity but also in the qualifications and skills they possess. Where labour resources are a major influencing factor some industries tend to locate in areas which have a tradition in that industry.

GOVERNMENT
POLICY

We saw in Chapter 1 that Britain has a 'mixed' economy whereby the government exerts considerable influence on the economy. This influence includes the location of industry. Apart from direct influence in the location of state controlled industries, the government can also influence the location of privately owned industries.

The main reason the government may wish to influence the location of industry is to improve the regional balance of employment. In other words, to draw production into regions of high unemployment and areas where industry has declined. Such areas are sometimes referred to as 'depressed' or 'problem regions'. These can be distinguished by the following:

- Unemployment rate higher than national average.
- Average income of residents is below the national average.
- Large numbers of workers are leaving the area.
- Workforce generally retains outdated skills.
- There is less industry than in other regions.
- Factories, housing, hospitals, roads, etc. are generally outdated.

The ways in which the government can influence the location of industry include offering grants, subsidies, relief from taxes, or prohibiting industrial development in other areas.

REGIONAL
DEVELOPMENT
GRANTS

Over the years the Government has created areas where grants are available as incentives to businesses. Currently these are defined in the following way:

Development areas

These are areas of high unemployment and declining basic industries. Grants are available to firms to contribute to new buildings and creation of new jobs. The grants are particularly for manufacturing industry, although some service industries also qualify.

Intermediate areas

These are areas where unemployment is high, but not as high as in development areas. Often there are indications that unemployment is increasing. The grant in an intermediate area will vary with the type of project but can include cheap rents on government-built factories and training grants for workers.

Enterprise zones

These are small geographical areas where businesses of all types are encouraged to locate or expand. Enterprise zones are particularly identified in run-down inner city areas where economic decay is particularly problematic. These areas offer incentives such as:

- rate free accommodation (ten years)
- tax advantages to firms locating in zones
- simplified planning procedures.

In addition to the foregoing Government policies, local authorities also spend considerable funds encouraging businesses to locate in their areas, and back this up with local incentive schemes.

Economies of scale

The producer has to decide how to use the factors of production to the best advantage, because his chances of making a good profit depend on how effectively they are employed. He also has to decide on what scale to produce, in other words, which size of business. Obviously, the entrepreneur should aim for the scale of production which yields the greatest profit margin.

It is generally the case that larger firms achieve bigger profits because they enjoy 'economies of scale'. That is, unit costs fall as output increases. However, diseconomies of scale can also occur and these are reflected by unit costs increasing as output increases. Both of these possibilities can be examined by looking at the advantages and disadvantages of large-scale business.

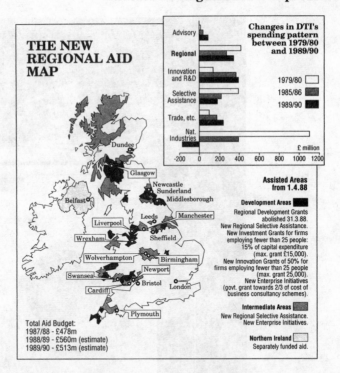

THE NEW
REGIONAL AID
MAP

**Changes in DTI's
spending pattern
between 1979/80
and 1989/90**

Advisory
Regional
Innovation
and R&D
Selective
Assistance
Trade, etc.
Nat.
Industries

1979/80
1985/86
1989/90

£ million
-200 0 200 400 600 800 1000 1200

**Assisted Areas
from 1.4.88**

Development Areas
Regional Development Grants
abolished 31.3.88.
New Regional Selective Assistance.
New Investment Grants for firms
employing fewer than 25 people:
15% of capital expenditure
(max. grant £15,000).
New Innovation Grants of 50% for
firms employing fewer than 25 people
(max. grant 25,000).
New Enterprise Initiatives
(govt. grant towards 2/3 of cost of
business consultancy schemes).

Intermediate Areas
New Regional Selective Assistance.
New Enterprise Initiatives.

Northern Ireland
Separately funded aid.

Dundee
Glasgow
Newcastle
Sunderland
Middlesborough
Belfast
Leeds   Manchester
Liverpool
Wrexham
Sheffield
Wolverhampton
Birmingham
Swansea
Newport
Cardiff
Bristol London
Plymouth

Total Aid Budget:
1987/88 - £478m
1988/89 - £560m (estimate)
1989/90 - £513m (estimate)

**ADVANTAGES OF
LARGE-SCALE
BUSINESSES**

- Large firms find it easier to raise large amounts of capital.
- More capital is available for
  - extensive advertising
  - research and development
  - employing specialist personnel
  - labour-saving machinery.
- Mass production allows greater possibilities of specialisation.
- Large firms can obtain special prices and discounts.

**DISADVANTAGES
OF LARGE-SCALE
BUSINESSES**

- Large organisations can become too complex to manage and lines of internal communication and management unwieldy.
- Customers may find the large organisation too impersonal.
- Employees may not feel they play an important part in the organisation.
- Mass production and specialisation can result in boredom for workers, vulnerability to production interruption and other disadvantages referred to in Chapter 1.

Technological change

Demand for material goods is continuously increasing, and many of these commodities are more sophisticated than ever before. The profit available to those who produce the goods and services demanded has always motivated organisations to look for the most economic way to meet this demand.

For hundreds of years man has looked towards implements and machines to make tasks and production easier and more effective. The

Technological change: use of microchip in control panel of a washing machine (copyright: Hotpoint)

relatively recent development and application of the silicon chip is possibly the biggest technological advance ever.

Many people are suspicious and apprehensive of this new technology, and only time will tell if it heralds the start of the bright new future forecast by some or the less attractive possibilities predicted by others. However, at various places in this book, we will see examples which illustrate some of the benefits that recent technological developments have brought about, particularly in respect of business applications.

WORD PROCESSORS AND COMPUTERS

The most far-reaching technological change currently affecting businesses is undoubtedly the dramatic increase in the use of word processors and computers.

A word processor is an electronic typewriter which allows a full text to be memorised and edited prior to printing. It consists of the following main unit parts:

Keyboard – electronic typewriter keyboard used to feed information into the system.

Visual display unit (VDU) – television-like screen used to display text prior to printing.

Central processing unit (CPU) – where processing of the information takes place.

Memory system – all word processors have a temporary internal memory, but this can be extended for long-term storage by recording data on to magnetic disks ('floppy disks').

Disk drive – used to feed in 'extended' memory from disks.

Printer – used to print out final text.

A computer is an electronic information processing machine. It can accept information from a user *(input)*, supply information to a user *(output)*, sort, select, store and retrieve information, and do calculations *(process)*. The information may be in words or numbers. Computers operate on instructions (called a *program*) given to them by the user.

COMPUTERS IN BUSINESS

Company registers – of shareholders are constantly changing as a company's shares are bought and sold, and the current holders of the shares must periodically be paid their share of the company profits. A computer helps a company to speedily update these records.

Stock records – automatic updating of records as stocks are removed from store. Warnings can be given when stock level falls too low, and valuation of stock is immediately available.

Banking – automated cheque clearing, keeping branch records, issue of bank statements and standing order payments, and operation of cash dispenser systems.

Payroll (wages system) – maintenance of payroll and personal records, automatic calculation of wages, income tax, national insurance, issue of P60, etc.

Word processing – computers can be used as word processors. Copies of letters, invoices, statements of account and other important paperwork can be typed into a computer and stored on magnetic disk or tape for later retrieval for review on VDU or line printer.

Accounts – issue of invoices, statements of accounts and maintaining records of customers' accounts.

Production line applications – many machines in factories are used to perform repetitive tasks, consequently it has not been surprising to find that there has been increasing use of computers to control production machinery.

RESULTS OF AUTOMATION

Automation is using sophisticated machinery which is electronically or computer controlled to carry out manufacture with minimal human intervention.

- Greater standardisation of production results in increased output and reduced prices.

- Business risk is increased because sophisticated, expensive machinery must be purchased well in advance of sale of products.
- There is a need for people displaced by automation to be redistributed to alternative occupations.
- Leisure time can be increased by a reduced working week and a lower retirement age.
- The need for tertiary services is greatly increased.

Demand and supply

All markets involving many buyers and sellers operate according to the law of demand and supply. That is, if demand for goods and services increases faster than supply of them, prices rise. If supply increases faster than demand, prices fall. In other words, the price of goods and services is determined by the interaction of the forces of demand and supply and this of course has a direct influence on production.

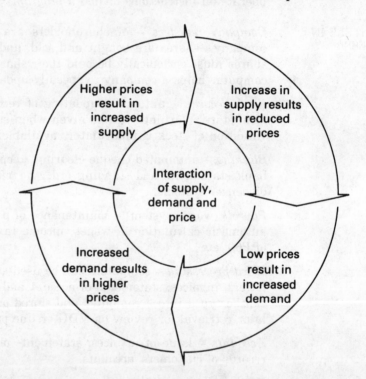

DEMAND   The demand for any commodity is the amount that consumers are prepared to purchase at a given price in a given period of time. For each price the demand is different. Usually the lower the price the higher the quantity demanded, and vice versa, although there are exceptions. 'Giffen goods' is a name given to those essential and relatively cheap goods for which demand is likely to increase following a rise in price. The term 'Giffen' is given after a nineteenth century economist of that name who noticed that when the price of bread increased, consumers bought more of it, being unable to afford to buy other more expensive alternatives such as meat and fruit.

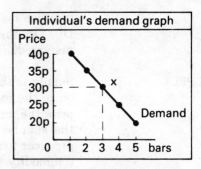

Individual's demand schedule	
Price of each chocolate bar	Quantity demanded at each price
40p	1
35p	2
30p	3
25p	4
20p	5

An individual's demand schedule and demand graph for chocolate bars at various prices. The point x on this demand curve indicates that at a price of 30p the person would be likely to buy three bars

The above table shows a possible demand schedule for a fictional commodity at various prices. A demand schedule can also be shown graphically by plotting the data on a demand curve.

This demand schedule and demand curve only refers to an individual consumer, but market demand consists of many people. A market demand curve is obtained by summing the demand curves of all individuals, so we can expect the market demand to behave in a similar way to individual demand.

Both the individual demand curve and the market demand curve express a relationship between the demand for a commodity and the price of it, but there are other determinants of demand.

Determinants of demand

- Price of the commodity
- Price of other commodities
- Income of the buyers
- Population or number of buyers
- Buyer's scale of preferences, i.e. how much the buyer values or prefers the items he wants in comparison with other commodities.

If one of the conditions of demand changes the demand curve moves to a new position. For example, a rise in income or purchasing power could

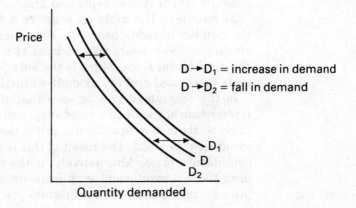

increase market demand and shift the demand curve to the right (D to D^1). On the other hand, if one of the determinants causes a fall in market demand the curve moves to the left (D to D^2).

SUPPLY

Supply is the amount of a commodity that producers are willing to put on to the market at various prices in a given period of time. For each price the amount supplied is different. Alternatively, we could say that the supply curve shows the price that is necessary to persuade the producer to provide output. Usually the higher the price the more of the commodity the producer will want to supply and vice versa, but in the same way as in the case of demand, there are some exceptions to this.

A supply schedule and graph can be constructed similar to that used to plot demand. Unlike the demand curve the supply curve usually slopes upwards to the right.

Market supply schedule	
Price	Quantity
10p	100
20p	200
30p	300
40p	400
50p	500

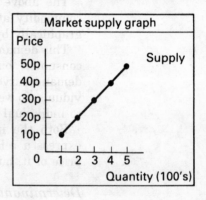

PRICE

From our examination of supply and demand so far, it should be clear to the reader that buyers want to buy at the lowest price they can, whilst sellers want to obtain the highest price they can for their goods. Whilst these may at first seem conflicting interests, closer examination shows that it is a combination of demand and supply that determines price.

When any two forces balance each other they are said to be in equilibrium. Under the conditions of a perfect market the price of a commodity is determined by the interaction of supply and demand. This can be made clearer by looking at a combined demand and supply schedule which is also expressed graphically for simple observation.

As shown in the table on page 29 it is only at the price of £3 that the number of teddy bears the consumers wish to buy is equal to the amount of teddy bears the producer is willing to supply. This is called the *equilibrium price*, which is the only price at which the amount willingly demanded and the amount willingly supplied are equal.

In the diagram it can be seen that the equilibrium price is at the intersection of the demand and supply curve. We can also see that if the price is above the equilibrium price, there is an excess of supply and insufficient demand. The result of this is that the price falls towards the equilibrium price. Alternatively, if the price is below the equilibrium price there is insufficient supply and excess demand. This results in the price rising towards the equilibrium price.

Price	Quantity demanded	Quantity supplied
£5	100	500
£4	200	400
£3	300	300
£2	400	200
£1	500	100

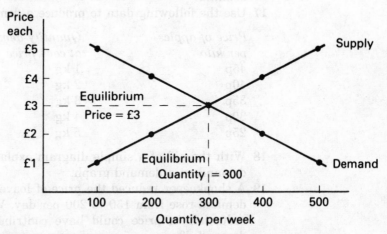

Market for teddy bears – amount demanded and supplied at various prices during one week

Our examination of the laws of demand and supply in this section has been very elementary although sufficient for our purposes. However, it should be understood that in reality the interaction of demand and supply is often more complex. The economist is particularly interested in investigating this interaction in greater depth.

MAKE A NOTE OF IT

1 What is the purpose of production?
2 Name the three primary human needs.
3 In your own words explain the difference between 'needs' and 'wants'.
4 Give a brief description of the factors of production.
5 Describe some of the factors that influence the supply of labour.
6 'Education and training make an important contribution to the quality of labour, but some skills cannot be taught.' Explain this statement.
7 Explain the difference between fixed capital and working capital.
8 What is the function of entrepreneurs?
9 Give an account of at least four factors that influence the location of industry.
10 What do you understand by 'economies of scale'?
11 What are the advantages enjoyed by large firms? Why do large organisations also have some disadvantages?
12 Why do you think some people are apprehensive about new technological developments?

13 Word processors are making a considerable impact on office work. What is a word processor? Briefly describe the functions of the main parts of a word processor.

14 What is a computer? Give four examples of the use of computers including at least one application to office work and one related to production.

15 Define automation. What are the possible results of automation?

16 What do you understand by demand? What are the determinants of demand?

17 Use the following data to produce a demand graph:

Price of apples per kilo	Quantity demanded at each price
45p	1 kg
40p	2 kg
35p	3 kg
30p	4 kg
25p	5 kg

18 With the aid of a simple diagram explain the effects of changes in demand on a demand graph.

19 A shopkeeper reduced the price of loaves of bread by 10p each and demand rose from 150 to 200 per day. What factors other than the reduction in price could have contributed to the extra quantity demanded?

20 Joe Bloggs is willing to pay £40 for a new raincoat. Why would he be unlikely to be prepared to pay £40 for the raincoat if he already had two of them?

21 A high street shop has reduced the price of sugar by 20 per cent. Has the shopowner done this to help the poor, or is there some other reason?

22 Translate the following market supply schedule into a graph:

Price	Quantity
£5	2000
£10	4000
£15	6000
£20	8000
£25	10000
£30	12000

23 Explain the relationship between demand, supply and price using simple diagrams to illustrate your answer.

24 Translate the following data into a combined demand and supply graph which clearly indicates equilibrium price:

Price each	Quantity demanded	Quantity supplied
£100	200	800
£80	400	600
£60	600	400
£40	800	200

3 Internal organisation of business

Business functions

The main aim of any business is to maximise profits in order to give the best possible return to the owners for the money they have invested in the company. Businesses achieve this aim primarily through the functions of production and marketing.

PRODUCTION

The broad function of production is to satisfy human wants. This is particularly evident in the efforts which are put into the production of commodities. But production not only encompasses industrial producers but also commercial producers. The term production not only includes those people directly involved in production, but also those members of the community such as bankers, transporters, insurers, teachers and doctors, etc., who increase the efficiency of those directly involved in production.

MARKETING

The marketing function of business aims to anticipate consumer demand in order that the right products are manufactured. Once the commodities have been produced it is the function of marketing to promote sales to the consumer. Marketing is not confined to goods alone, labour, capital, land and buildings must also be marketed as well as the many services that are needed.

EMPLOYMENT

A further function of business is the provision of employment. Theoretically, the more businesses that exist, and the more successful they are, the greater the number of personnel needed. However, in reality the provision of employment is far more complex than this simple view. Technological developments which lead to increased efficiency and growth can also result in a reduction in the number of employees needed in a particular industry.

The revolution in electronics has transformed many of the traditional areas of employment. For example, many of the functions of office workers have been by-passed by computers and word processors; many of the postal services are now being carried out more effectively by telecommunication; postal sorting has become increasingly automated; telephone communications are now very largely automated on a world-wide basis, and the workforce in these areas has been dramatically reduced. The automated factory, so long a part of science fiction, is now a reality.

However, the revolution in electronics has created a whole new industry in microelectronics, and our demands for material goods continue to increase making yet further demands for the production of consumer goods. There has also been a growth in the service industries which provide a wide range of support for industrial producers. The need for increased personnel in service industries will be likely to continue if the predicted increase in leisure time becomes a reality.

Internal structure

The internal structure of a business is influenced by its size. The small business is organised fairly simply, whereas the larger company has a more complex structure and more divisions.

SMALL FIRMS

Because they employ fewer people, small firms cannot easily be organised into separate units or departments. Consequently, the workers in the small firm tend to be less specialised and need to have a broader knowledge of the way that the firm is organised, and a wider range of skills to offer. This is because in the small firm the employee is required to undertake a wider variety of tasks, whereas in a larger organisation each task might be carried out by a single worker specialising in that activity. The variety of the work involved can make work in a small firm more interesting and satisfying.

LARGE ORGANISATIONS

Large organisations are generally private or public companies which are dealt with later in Chapter 4. This type of organisation is owned by shareholders and governed by a board of directors elected by the shareholders. The board appoints a managing director to oversee the day-to-day running of the business and to ensure that policies formulated by the board are carried out effectively. A company secretary is also appointed to deal with legal matters.

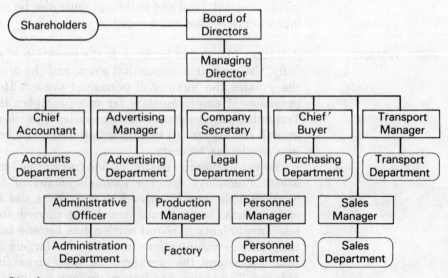

Simple company structure

ACCOUNTS

Records all payments in and out of the firm. It is particularly concerned with incoming and outgoing invoices, and maintaining the firm's money flow. Payment of wages is frequently included in the responsibilities of this department. The modern accounts department has an extensive data processing system backed up by computers.

SALES

To plan and organise the selling of goods or services offered by the firm. This department is one of the most essential because without it other departments would not be needed. Sales representatives provide an important link between the company and potential customers.

LEGAL

Most legal matters are dealt with by the company secretary, although a very large organisation might have a legal department. The department's activities include legal matters such as contracts, guarantees, insurance, compensation, etc.

ADVERTISING

May be a separate department or it can be incorporated into the sales department. The aim of this department is to make potential customers aware of the goods or services the company offers and to encourage custom. Smaller firms may employ the services of an advertising agency to carry out this work for them.

PURCHASING

The purchasing or buying department is responsible for all items bought by the firm. It obtains quotations from suppliers and issues orders, ensuring delivery is made on time. It also checks that prices, quality and quantity delivered correspond with the quotation and order. This department also deals with 'requisitions' which are written requests for supplies from other departments in the firm.

TRANSPORT

May operate the company's own fleet of vehicles, or alternatively it organises other forms of transport using agencies outside the firm. The function of this department is to arrange for delivery of goods to customers on time, in good condition, at home or overseas, and by the most economical method and route applicable.

ADMINISTRATION

Many firms have a general office concerned with co-ordinating the activities of the various departments of the firm. The administration department may include back-up facilities such as centralised filing, typing pool, mail room, reprographics and data processing. The administration department is frequently closely related to the managing director.

PRODUCTION

Where the company is involved in production of some commodity, a production department may be used to co-ordinate the work of the factory unit. 'Progress chasers' may be employed to ensure that delivery schedules are adhered to, and 'quality controllers' can be used to maintain production standards and investigate complaints or deal with goods returned as faulty.

PERSONNEL

Concerned with finding the right person for vacant jobs, dismissing unsuitable workers, dealing with resignations and providing references. It is involved directly in any induction training or staff training school the company operates. It maintains personal records of all employees and is involved in the welfare and happiness of all personnel.

The departments of a large firm

DEPARTMENTAL
ORGANISATION

One of the advantages enjoyed by large firms is that because of their size such companies are able to divide their organisations into separate specialist departments. The number and type of departments vary depending on the type of firm, but page 33 shows typical examples of the type of departments frequently included within the large organisation.

Business growth

It is logical for firms to try to increase in size. Increased capital resources, obtained from new capital or plough back of profits, provides capacity to expand the business and increase output and profits. Increased size may be achieved through internal growth, but also by combining with other firms to form a larger organisation.

MERGERS

Mergers or amalgamations occur when one or more firms combine to operate under a single name and control. The most familiar way in which a merger takes place is for one company to absorb the other by a 'take-over' bid. A bid is made to take control of another company by offering money, or money and so many shares of the bidding company, in exchange for shares of the firm being taken over.

To make the task of obtaining control of another company easier, the firm seeking control of another may buy up the voting shares on the open market until it has voting control, or until it owns sufficient to make a strong take-over bid. Once the take-over has been effected the firm may well be in a stronger trading position and enjoy greater economies of scale.

MULTINATIONALS

It is not unusual for mergers to take place across international borders. In other words, companies sited in different countries may combine to form a multinational company. A multinational company can also be formed by a parent company expanding into other countries and setting up subsidiary companies.

MONOPOLY

A possible result of the merger of organisations is that they may end up in a monopolistic position. A monopoly arises when a firm has so much control over the supply of a commodity or service, that it is able to also control the price. Whilst such a situation is beneficial to the firm, it can be to the detriment of the consumer if the firm abuses its power.

Effects of growth on an organisational structure

• Increased capital investment available
• More personnel can be employed
• Greater specialisation or division of labour can be employed
• Increased internal communication and control are necessary to operate the business.

MAKE A
NOTE
OF IT

1 What is the main aim of a business?
2 What is the function of production? Differentiate between industrial producers and commercial producers.
3 Why is marketing just as important as production?
4 'The more businesses that exist should theoretically mean more employment, but this is not necessarily the case'. Explain this statement.
5 Give a detailed comparison between small firms and large organisations.
6 Why are large firms more able to organise into departments than small businesses?
7 Describe the functions of six departments of a large company.
8 Why is it logical for firms to increase in size?
9 What is a merger and how might it take place?
10 What is 'multi' about multinational companies?
11 Define the term monopoly. What are the dangers of a monopoly from the point of view of the consumer?
12 List the effects of growth on an organisation.

4   Types of business

Private and public enterprise

Britain is said to have a 'mixed' economy because it consists of both private enterprise and public enterprise.

Private enterprise refers to businesses that are owned by private individuals (some of the public) engaged in the production of goods or services. There are four main forms of business ownership in the private sector of the economy:

1 Sole traders
2 Partnership
3 Private limited companies
4 Public limited companies.

There are also some private organisations which have a special relationship with the owners of the business. Co-operative societies and holding companies are examples of these special forms of private enterprise.

Public enterprise refers to industries and services owned by the state (all of the public) and run by central or local government.

Limited liability

The business entrepreneur faces many risks of participating in business activity, especially if the firm has unlimited liability. This means that if the business goes bankrupt and cannot pay its creditors, the owner's personal possessions such as car or home and its contents can be taken and used to pay the debts owed.

Although many small firms do have unlimited liability, larger organisations face so much greater risks that only some form of security for personal assets encourages people to invest and accept the greater risks involved.

The status of limited liability allows people to invest in a business without having to face the risks of unlimited liability. Limited liability indicates that the liability of shareholders for the debts of a business is limited to the amount they have invested in the business and not their personal assets.

Limited liability can be applied to the shareholders of a private or public limited company and a limited partnership. The private company and limited partnership must show the letters Ltd at the end of the company title. The public company must indicate limited liability by the letters PLC (Public Limited Company) at the end of the company title.

Limited companies are said to have a 'separate corporate identity'. In other words, an identity separate from their shareholders. They can sue and be sued in their title name.

Sole traders

This type of firm is owned by one person who provides all of the capital needed to form, operate, or expand the business. The sole trader is the simplest and most common type of enterprise. It is the easiest form of business to set up and it is also more likely to fail than any other.

ADVANTAGES
- The small size of this type of business requires a relatively small amount of capital for formation.
- The owner does not have to consult with anyone else when making decisions.
- The owner does not have to share profits with anyone else.
- The owner will be familiar with all aspects of the business.

DISADVANTAGES
- The owner's personal assets are at risk because the business has unlimited liability.
- There can be difficulty in continuing business (lack of continuity) if the owner is on holiday, ill, or dies.
- Division of labour may be difficult to organise because of small size of business.
- Shortage of capital can occur because all capital has to be provided by one person.
- This type of business finds it more difficult to borrow money than others.

Partnerships

Some of the problems faced by the sole trader can be overcome by incorporating more owners into the business to form a partnership.

Partnerships are regulated by the Partnership Act. This Act allows partnerships to have from two to twenty members although there are two exceptions to this rule.

1 Banks which operate as a partnership are not allowed to have more than ten partners.
2 Some professional partnerships are allowed to have more than twenty partners, (e.g. accountants, solicitors, members of the Stock Exchange).

A deed of partnership sets out the rights of each partner, such as the way in which profits are to be divided. Where no deeds exist it is assumed that the profits are shared equally.

All partners are equally responsible for the debts of the business. A 'sleeping' partner is one who invests in the business but takes no active part in running it, but such a partner is fully liable with other partners for debts incurred by the business.

It is possible to have a limited partnership but at least one partner must accept unlimited liability. Consequently, limited partnerships are relatively rare.

Some professional bodies prohibit their members from forming a limited company and, therefore, the partnership is particularly suitable for them. Solicitors, doctors and accountants are examples of professions that are not allowed to have limited liability status.

Advantages	*Disadvantages*
• Easily formed	• Generally unlimited liability
• Greater continuity than sole trader	• Possible conflicts between partners
• More people are available to contribute capital to the business	• Each partner is fully liable for the debts of the business
• Expenses and management of the business are shared.	• Membership limit of twenty restricts resources of business.

Private limited companies (Ltd)

Any company which is not registered as a public company is a private limited company. This type of business must include Limited (or Ltd) in its title name.

Both private and public limited companies are sometimes referred to as joint stock companies. This is because the money contributed by many shareholders is combined to form a joint stock of capital assets, which is used in some form of business enterprise to generate further wealth or profit which is divided between the shareholders.

The private company is allowed from two to an unlimited number of members (shareholders). The capital of the firm is divided into shares, but the shares are not sold on the Stock Exchange and they cannot be advertised for sale publicly. Consequently, shares have to be sold privately – hence the name 'private'.

Some firms may wish to keep ownership within a particular group of people, for example, within a family or a religious group. The private company may restrict share transfer if it wishes by writing a rule into its articles of association requiring members to offer shares to existing shareholders before attempting to sell them to non-members.

ADVANTAGES
- Has more people contributing capital than a sole trader or partnership.
- Has greater continuity than smaller businesses.
- Has limited liability.

DISADVANTAGES
- Capital raising possibilities are limited because shares cannot be offered for public sale.
- Capital raising may be further limited if the company decides to restrict share transfer.
- Audited accounts have to be available for inspection.

Public limited companies (PLC)

The public limited company must indicate its public status by including the letters PLC (public limited company) in the title name.

The public company in formation must have at least the minimum amount of share capital laid down in the Companies Act, 1985. It is allowed from two to an unlimited number of shareholders, and it can advertise shares and debentures for public sale. Capital raising is also helped by the fact that public company shares are listed on the Stock Exchange. This encourages people to contribute to the original share capital because they know they can easily sell their shares second-hand on the stock market. Consequently, this type of business organisation can raise almost limitless funds.

When one investor buys shares in a limited company he becomes a part owner. This not only entitles him to a share of the company's profits, but also gives him the right to some say in the way that the company is operated. It is usual for the shareholders of a company to elect a small committee called a board of directors to decide overall company policy on behalf of the shareholders. A chairman is also elected to regulate board meetings.

Even a board of directors consists of too many people to take an active part in the day-to-day operation of the firm so the board appoint a managing director to carry out this function. Both private and public companies elect a board of directors and a chairman and appoint a managing director.

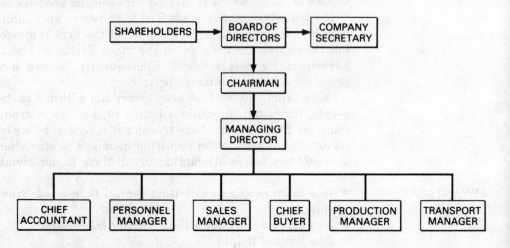

ADVANTAGES
- Has limited liability.
- Enjoys maximum continuity.
- Can raise large sums of capital.
- Large size enables them to enjoy 'economies of scale', such as being able to buy supplies in bulk.
- Size allows them to buy special equipment which will save in labour and expense.
- Find it easier to borrow money than smaller businesses because they are less risk than smaller firms.

DISADVANTAGES
- Formation involves considerable documentation and expense.
- Company, employees and shareholders become too detached from one another because of large size.
- Ease of transfer of share ownership can lead to 'take-over' bids for company.
- Tend to develop too many rules ('red tape').
- The annual accounts of the company are open to public inspection which reduces confidentiality of the firm.

Forming a limited company

All types of private businesses, including sole traders, partnerships, private and public companies, must register with the Registrar of Business Names if they wish to operate under a name other than that of the owner.

When a limited company is being formed it must register with the Registrar of Companies. This registration is carried out mainly by presentation of two completed documents, the memorandum of association and the articles of association, by those initially forming the company. Both the private and the public company follow a similar procedure, except that the private company passes through fewer stages than the public company.

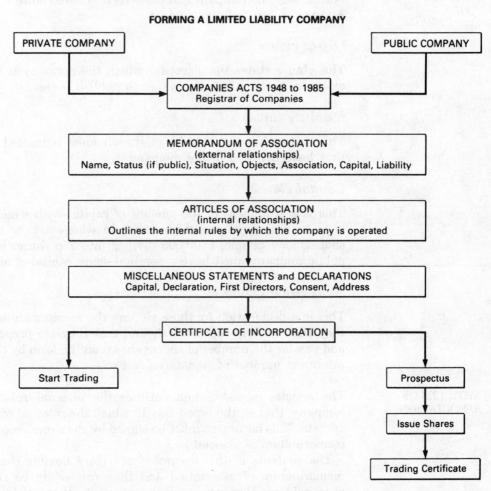

FORMING A LIMITED LIABILITY COMPANY

PRIVATE COMPANY

PUBLIC COMPANY

COMPANIES ACTS 1948 to 1985
Registrar of Companies

MEMORANDUM OF ASSOCIATION
(external relationships)
Name, Status (if public), Situation, Objects, Association, Capital, Liability

ARTICLES OF ASSOCIATION
(internal relationships)
Outlines the internal rules by which the company is operated

MISCELLANEOUS STATEMENTS and DECLARATIONS
Capital, Declaration, First Directors, Consent, Address

CERTIFICATE OF INCORPORATION

Start Trading

Prospectus

Issue Shares

Trading Certificate

MEMORANDUM OF ASSOCIATION

This document states the external relationship of the company, for example, the relationship between the company and others. The memorandum of association consists of a number of clauses.

Name clause

This states the trading name of the company. The Registrar of Companies ensures that no two companies are formed bearing the same name.

Status clause

The memorandum of a public company has to state that it is to be a public company. The public company indicates its status by the letters PLC (or plc) at the end of its title name, whereas the private company ends its title with Limited (or Ltd).

Situation clause

This identifies the country where the registered office of the company is situated. The company can move its registered office within the stated country.

Object clause

This clause states the object for which the company is established, for example, to manufacture toys, or to publish books.

Liability clause

This states that the liability of shareholders is limited to the amount they have invested in the company.

Capital clause

This is a statement of the amount of capital with which the company is to be registered and the manner in which it is to be divided into shares, for example, £500 000 divided into 25p shares or £1 shares. A public company must have a nominal share capital of at least £50 000.

Association clause

This is a declaration by those signing the memorandum implying that they wish to form the company and that they are prepared to take up and pay for the number of shares shown on the form by their name. The minimum number of signatories is two.

ARTICLES OF ASSOCIATION

The articles of association outlines the internal relationship of the company, that is, the broad way in which the internal organisation will operate. This document must be signed by the same people who sign the memorandum of association.

The contents of this document are more flexible than those of the memorandum of association and they can easily be changed by the shareholders. However, any alterations to the articles of association must not conflict with the memorandum of association.

Contents of the articles of association

- The rights of shareholders
- Methods of election of directors
- The manner in which meetings are to be conducted
- Division of profits.

MISCELLANEOUS STATEMENTS AND DECLARATIONS

In addition to the memorandum of association and the articles of association the promoters of a company must also make the following statements and declarations to the Registrar of Companies.

Statement of nominal capital

This shows the amount of registered capital and the manner of its division into shares (similar to the capital clause in the memorandum of association).

Declaration

A statement made under oath by the company secretary or a director confirming that all the requirements of the Companies Act have been met.

List of first directors

The names of the first directors of the company are listed.

Statement of consent

Signed by each of the proposed directors confirming that they are willing to act in this capacity.

Address of registered office

This states the precise registered address of the company. Any changes in this address must be notified to the Registrar within twenty-eight days of change.

If the Registrar of Companies is satisfied that all the requirements have been met, a certificate of incorporation is issued. The business now has an identity separate from that of its owners. A private company can now start trading and a public company proceed to raise capital.

RAISING CAPITAL FOR A PUBLIC COMPANY

The directors of the public company now attempt to raise the capital stated in the capital clause of the memorandum of association. This is done by issuing a prospectus, which is a printed circular or an advertisement, giving a frank outline of what the company hopes to do, and detailing the amount of capital required to start trading.

When the Registrar of Companies is satisfied that the company's share capital is not less than £50 000, and that at least a quarter of the nominal value has been paid on each share, a trading certificate is issued allowing the company to begin trading.

Special business relationships

FRANCHISING

In franchising, a company allows someone to buy the right to use their products or techniques under their trade names. This is one of the fastest growing sectors of the economy and over 20 per cent of retail sales is accounted for by this form of trading, and the trend is growing each year.

Franchising offers a 'ready-made' business opportunity for those who have the capital and are willing to work hard. The potential entrepreneur or franchisee pays to use the name, products, or services of the franchiser who receives a lump sum and a share of the profits of the business.

The franchisee receives the majority of the profits, but must also meet most of any losses. In return for the money they receive, in addition to allowing use of their name, products, techniques, or services, franchisers usually provide an extensive marketing back-up.

Fast food giants such as Wimpy, Kentucky Fried Chicken and Burger King are particularly well known in the franchising sector, but the range of franchise activities is much wider than just fast food, and the following are a few other examples of this type of business.

- developing and printing films
- home tuning of car engines
- drain clearing
- door to door ice cream sales
- bakeries.

CO-OPERATIVES

Co-operation sometimes develops in production when small units of agriculture or manufacturing owned by people with small and limited amounts of capital combine together for the purpose of sharing labour and buying or hiring equipment which individually they would be unable to afford.

By co-operating in this manner the members of the co-operative not only have access to the economic use of equipment purchased or hired through their pooled resources, but they can also enjoy economies of scale such as bulk purchasing of supplies and wider advertising and marketing possibilities.

Productive co-operation is less familiar in Britain than it is in many other European countries, and in this country most examples of co-operatives are found in distribution (*see* Chapter 12) rather than in production.

HOLDING COMPANIES

For a variety of reasons, businesses sometimes form a temporary or permanent combination to achieve a certain aim. For example, the combination of three or four businesses might usefully bring together several separate processes into one production unit.

This kind of partnership of companies is usually incorporated as a holding company. Each member company retains its legal entity, but overall control lies with the holding company.

Building societies

Building societies are a further example of a special business relationship. They operate on a non-profit-making basis. They are concerned with personal rather than business matters and, consequently, they are considered to be on the fringe of commercial activities.

Building societies are intermediaries between 'small' savers who wish to invest funds and people who wish to borrow money to purchase or improve property. Building societies lend by means of a *mortgage* which is a long-term loan, often repayable over a period of twenty years or more. Most of the deposits to building societies are lent out in this manner, but some of their funds must of course be retained to meet demands for cash withdrawals.

It is usual for the deeds of the property purchased by a borrower to be held by the building society until the mortgage has been repaid. If the borrower defaults in repayment of the mortgage, the society can sell the property to recover the debt.

Building societies have always competed with the commercial banks to obtain deposits from savers. Since the Building Societies Act, 1987 the societies have been allowed to compete more openly with the banks, offering many of the financial services that have traditionally only been provided by the banks. The range of services the societies offer remain relatively limited, and the Act ensures that they keep primarily to their traditional areas of business. At least 90 per cent of every society's commercial assets has to consist of first mortgages on residential property. Some banks have also begun to provide mortgages and these developments are providing the basis of healthy competition between building societies and banks.

Public enterprise

Public enterprise refers to the various forms of business organisation in public ownership. These fall into two broad categories: municipal undertakings and state undertakings.

MUNICIPAL UNDERTAKINGS

Municipal undertakings are businesses or services operated on a commercial basis by local authorities. They are financed by local rates and charges made for the use of the service. Sometimes municipal undertakings are subsidised by grants from central government. Examples: sport centres, theatres, bus services, conference halls, art galleries, museums and street markets.

STATE UNDERTAKINGS

State undertakings, state ownership, public ownership, public enterprise, public corporation and nationalised industry are all terms that are used to refer to a variety of businesses that are operated by the government on behalf of the public.

Each public corporation is set up by an Act of Parliament to provide commercial or industrial functions, often in a monopolistic position. Each corporation has a legal identity separate from the government.

Sports centres are a typical municipal enterprise. What municipal enterprises can you identify in your locality?

In effect, a public corporation is owned by all the public. General overall policy is decided by the government in consultation with the corporation board, which is selected by the government.

Financially speaking, corporations are expected to at least break even. However, sometimes other priorities may be decided as more important than making a profit.

British Rail is a state undertaking

Profits are used in three ways:

1 to pay interest on capital borrowed;
2 set aside for future repayment of loans;
3 reinvested to improve or expand the industry.

Losses must be met by the Treasury, which in effect means the taxpayer.

Nationalisation and privatisation

Some public corporations have been set up by the government in the first place (e.g. the Post Office and the BBC), others have at one time been in private ownership (e.g. British Rail) and have been taken into state ownership (nationalised). When nationalisation takes place the original owners are paid compensation.

When a publicly-owned business is sold back to the private sector it is said to have been *privatised*. There are many reasons why the government might return a state-owned business to the private sector. Obviously the sale will raise revenue for the government, but it can also result in increased choice and improved quality for consumers.

In the past Labour governments have favoured nationalisation whereas Conservative governments have preferred private ownership of industry.

Reasons for public ownership

- To take a monopoly out of private ownership.
- To keep a natural monopoly (e.g. water) in public ownership.
- Sometimes the initial capital cost of setting up an industry may be too high for private enterprise.
- Some forms of enterprise may be essential to our welfare but uneconomic for private business.
- National security may have to be protected through state ownership (e.g. atomic energy).
- To standardise equipment and avoid duplication of services (e.g. British Rail).
- To save an ailing industry and protect jobs.

Examples of public corporations

Atomic Energy Authority, Bank of England, British Rail, Central Electricity Generating Board, British Coal.

Advantages of public ownership

- Government has the resources to fund a vast industry, even if it is uneconomic.
- Will ensure provision of essential services.
- Reduces possible duplication of equipment.
- Enables large sections of the economy to be planned towards a single strategy.
- Profits benefit the whole nation as opposed to a limited number of private individuals.
- Large size of public corporations allows them to enjoy maximum economies of scale.
- Personnel are appointed and promoted because of proven ability as opposed to personal contact or share of business owned.

Disadvantages of public ownership

- Can be over-cautious due to the fact that they are answerable to the public.
- Bosses are politicians who may not have the necessary business expertise.
- Local issues may be disregarded in favour of policies of national importance.
- State monopoly can lead to inefficiency and insufficient profit motive.
- Losses have to be met by taxpayer.

MAKE A NOTE OF IT

1 Why is Britain said to have a 'mixed' economy?
2 What is limited liability?
3 What do the letters PLC stand for?
4 Why is the sole trader the most common form of business? List the advantages and disadvantages of this form of business organisation.
5 What would be the advantages of a sole trader converting his business into a partnership?
6 Give a brief description of the form a partnership might take. Why is the limited partnership relatively unusual?
7 List the advantages and disadvantages of partnerships.
8 Give a detailed comparison between private and public limited companies. Include a list of the advantages and disadvantages of each of these forms of business ownership.
9 In what way do sole traders, partnerships, private companies and public companies differ in the way they raise capital and deal with profits and losses?
10 Give a detailed description of the process followed in forming a limited company.
11 What is franchising? Give four examples of typical products or services likely to be marketed in this way.
12 Compare the productive co-operative with the retail co-operative.
13 What is a holding company?
14 In what ways are building societies different from the commercial banks?
15 Briefly explain the difference between municipal undertakings and state undertakings.
16 Give four examples of public corporations. Explain how their profits are used and the manner in which losses are met.
17 What is nationalisation? Why might the government decide to nationalise an industry?
18 List the advantages and disadvantages of public ownership.

DATA RESPONSE QUESTIONS
1

BUSINESS STRUCTURE AND ORGANISATION

Going it Alone

There has never been a better time to start a business of your own, but our Business Correspondent Amira Shah reports, it's a rocky road before you can hit the big time.

Instant success is rare in business and budding entrepreneurs need to be aware of the five stages of growth of a business:

Existence At the existence stage the founder is technically orientated and using all the energy to design and manufacture a product (or provide a service). The business is run by the owner who often performs all the managerial functions.

Survival At the survival stage the business becomes more aggressive in seeking new customers and a small standardised product line appealing to a wider set of customers is developed. The number of employees starts to expand and the ⋅owner becomes much more burdened with management responsibilities.

Success At the success stage the business credibility and technical feasibility has been established. Economies of scale are introduced in the production process. The owner has to make a decision, either to concentrate all his or her energies on expanding the company with the consequent risks or to. keep the company stable and profitable and provide a basis for alternative interests.

Take off If the owner decides on the expansion route and is successful then he or she should reach the take off stage. At this stage there are multiple product lines and a divisionalised organisation structure to cope with the increasing complexity of the business.

Resource maturity At the resource maturity stage, the business is now very well established. It is successful and the owner and the business have become quite separate financially and operationally. However it can become very bureaucratic and stifle innovation.

One of the major challenges for independent business people is that both the problems faced and the skills necessary to deal with them change as the business grows. You need to anticipate these changing factors based on the stage of development of your business.

Similarly at the success stage, you have to decide whether or not to commit all your time and risk everything you have worked for to date in order to grow further.

(a) Explain the words 'founder' and 'entrepreneur' used in this newspaper article. (2)

(b) Why does the owner of the business tend to be carrying out all the managerial functions at the 'existence' stage of business development? (2)

(c) Advertising tends to become an important feature of a business at the 'survival' stage. Why is this so? (3)

(d) What does it mean in the article when it says that the business 'creditability and technical feasibility has been established' at the 'success' stage? (3)

(e) What 'economies of scale' are likely to be introduced during the 'success' stage of development? Why are these not likely to be introduced earlier in the development of the business? (4)

(f) Why do the skills required of a businessperson change as the business grows? (6)

2

Dai Evans holds a majority shareholding in Easy Electronics plc, a company that owns a large chain of shops that sell a wide range of household electrical goods. Hightec Electrical plc produces a range of electrical items such as kettles, irons, hairdryers, etc. Hightec have been trying to take over Easy Electronics for some time. They have been openly buying ordinary shares on the Stock Exchange over the last year, but they have not managed to obtain sufficient shares in order to make a bid for the company. They have now offered to buy Dai Evans shares at a price above the current market price.

(a) What do the letters plc stand for? (1)

(b) What implications do the letters plc have for companies? (2)

(c) What is meant by the wording 'Dai Evans holds a majority shareholding'? (2)

(d) What do you understand by the term 'take over' as used here? (2)

(e) State at least three ways that the takeover could affect the workers of Easy Electronics if it were to take place. (3)

(f) What factors might Dai Evans take into account before agreeing to sell his shares? (4)

(g) Suggest reasons why Hightec would want to take over Easy Electronics. (6)

Developing a New Machine

Where the time and money goes...

Companies invest so as to be able to carry on their business effectively in the future. This investment takes many forms. A more powerful computer. A more convenient factory. More productive machines...

This diagram analyses the investment that must be put into the development of one such machine by a company, before other companies can themselves invest in its purchase. The machine in our example is used to shape metal cans for soft drinks. It sells for about £130,000: its development from first discussions through to its launch in the market cost £750,000. But to give the diagram a more general application, we are showing *percentages* of the total money and time involved.

Several points ought to be noted. The whole process generally falls into three stages, as shown. In stage one, the 'market opportunity' for a new machine has to be defined: the main features of a new machine likely to be successful have to be described. In the next stage, the actual engineering of the new machine is developed through design calculations, drawings, prototypes and early production examples. Stage three sees the first production batch made, together with preparation of publicity, selling resources, and trials in a potential customer's factory. Stage three ends with the general launch of the product on the market. Throughout run the two threads of engineering and marketing.

1st stage

MARKET RESEARCH

Identify the market: estimate its size. Identify likely customers, their needs and cost expectations. Assess all competitors. Explore materials and ancillary equipment. Research other issues, e.g. energy saving, usage improvements. Budget costs, time-scale and return on the investment.

PRODUCT BRIEF

Provide development team of engineers with exact data on what the machine must achieve, e.g. its range of outputs; size and shape of its finished products; materials to be handled.

Ensure development team know the cost and time targets.

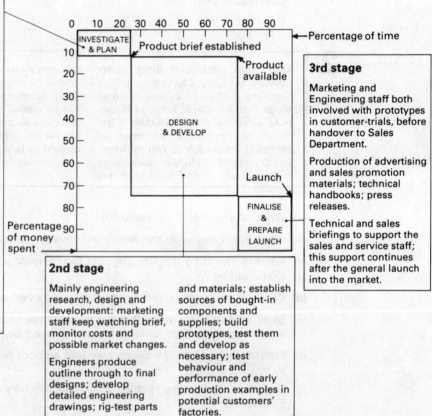

3rd stage

Marketing and Engineering staff both involved with prototypes in customer-trials, before handover to Sales Department.

Production of advertising and sales promotion materials; technical handbooks; press releases.

Technical and sales briefings to support the sales and service staff; this support continues after the general launch into the market.

2nd stage

Mainly engineering research, design and development: marketing staff keep watching brief, monitor costs and possible market changes.

Engineers produce outline through to final designs; develop detailed engineering drawings; rig-test parts and materials; establish sources of bought-in components and supplies; build prototypes, test them and develop as necessary; test behaviour and performance of early production examples in potential customers' factories.

Source: Industry in Perspective

Industry in Perspective is a publication issued for use in schools and is sponsored by a group of major companies and the Department of Trade and Industry.

3 Look at the article on page 52, and then answer these related questions.

(a) Which aspect of the development of a new machine takes up the most money? (1)

(b) What do you understand by investment in the way that it is used in this article? (2)

(c) In your own words briefly explain the purpose of market research. (2)

(d) Why is the product brief only completed after market research has been carried out? (3)

(e) Re-present the data shown in bar chart form to illustrate both the time and money elements of product development. Be sure to label chart parts clearly. (4)

(f) Why do the production and marketing sections of a firm have to work in close co-operation. Use examples from the data shown to illustrate your answer. (8)

4 Look at this photograph taken in a factory and answer the questions that follow it.

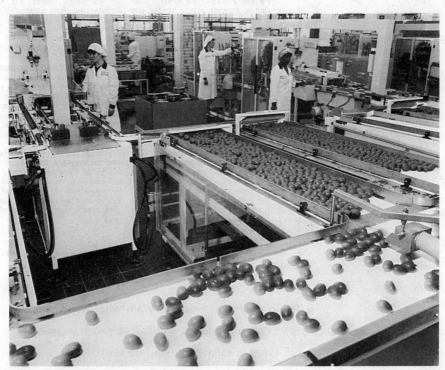

(a) What is being produced? (1)

(b) Name two factors of production that can be identified in the photograph. (2)

(c) The system of production illustrated is called 'division of labour by process'.
  • Explain what is meant by 'division of labour by process'. (2)
  • Describe one example of this process that operates within your school or college. (2)

(d) Many firms have introduced new technology into their production process, and increased the productivity of their work force.
- Define the terms 'new technology' and 'productivity' (2)
- State two costs and two benefits new technology can bring to a work force. (4)

(e) One of the possible disadvantages of division of labour by process is that it can result in alienation of the work force. What do we mean by 'alienation' and what methods might a firm use to combat it? (7)

5

Franchising can offer success in self-employment

FRANCHISING is a method starting up on your own by buying, not a business as such, but a licence from a franchisor to use his name and his tested operating methods and the exclusive rights to sell his products or service in a privileged territory for a fixed but renewable period of time.

The idea is that if you follow the methods that he lays down and that other franchisees have followed, you will achieve a predictable level of results.

The start-up costs vary from under £10,000 to over £250,000, but the average is around £40,000-£50,000 and profit projections generally show that you should get your money back in 3-4 years. Furthermore you can borrow up to 70% of the cost of an approved scheme from the bank.

There are about 350 franchises on the market and a number of them are household names: Tie Rack, Prontaprint, Pizza Express, Budget Rent a Car and Body Shop, are just a few.

Rapid expansion

In the USA, franchising accounts for 30% of all retail sales, and though it has a long way to go to reach anything like that figure here, it is expanding ever more rapidly. Latest figures show that annual UK sales are at £2.2 billion and that they are expected to top £5 billion comfortably by the end of 1990.

Franchising is seen by the banks and, increasingly, the government, as one of the major avenues into self-employment, because using a business format in this way has proved to have a high success rate as compared to starting out entirely on your own.

Source: Executive Post *June 1988*

(a) In your own words explain what franchising is. (2)

(b) Explain the terms franchisee and franchisor. (2)

(c) What is meant by 'start-up costs'? (3)

(d) The article says that profit projections generally show that franchisees should get their money back in 3–4 years. What are 'profit projections'? (3)

(e) State four disadvantages of being a franchise holder. (4)

(f) Why is a franchise business seen by banks as more likely to be successful as a form of self-employment than starting out on your own? (6)

Part 1

BUSINESS STRUCTURE AND ORGANISATION

1 Consider the extent to which siting of your local businesses can be seen to be influenced by local or national government.

2 Consider any new business which might wish to locate in your area and examine different factors helping them to decide which of two contrasting sites to choose from.

3 Take any vacant business premises in your locality and put forward rational arguments for starting a new type of business in those premises.

4 Make a survey of all (or a section of) the businesses in your High Street and discuss the appropriateness of the various legal forms for the nature of the business enterprise.

5 Make a survey of municipal undertakings in your locality and assess to what extent it would be more appropriate if they were in private ownership.

6 Make a study of any local issue which has implications for businesses, e.g. introduction of a one-way system or parking restrictions.

7 Make a diagrammatic 'map' of the organisation structure of a small and a medium-sized local firm with which you are familiar. Comment on the differences observed.

8 Make a comparative study of the organisation structure of a local department store and that of a local manufacturing unit.

9 Select two competing businesses situated within your locality and show:
   (a) how they compete
   (b) why they are both able to survive in spite of the competition they are part of.

10 Use demand curve construction to illustrate an analysis of the demand for a particular good or service.

11 Make a survey of all the businesses within a clearly defined area in your locality and identify the legal structure (legal identity) of each. Present the information collected in some appropriate diagrammatic form (with a 'key' if necessary). To what extent are the firms investigated reliant upon the local transport network?

12 Locate a well-established local entrepreneur who started his or her business from 'scratch'. What factors can you identify as making important contributions to its apparent success?

13 Use a relatively local map to illustrate the main area of location of primary,

secondary and tertiary production. Make observations on the reasons for site choice in each case.

14 Make a survey of small production industries in your area (perhaps on an industrial estate). Present the survey on a simple colour coded diagram/map to show different categories of production. See if you can identify any relationship between the size of premises and the legal identity of the firm. Comment on your findings.

15 Make a survey of all the public sector activities within your locality. Which are controlled by a public corporation, central government, or local government? To what extent do you consider the source of control appropriate to local needs?

16 Choose one of the nationalised (or one that has been privatised) industries and trace its development from the time of nationalisation to its present status.

17 Using library resources make a comparative study of the USA, the USSR and the UK as illustrations of different types of economy. To what extent, if any, do you feel these are changing?

18 Your school art department has decided to start a mini-enterprise which will produce ornamental pottery for marketing locally. A local bank has offered to finance the rent of a small shop in the town, if it is not too expensive.

What are the cheapest but most practicable premises you can identify. Give reasons for your choice.

19 Interview the owners of any recently established business in your locality:
    (a) Discover what were the main problems faced by the owners.
    (b) How did they overcome the difficulties?
    (c) What problems are they still faced with?

20 Imagine that you are a skilled craftsman who has recently been made redundant and you have been awarded £20 000 redundancy pay. What local help is available to assist you to set up your own business?

21 Visit a local factory that has a production line and find out the following information about the organisation of production:
    (a) What elements of the manufacturing process are done on the production line and which are not?
    (b) To what extent does the factory employ 'modern' technology?
    (c) How do wage rates differ between workers within the firm and why does this occur?

Part 2
MONEY, CAPITAL AND FINANCE

5 Structure of the banking system

The British banking sector includes the following institutions with the Bank of England playing the prominent role as the country's central bank, and at the hub of most banking activity.

Bank of England

Most major countries today have a single central bank which plays a major role in controlling the monetary system. As our central bank, the Bank of England (the Bank) is the heart of the British banking system, exerting a considerable influence on other parts of the banking sector.

The Bank of England was nationalised in 1946 and is controlled by a court of directors appointed by the state. This court consists of a governor, a deputy governor and sixteen directors.

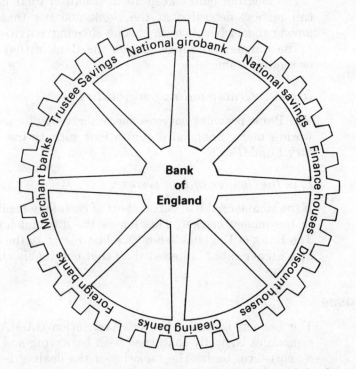

The Bank of England is at the centre of the British banking system

It is the government's bank

This is the major function of the Bank. In this respect it manages the government's banking accounts, for example, for the Exchequer and other government departments.

The Bank advises the government on formulation of monetary policy and assists the government in carrying out the monetary policy.

The Bank also handles the arrangements for government borrowing:

- short-term – principally through the sale of Treasury bills,
- long-term – management of government stocks which form the bulk of the national debt.

Management of the exchange equalisation account is also carried out by the Bank and it is through this that the Bank can influence the value of sterling by selling or buying pounds to affect the foreign exchange market prices.

It controls the note issue

The Bank has the sole responsibility for the issue of bank notes in England and Wales.

It is the bankers' bank

Each of the clearing banks has an account with the Bank, and during the process of cheque clearing (*see* Chapter 6) debits and credits are made to these accounts as a means of interbank settlement.

The clearing banks keep about a half of their liquid reserves (short call money) deposited at the Bank and use these for settling debts among themselves (e.g. in cheque clearing activities).

The commercial banks rely on the Bank if they run short of money or require loans.

It has international responsibilities

The Bank provides services for other central banks and some of the world's major financial organisations such as the International Monetary Fund (IMF).

It is the 'lender of last resort'

If the commercial banks run short of cash they recall deposits they have in the money market. This leaves the discount houses short of funds. The Bank of England 'lends as a last resort' to the discount houses, but at a higher rate of interest than that obtainable elsewhere in the City.

Discount houses

The London Discount Market Association (LDMA) consists of twelve companies basically concerned with borrowing and investing money on a short-term basis. The majority of the dealing is carried out by telephone and personal contact.

The main functions of the discount houses can be summarised as follows:

- accepting very short-term deposits from businesses, particularly banks, in return for a low rate of interest;
- using funds raised in this way to purchase a variety of assets, for example, Treasury bills, bills of exchange and gilt-edged securities;
- providing immediate finance for companies by discounting reliable bills of exchange, that is, buying them for less than their face value and holding them until they mature to obtain the full value, or reselling them and charging a higher rate of discount to achieve a profit.

Clearing banks

'Clearing' banks are so-called because they handle the exchange and settlement of cheques through the clearing house system (refer to Chapter 6 for explanation of the clearing house system).

The clearing banks consist of:

- the Northern Ireland clearing banks
- the Scottish clearing banks
- the London clearing banks:

  1 Barclays
  2 Lloyds   } Sometimes referred to
  3 Midland   as the 'big four'
  4 National Westminster
  5 Coutts & Co (owned by National Westminster)
  6 Co-operative Bank
  7 Trustee Savings Bank
  8 National Girobank.

The functions of clearing banks are dealt with in detail in the next few chapters but they can be summarised as follows:

- acceptance of deposits of money,
- providing a system of payments mechanism,
- supply of finance,
- provision of a wide range of services.

Can you identify the logo that belongs to each of the 'big four' banks?

TRUSTEE SAVINGS BANK (TSBs)

The TSBs have moved away from providing simple savings facilities towards becoming fully fledged banks. The holding company, TSB Group plc, has offered shares in ownership to depositors as part of a major restructuring programme to enable them to become full banking institutions. They now offer the following variety of services similar to those of the other clearing banks, and aimed at the personal customer.

- current, deposit and savings and investment accounts;
- credit transfer facilities;
- overdrafts, personal loans and mortgage loans;
- combined credit and cheque guarantee card (TSB Trustcard);
- travel cheques and foreign currency.

State banks

NATIONAL SAVINGS BANK

The National Savings Bank is operated through the Post Office. There are two types of account, ordinary and investment. Interest is paid on both types of account, but the investment account receives a higher rate of interest and requires one month advance notice for withdrawal. National Savings Bank funds are invested in government securities.

NATIONAL GIROBANK

The National Girobank is a state-run bank and is a part of the business of the Post Office, but is financially independent from it. There are plans to privatise the bank. The bank was originally established to provide a simple money transmission service operated through the postal system, and cash facilities through Post Offices. The scope of National Girobank has now been extended considerably to include all the following activities:

- current, deposit and budget accounts,
- foreign currency and travel cheques,
- loans and overdrafts,
- cheque guarantee card,
- postcheques (cashable in post offices abroad),
- credit transfer services.

Merchant banks (acceptance houses)

These are not banks in the commonly understood sense but private firms that offer highly specialised services almost exclusively for business customers. The main activities of merchant banks can be divided into accepting house activities, issuing house activities and capital market activities.

ACCEPTANCE HOUSE ACTIVITIES

The traditional activity of merchant banks is 'accepting' (i.e. lending their name to) a bill of exchange issued by less well-known traders, so that it becomes more acceptable because of the bank's good reputation in the financial world. By endorsing the bill, the accepting house guarantees payment of the bill should the drawer default (*see* Chapter 15 for application of bills of exchange in finance of international trade).

ISSUING HOUSE ACTIVITIES

Merchant banks play a major role in assisting in raising company finance by sponsoring first issues of company shares on behalf of their clients, or acting as intermediaries between companies seeking capital and those willing to provide it. It should be noted that not all issuing houses are merchant banks (*see* Chapter 9 for notes on share issue).

CAPITAL MARKET ACTIVITIES

In addition to raising capital for companies by their issuing house activities, merchant banks are also involved in a wide range of other capital market operations, some of which are as follows:

- operate some current account services for customers;
- accept larger (e.g. £25 000+) deposits, generally for one year or more;
- offer consultancy services to businesses wishing to become limited liability companies;
- advise on company problems such as capital reorganisations, dividend policy, mergers and takeover bids;
- provide finance for hire-purchase, local government and industry;
- operation of unit trust (*see also* Chapter 9);
- assistance in investment of trustee funds for large institutions;
- act as agents to companies establishing branches overseas;
- dealing in the precious metals market.

Foreign banks

There are now about 400 foreign banks (particularly from European countries) in London existing to give service and credit to companies from their own countries operating in Britain. A number of these banks have expanded their activities and they now make substantial sterling loans to British borrowers.

Finance houses

The Finance Houses Association (FHA) consists of forty-three member companies who control 80 per cent of the instalment credit business in the UK.

Monetary control

The Bank of England is responsible for carrying out the monetary policy of the government. This particularly involves the Bank in exercising control of the money supply and the lending activities of the banks. It does this in a number of ways.

OPEN MARKET OPERATIONS

The Bank seeks to keep interest rates within an unpublished band through its bill dealing with the discount houses. By buying and selling bills from and to discount houses the Bank influences the amount of funds available to the banking system as a whole.

Basically, this action influences short-term interest rates, but leaves the influence of long-term rates to market forces.

MINIMUM LENDING RATE (MLR)

The use of MLR has currently been suspended by the Bank, although it can be reintroduced at some future date, maybe temporarily. When in operation, MLR is the minimum rate of interest at which the Bank will normally lend to the discount houses. All other interest rates tend to follow MLR movement when used in this way.

CASH AT THE BANK

The Bank requires all institutions in the monetary sector with eligible liabilities of £10 million or more to keep ½ per cent of their eligible liabilities in non-interest earning balances at the Bank of England. Eligible liabilities are the liabilities of the banks *less*

(a) funds lent by one institution in the monetary sector to any other;
(b) money at call (can be withdrawn on demand) placed with money brokers and jobbers in gilt-edged in the Stock Exchange, and secured on gilt-edged stocks, Treasury bills, local authority bills and eligible bank bills (e.g. bill of exchange).

MONEY AT CALL

Each bank whose bills are recognised as eligible is required to maintain:
(a) 6 per cent of its eligible liabilities with members of the London Discount Market Association (LDMA) and/or with money brokers and gilt-edged jobbers;
(b) the proportion held with members of the LDMA must not fall below 4 per cent on any one day.

SPECIAL DEPOSITS

Banks and deposit-taking institutions with eligible liabilities of £10 million or more can be called on to deposit a percentage (decided by the Bank) of their liabilities with the Bank, which earns interest at a rate close to Treasury bill rate. This process can be used as a means of withdrawing cash from the money market.

LENDER OF LAST RESORT

(Refer to the earlier section on the functions of the Bank.) If the commercial banks run short of cash they recall their loans made to the discount market. Consequently, the members of the discount market are forced to borrow funds from the Bank which charges a rate of interest higher than that charged anywhere else in the City.

MAKE A NOTE OF IT

1 Name the institutions which make up the British banking sector.
2 What do we mean when we say that the Bank of England is a central bank?
3 State one way in which the Bank of England influences the value of sterling.
4 Briefly describe the functions of the Bank of England and say how they differ from the functions of the commercial banks.
5 What is the London discount market?
6 What are the main functions of discount houses?
7 Why are commercial banks sometimes referred to as 'clearing' banks?
8 Name the London clearing banks and identify the 'big four'.
9 What are the four main functions of the clearing banks?
10 Briefly explain the difference between the two types of National Savings Bank accounts. What happens to money whilst it is invested in these types of account?

11 In what ways does National Girobank differ from other banks?

12 Why are merchant banks sometimes referred to as acceptance houses?

13 In what way does a merchant bank help in raising capital for businesses.

14 List six other services which are provided by merchant banks for businesses.

15 Name the form of business that controls the majority of the UK instalment credit business.

16 What is the purpose of the Bank of England's open market operations?

17 What do the letters MLR stand for? What is the purpose of MLR?

18 Briefly describe what is meant by 'money at call'.

19 What are 'special deposits'?

20 In what way does the Bank of England act as 'lender of last resort'?

6　Budgeting and bank accounts

Budgeting

THE NEED TO
BUDGET

How much wages or pocket money do you receive each week? How do you decide which of the many items you want you will buy with the limited income you have available? Whatever you decide to do with your limited income, the decisions you take will involve budgeting.

Budgeting means having a plan for systematic spending. This involves ensuring that, over a given period of time, spending does not exceed income.

All people and organisations find it necessary to budget and to strike a balance between income and expenditure. The Chancellor of the Exchequer is continually engaged in trying to balance the nation's income and expenditure. Companies face the risk of bankruptcy if they allow expenditure to continually exceed income. Ideally, family and personal budgeting should follow a similar process on a smaller scale if maximum use is to be made of resources.

PERSONAL
BUDGETING

If you were to ask fifty people to make a detailed list of their income and expenditure for one month, it would be quite remarkable if any two of them had the same budget. The reason is quite simple. Even though two people may have the same income, they will have different tastes and priorities for spending their money. But whatever one's tastes and priorities, personal budgeting is important if future money problems are to be avoided.

Imagine you receive £100 per week in wages and this week you have to pay a telephone bill of £45 and a £65 gas bill. How can you pay these bills and also meet other expenses such as fares and food for the week? The answer is to plan ahead, preferably for twelve months, to form a personal budget. This is done by working out your total expected annual expenses on things like rent, gas, electricity, telephone, etc., and divide the total by twelve. You must then save this amount every month if you are to be able to pay your bills as they arrive. The part of your wages left over after saving towards your budget can be used firstly for daily expenses such as food and travel, and any remainder can be used for luxuries or investment.

BUDGET
ACCOUNTS

Banks operate budget accounts on a similar principle to the personal budget described above and the aim is to help even out annual household expenses. On payment of an agreed weekly or monthly amount the bank gives the account holder permission to draw cheques, standing orders or direct debits up to a given credit limit. The limit is calculated proportionate to the regular inpayment. While the account is in credit, the money earns interest, and interest is charged when the account is overdrawn. There is also a charge for each cheque or other withdrawal.

The bank budget account is particularly useful for someone who finds it difficult to organise and stick to their own personal budget plan.

Deposit account (savings account)

The bank deposit account is used by individuals and businesses for safe-keeping of funds not needed for immediate use. Credit slips are used to pay money, cheques, postal orders, etc. into the account.

No cheque book is issued with this account and, therefore, transfer of sums of money from the deposit account is normally in the form of cash. The bank can request seven days' notice of withdrawal of money from the account, although this rule is usually waived, especially for relatively small amounts.

Depositors are paid interest on money left in the account, and the bank then lends the money to borrowers who are charged a higher rate of interest. A statement of account is issued periodically to the account holder. The account cannot be overdrawn (*see* later).

Current account (cheque account)

This type of account is used by individuals and businesses for safe-keeping of funds needed for current use. In other words, funds which are required to be immediately available.

The current account can be opened with a small deposit, a specimen signature and a reference from someone acceptable to the bank.

Credit slips are used to pay deposits into the account and cheques are used to draw cash or transfer funds to others. Funds can also be withdrawn from the account twenty-four hours of the day through a cash dispenser.

Interest is not always paid on this type of account although some banks have experimented in paying interest on maintenance of a minimum balance. Bank charges may be incurred if a minimum balance is not maintained.

A statement of account is issued to the account holder periodically or on request, and a current balance figure can also be obtained twenty-four hours a day through a cash dispenser.

With the permission of the bank the current account may be 'over-drawn', that is, the account holder will be allowed to draw on more money than is in the account. This is examined in more detail in the next chapter.

A 'joint' account may be shared by two or more persons. In the case of a joint account or a business account, the account holders can make a variety of arrangements for signing cheques, for example, signed by any one, or any two of a number of authorised signatories.

National Girobank

National Girobank is a separate business currently within the Post Office Corporation. There are plans to privatise the bank. Account records are held at the Girobank's headquarters and operational centre in Bootle, and the bank's regional offices throughout the country have access to this information by computer links.

National Girobank accounts can be opened (there is lower age limit of 15 years) with an initial deposit of £10. Application forms are available at all post offices. No bank charges are made while the account is in credit, but transaction charges are made while the account is overdrawn.

Two basic types of account are available, private accounts and business accounts. As the names imply, the private account is for individuals whereas the business account is intended for firms, local authorities, public corporations and government departments, etc. Individuals normally deal through post offices throughout the country whereas business accounts deal directly through the head office.

WITHDRAWALS

Cash can be withdrawn at post offices by completing a Girobank cheque ('Girocheque') made payable to 'self'. The account holder can withdraw up to £50 on every working day from either of two post offices named when opening the account, or from any post office when using a Girobank cheque guarantee card. Before larger amounts can be withdrawn, or before money can be withdrawn from a post office other than those named, cheques have to be first sent to Bootle for clearance.

OTHER GIROBANK FACILITIES

Girobank includes many facilities similar to the commercial banks, e.g. cheque books, cheque guarantee card, credit transfer and standing order, deposit accounts, budget accounts, loans and overdrafts. But overall the range of services offered by Girobank is limited when compared with those provided by the commercial banks.

GIROBANK SERVICES FOR NON-ACCOUNT HOLDERS

People who do not hold a Girobank account can use the system to pay people and organisations who do have accounts. This conveniently allows them to make payments but avoids the cost of envelopes and

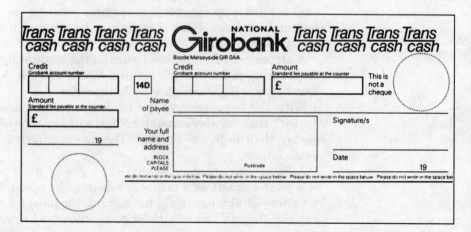

postage. Payments can be made at any post office by filling in a Trancash form similar to the illustration shown on page 68. Many organisations include an in-payment form with their bills.

Using the service

- In-payment must be made using a Girobank Transcash form, or one provided by the account holder.
- The form has to be completed with details of the payer and also the payee.
- In-payment must be made in cash. Cheques are not acceptable.
- A small nominal charge is payable by non-customers, except where the account holder has provided an in-payment form.
- The reverse of the Transcash form has a space for messages, such as details of the outstanding account being paid.

Cheques

A cheque is a written instruction to the bank (the *drawee*) to pay money to the account holder (the *drawer*) or to another person (the *payee*). Most cheques are *order* cheques, which means they must be signed (*endorsed*) on the reverse by the named payee if they wish to pass it on to someone else.

Although today we recognise cheques as special slips of printed paper, these are only issued by banks for both the convenience of their account system, as well as to help account holders. However, there is no reason why the instruction to the bank cannot take the form of a letter, or even a less formal message. There have been occasions when, for a variety of reasons, these instructions have been written on such widely diverse items as a door, a paving slab, various items of clothing and even a fish.

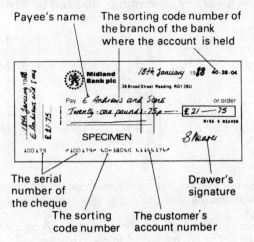

Payee's name

The sorting code number of the branch of the bank where the account is held

The serial number of the cheque

The sorting code number

The customer's account number

Drawer's signature

The bank will ensure that the cheque:
- *has been written out correctly*
- *has not been altered*
- *has a valid date*
- *signature compares with the specimen held.*

THINGS WRITTEN
ON A CHEQUE

- The date from which the value of the cheque is payable (a post-dated cheque is one dated for sometime in the future).
- Name of payee (person cheque is to pay).
- Amount to be paid in words.
- Amount to be paid in figures.
- Signature of drawer (person from whose account funds are to be withdrawn).

OPEN CHEQUE
(UNCROSSED)

The open cheque does not have two parallel lines drawn across it. It is 'uncrossed'. The payee of an open cheque can:

- Pay the cheque into his own account.
- Pass it to someone else by endorsing it.
- Exchange it for cash at the bank on which it is drawn.

The open cheque can be paid out to whoever presents it at the bank, and, therefore, it is not very safe. Banks prefer their customers to use crossed cheques and open cheques are used far less frequently than crossed cheques.

CROSSED CHEQUE

A crossed cheque has two parallel lines drawn vertically across it. This type of cheque must be paid into a bank account and cannot be exchanged for cash except by the drawer at his own bank, or at another bank with the use of a cheque card. These rules help to eliminate fraud in the use of cheques.

If you look at the cheque shown you will see that it has a 'general' crossing; there is nothing written between the lines of the crossing. This means that the cheque must pass through a bank account and cannot be exchanged for cash. However, a cheque with this sort of crossing can still be endorsed and passed to someone else, and such a cheque is still open to fraudulent use, although less so than the open cheque.

There are a variety of wordings that can be written between the lines

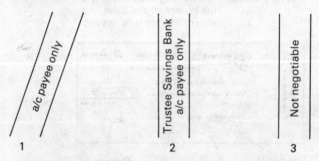

1 *This crossing ensures that the cheque can only be paid into the account of the payee, although they can pay it into their account through any branch they wish.*
2 *This means the same as the above crossing except that the cheque can only be paid in at the branch stated in the crossing.*
3 *When written as a cheque crossing this warns anyone other than the payee accepting the cheque that they do so with some degree of risk. The risk they face is that if the cheque has been stolen or fraudulently used, then the person accepting it is liable to refund the rightful owner with the amount shown on the cheque.*

of a cheque crossing to give more specific instructions on how the cheque may be used, and to make it safer. The three most frequently used 'special' cheque crossings are shown on page 70.

DISHONOURED
CHEQUES

Cheques which are not passed for payment by the drawer's bank are said to have 'bounced' or been dishonoured. When a cheque is refused for payment the drawer's bank will write 'refer to drawer' or R/D on the cheque and return it to the payee who must find out from the drawer why the cheque has not been honoured.

Reasons why a cheque might 'bounce'

- Cheque contains an error or is unsigned
- Cheque is 'stale' (more than six months old)
- Signature differs from specimen held at bank
- Drawer does not have sufficient funds in account
- Cheque has been altered
- Cheque is post-dated
- Cheque has been 'stopped' by the drawer (drawer has instructed bank not to make payment).

Bank statement of account

The bank statement of account is issued to the account holder periodically or on request. The account holder can also obtain a figure to show

Midland Bank plc

MISS A. N. OTHER

COVENT GARDEN BRANCH
16 KING STREET LONDON WC2E 8JF

Statement of Account

1988	Sheet 42 Account No. 51149903	DEBIT	CREDIT	BALANCE Credit C Debit D
AUG 5	BALANCE BROUGHT FORWARD			62.08 C
AUG 8	AUTOBK COVENT GDN2	10.00		52.08 C
AUG 9	100142	35.00		17.08 C
AUG10	100146	10.30		
AUG10	100147	8.15		
AUG10	AUTOBK NATW 601533	10.00		11.37 D
AUG15	100148	10.00		21.37 D
AUG16	100144	5.00		26.37 D
AUG19	100149	10.00		
AUG19	PITMAN PUBLISHING		506.33	469.96 C
AUG22	AUTOBK NOTT HLL GT	15.00		
AUG22	SUNDRIES		65.00	519.96 C
AUG23	100473	41.00		
AUG23	AUTOBK NATW 503021	60.00		418.96 C
AUG24	100150	80.00		
AUG24	100474	160.00		
AUG24	AUTOBK NATW 503021	10.00		168.96 C
AUG30	AUTOBK COVENT GDN2	10.00		158.96 C
AUG31	100475	38.40		
AUG31	AUTOBK COVENT GDN	20.00		
AUG31	AUTOBK NATW 503021	45.00		55.56 C
SEP 2	AUTOBK NATW 503021	10.00		45.56 C
SEP 6	AUTOBK NATW 503021	10.00		35.56 C
SEP 6	BALANCE CARRIED FORWARD			35.56 C

A bank statement

the current balance in the account from the bank cash dispenser which will provide information and cash twenty-four hours of the day. The statement sums up all the transactions which have taken place since the last statement was issued and shows the current balance held in the account.

Amounts which reduce the balance (e.g. cheques issued) in the account are shown in the payments column, and amounts which increase the balance in the account are shown in the receipts column. As each payment or receipt is recorded a new balance figure is shown in a third column.

Cheque clearing

The reader's attention is directed again to the point made earlier that a cheque is an instruction to their bank by the drawer of the cheque. Consequently, when a payee deposits a cheque into their account it does

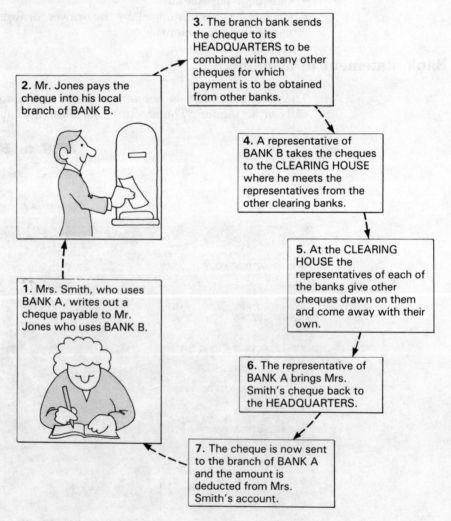

3. The branch bank sends the cheque to its HEADQUARTERS to be combined with many other cheques for which payment is to be obtained from other banks.

2. Mr. Jones pays the cheque into his local branch of BANK B.

4. A representative of BANK B takes the cheques to the CLEARING HOUSE where he meets the representatives from the other clearing banks.

1. Mrs. Smith, who uses BANK A, writes out a cheque payable to Mr. Jones who uses BANK B.

5. At the CLEARING HOUSE the representatives of each of the banks give other cheques drawn on them and come away with their own.

6. The representative of BANK A brings Mrs. Smith's cheque back to the HEADQUARTERS.

7. The cheque is now sent to the branch of BANK A and the amount is deducted from Mrs. Smith's account.

The lifecycle of a cheque

not mean the transfer of funds has taken place. The instruction is to the drawer's bank, and transfer cannot be carried out until the drawer's bank has received the instruction. In the meantime the payee cannot draw on the amount stated on the cheque. The process by which cheques are passed for payment is known as the *clearing system*.

A cheque can only be 'cleared' for payment at the bank on which it is drawn. If the drawer and payee use the same branch bank then, so long as the drawer has sufficient funds, a simple paper transfer is carried out within the branch bank. If the drawer and payee use the same bank but different branches the system of clearing the cheque for payment is still relatively simply carried out through the headquarters of the bank.

If the drawer and payee have accounts with different banks the cheques are cleared through the *Bankers' Clearing House* where representatives of all the clearing banks meet daily to exchange cheques they have received belonging to other banks.

At the Clearing House the representative from the headquarters of each clearing bank meets the representatives of the other banks and gives them cheques drawn on their banks and accepts cheques drawn on his bank. During this process an account is kept of the value of the cheques changing hands. The difference between the value of the cheques received and handed over shows how much each of the banks owes the other. This information is used daily to credit or debit the balances of the clearing banks which are kept at the Bank of England.

The cheque passes through a complete cycle, from the time the drawer writes out the cheque until the drawer's bank has released the payment to the payee takes just three days.

Postal orders

Postal orders provide a convenient way of safely sending funds from one person to another by a means that can easily be turned into cash. They are sold by the Post office in varying amounts of 5p up to a maximum of £20. The value of a postal order can be increased to specific amounts by adding postage stamps up to a maximum of 9p. For example, a £1.00 postal order can be increased to £1.03 by adding a 3p stamp. A charge (called 'poundage') is made on each order by the Post Office. They may be cashed at any post office or paid into a bank account.

The postal order is filled in by the drawer with the name of the payee and the post office of payment. It has a counterfoil which is retained in case it is necessary to claim a refund for non-delivery or loss.

Similar to a cheque, the postal order may be crossed for deposit into a bank account, and it also has a life of six months.

MAKE A NOTE OF IT

1 Why is careful budgeting as important to individuals as it is to the whole country?
2 How might someone organise their own personal budget?
3 Compare a bank budget account with a personal budget.
4 Give a brief description of the deposit account.

5 How does the function of a current account differ from that of a deposit account? How is a current account opened?

6 Which public corporation operates the National Girobank? How can a National Girobank account be opened?

7 Name the two basic forms of National Girobank accounts. Describe the methods of deposit and withdrawal for these accounts.

8 What is a cheque? List the five things written on a cheque by the drawer.

9 Who is the drawer, the payee and the drawee of a cheque?

10 How is a cheque endorsed? What is the purpose of doing this?

11 In what way will a bank examine a cheque before passing it for payment?

12 Explain the difference between an open cheque and a crossed cheque.

13 Use simple diagrams to help you to explain the special ways a cheque may be crossed to make it safer.

14 What is a dishonoured cheque? Why might a cheque be dishonoured?

15 What is the function of a bank statement of account?

16 Explain clearly how the bankers' clearing system works.

17 What is a postal order and why is it a convenient way to transfer money? How long is the life of a postal order and how can it be made safe?

7 Banking services

There are a wide range of services that are provided by the commercial banks, National Girobank, and increasingly by the building societies. These assist businesses and individual consumers by making it easier to make payments.

Standing order

Imagine that a company has purchased an item of equipment on hire purchase. This could mean that every month someone in the firm has

STANDING ORDER MANDATE			
TO _Lloyds_ Bank PLC			
ADDRESS _16, Waterend Rd, Kendal, Cumbria_			

	BANK	BRANCH TITLE (Not address)	SORTING CODE NUMBER
Please pay	Midland	Bridge Rd	40 – 15 – 20
	BENEFICIARY'S NAME		ACCOUNT NUMBER
for the credit of	Sally Carstairs		1 0 0 9 2 3 4 1
	AMOUNT IN FIGURES	AMOUNT IN WORDS	
†the sum of	£		

DATE AND AMOUNT OF FIRST PAYMENT			DUE DATE AND FREQUENCY
commencing	*NOW	£ 100	and thereafter every _month_
	DATE AND AMOUNT OF LAST PAYMENT		
*until	—	£ —	*until you receive further notice from me/us in writing
quoting the reference	—		and debit my/our account accordingly.

*Delete if not applicable
†if the amount of the periodic payments vary they should be incorporated in a schedule overleaf

THIS INSTRUCTION CANCELS ANY PREVIOUS ORDER IN FAVOUR OF THE BENEFICIARY NAMED ABOVE, UNDER THIS REFERENCE.

SPECIAL INSTRUCTIONS

ACCOUNT TO BE DEBITED	ACCOUNT NUMBER
current account	7 1 2 4 6 0 8 1

SIGNATURE(S) _J. C. Carstairs_   DATE _6.4.19X8_

NOTE: The Bank will not undertake to   (i) make any reference to Value Added Tax or other indeterminate element
      (ii) advise payer's address to beneficiary
      (iii) advise beneficiary of inability to pay
      (iv) request beneficiary's banker to advise beneficiary of receipt

Standing order form

to remember to write out a cheque and covering letter, and address an envelope and post it to the hire-purchase company.

This is not only time-consuming and inconvenient, but there is the danger that the payment could be overlooked, perhaps damaging the firm's reputation for paying debts promptly. The bank standing order service solves this problem, for individuals or organisations, by making regular payments of a set sum from one bank account to another on behalf of the customer.

This service is available to current account holders and it saves the bank customer the need to remember, and to post off, payments. The service is only useful if the amount to be transferred does not change.

Direct debit

This is a variation of the standing order service. Instead of instructing the bank to make regular payments on their behalf, customers fill in and sign a form which gives permission for a payee to withdraw regular amounts from their account. The amount may be varied by the payee and notified to the account holder at some later time. This service is suitable for repayments of forms of credit where the repayment amount may vary due to changes in interest rates.

The standing order and the direct debit have dual roles in respect of business application. They not only make it easy for the business to make regular payments, but they also enable businesses to receive regular payments from their customers.

Bank giro

The bank giro is a method of transfer (credit transfer) of funds directly into the account of someone else, who may hold his account at another branch or even a different bank to the person making the payment. The person making the payment does not have to hold a bank account as in-payment can be made with cash or cheque. There are two basic methods of credit transfer that are generally used, the single transfer and the multiple transfer.

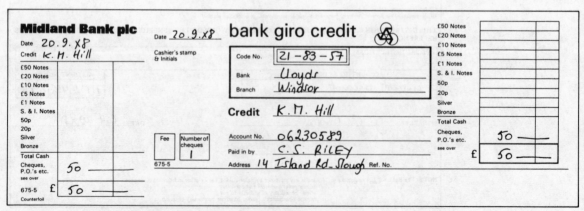

Single transfer bank giro form

SINGLE TRANSFER	A bank giro form similar to that on page 76 is filled in to make a single payment directly to a stated bank account. Most of the state-owned domestic suppliers such as gas, electricity and water boards help their customers to use the system by printing bank giro credit forms at the bottom of their bills.
MULTIPLE TRANSFER	Using this method the payee only writes out a single cheque to pay several bills or a number of different people.

Using this method the payee only writes out a single cheque to pay several bills or a number of different people.

A list or schedule is passed to the bank showing details of a number of different accounts to be credited by direct transfer. The account holder writes out a single cheque in favour of the bank itself and the bank credits each payee, saving the account holder the necessity of writing out many cheques.

The system can be used to pay the bills of several traders but it is particularly useful in paying the wages of many employees.

Bank cards

It is sometimes said that we have become a largely 'cashless' society. This not only refers to the cheque and giro systems of money transfer already examined, but also to the function of some of the bank cards that are now being used, often reducing the need for cash transactions. Three of the main bank cards are now examined, but it should be remembered that there are card systems apart from those issued by the banks (e.g. retailers' charge cards, telephone credit card and others discussed in other chapters) which also contribute to the conception of a 'cashless' society.

CHEQUE CARD

Cheque cards are issued by banks to reliable, well-established customers. The card is used to guarantee payment of a cheque up to a maximum amount which is stated on the card. The card shows an identification number and a specimen signature, and payment of a cheque cannot be stopped if a cheque card has been used to guarantee it.

CREDIT CARD

Credit cards are a financial service run by the commercial banks. The card shows the identification number and specimen signature of the rightful owner who can use it for purchasing without using cash or cheque.

The card holder signs for goods or services and presents the card to the trader. The bank pays the trader and the customer later pays the money to the bank. The system is used by account holders for shopping, travel, garages, restaurants, etc.

- A monthly statement is sent to the account holder.
- No interest is charged if the account is paid immediately.
- Interest is charged on balances left outstanding.

Note: Companies other than banks issue credit cards, e.g. American Express and Diners Club. Barclaycard is an example where a credit card and a cheque card are combined in a single bank card.

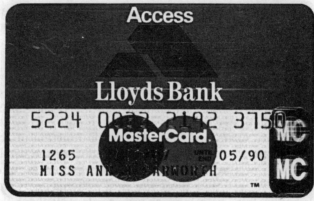

CASH DISPENSER CARD

The bank customer is issued with a card and a secret personal identity number (PIN) known only to them and the bank. The cash dispenser card also has its own separate identity code incorporated into it.

A cash dispensing machine is set into the wall outside the bank and is connected to the bank computer. The card holder feeds his card into the machine and 'keys in' the PIN.

If the card data and the keyed in PIN match up with the record the bank computer holds, the dispenser issues the money requested up to a daily individual limit. The customer's account is immediately automatically debited with the amount withdrawn.

The machine operates twenty-four hours a day and it will also provide information such as current account balance.

ELECTRONIC FUNDS TRANSFER

One of the most recent money transfer systems to be developed is the movement towards a national electronic payments system. This refers to a system known as EFT (Electronic Funds Transfer) and EPOS (Electronic Point of Sale). These are computer-controlled payment systems.

While a checkout till operator in a shop is totalling up the customer's purchases using a computer (EPOS) the customer inserts a bank card into a machine linked to their bank, building society, or credit card company. Their PIN (personal identification number), is keyed in and verified by the terminal computer. The computer will authorise the payment immediately (EFT) and debit the customer's account if sufficient funds are available; the transaction may be rejected if there are not enough funds available.

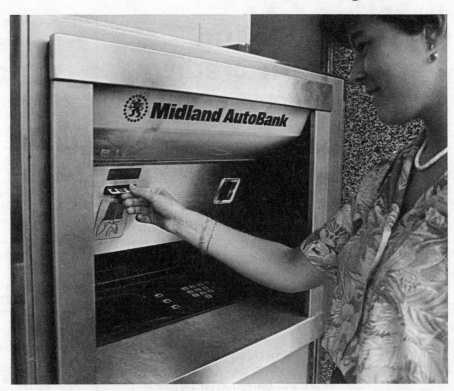

Borrowing from a bank

There are three main methods of borrowing from a bank, overdraft, loan and bridging loan. Banks often require some form of security (called 'collateral') to safeguard against possible non-repayment of the amount loaned. Collateral might take the form of property deeds, stocks and shares, or other items of value that can be sold by the bank in the event of default by the borrower.

The bank manager takes the following information into account before agreeing to allow a customer to borrow from the bank:

- income of the individual or organisation
- debts and commitments of the borrower
- assets owned by the borrower
- past banking record of the borrower.

Note: Interest is the 'price' of borrowing money or the 'reward' for leaving money in the bank.

OVERDRAFT

With permission of the bank the current account holder may write out cheques for more money than there is in the account. When this happens the account is said to be overdrawn or 'in the red'. The actual amount the account is overdrawn by is known as the *overdraft*.

Irrespective of what overdraft facility is granted, the customer is only charged interest (calculated daily) on the actual amount overdrawn. Any deposits made to the account while it is overdrawn have the effect of reducing the overdraft, while any cheques paid out increase it.

Buying on credit

Most people need to buy on credit at some time in their life, particularly when purchasing consumer durables which become increasingly important once we set up a home of our own.

There are times when we need to purchase something essential, such as a cooker, which is beyond our immediate means. But advertisements frequently tell us that 'credit facilities are available'.

If you want to purchase a modern cooker, you may well have to pay £400. Often you will be required to pay a deposit calculated as a percentage of the cash price. The balance would be required to be repaid in regular instalments over a period of time.

If you are under 18 years of age you will be unable to undertake a formal purchase on credit due to a law that prevents this. However, your parents could act as guarantor on a credit purchase made by you.

(a) What does the term 'credit' mean?

(b) How does a parent acting as 'guarantor' make it possible for someone under 18 years of age to enter into a credit agreement?

(c) What is meant by the 'cash price' in relation to a credit purchase?

(d) Why do 'consumer durables' become increasingly important once we set up a home of our own?

(e) Explain how the bank standing order service assists someone making repayments against a credit agreement

(f) Complete the following table of data related to purchase of a cooker on credit.

Cash price	£400.
Minus 10% deposit	?
Plus interest	120.
Balance	?
12 payments of	?

(g) How does a credit sale agreement differ from a hire purchase agreement?

The overdraft tends to be used for temporary or short-term borrowing when the borrower is not sure exactly how much is needed, or for how long it is needed.

LOAN

In the case of a bank loan, the total amount requested is transferred to the customer's account and, therefore, the customer is required to pay interest on the total amount borrowed, even if all the money is not used immediately.

The loan is repaid in regular fixed amounts, including interest, over a specific period of time agreed between the bank and the customer.

The bank loan tends to be used for a particular purpose when the amount required and length of repayment time is known, because the annual rate of interest on a loan is likely to be less than that of an overdraft.

BRIDGING LOAN

A bridging loan is provided by a bank as a temporary measure for a very short period (a few days or weeks) until other expected funds become available.

Miscellaneous bank services

NIGHT SAFE

This facility is provided by banks to enable customers to deposit money when the bank is closed. Cash for depositing is placed in a special cash wallet together with a credit or paying-in slip. The wallet is dropped into the bank through a trap in the wall, and the amount enclosed is credited to the customer's account on the morning of the next bank working day. This service is particularly used by traders wishing to make deposits at the end of a day's trading.

SAFE DEPOSIT BOX

This is a secure box kept in the bank's vault for the customers for the safe-keeping of valuables, important documents, etc.

TRAVELLER'S CHEQUES

These are special cheques charged against a bank and, therefore, guaranteed by the bank. This makes them acceptable throughout the world and useful to the business person or the individual when travelling. They can be purchased at the local bank for use abroad to obtain foreign currency. The cheques are 'safe' because if they are lost or stolen abroad they can immediately be cancelled and the bank will replace them. A further safeguard requires those encashing the cheques to sign in front of those cashing them, having first produced proof of identity (e.g. passport).

BILL OF EXCHANGE

A method of payment whereby the seller draws up a document and the buyer signs it (the opposite of the normal cheque transaction) agreeing to pay at some future date. The bill of exchange can be kept until payment is made, sold to someone else at a discount (*discounted*), or used as collateral against a loan (*negotiated*). These bills are particularly evident in international trade where exporters use them to guarantee payment for goods prior to despatch.

BANK DRAFT

This is a cheque drawn on a bank instead of a person's account. A bank draft is guaranteed by the bank (which makes it as good as cash) because the customer pays the value of the draft in advance.

Banks also render a wide variety of services too numerous to deal with fully here, these include:

- investment advice
- wills and trustee advice
- sale of foreign currency
- taxation guidance

MAKE A NOTE OF IT

1 Compare the standing order and direct debit services.
2 Give a description of the bank giro service.
3 Briefly say why it is sometimes said that we have become a largely 'cashless' society.
4 Clearly explain the difference between a cheque card and a credit card.
5 What is the purpose of a cash dispenser card? What safeguards are there to prevent dishonest use of this service?
6 Explain the difference between a bank loan and a bank overdraft.
7 What factors does a bank manager take into account before agreeing to allow a customer to borrow from the bank?
8 How does a bridging loan differ from other forms of bank loan?
9 Why is the bank night safe service of particular use to retail traders?
10 What is the purpose of traveller's cheques? What makes them readily acceptable as well as 'safe'?
11 Why are bills of exchange particularly evident in international trade? Explain the difference between discounting and negotiating a bill of exchange.
12 Why would a bank draft be more acceptable than a cheque for making a large payment?

8 Business finance

Balance sheet

The primary aim of a business is to make a profit for its owners or shareholders. How successful the business is in achieving this aim depends upon how efficiently the capital or assets (things owned) are employed. It is possible to get an idea of how 'healthy' a firm is by examining the financial facts and figures which show how efficiently the assets are being used. A balance sheet provides a basis for understanding the financial position of a firm.

Balance Sheet **Daly Designs plc** as at 31 December 19––			
Liabilities	£	*Assets*	£
Capital owned	100 000	*Fixed assets*	
Long-term liabilities		Land & Buildings	80 000
Mortgage	44 000	Equipment/Fittings	20 000
		Vehicles	10 000
Current liabilities		*Current assets*	
Tax to be paid	2 400	Stock*	32 000
Bank overdraft	5 600	Debtors	12 000
Creditors	8 000	Bank balance	5 400
		Cash float	600
	£160 000		£160 000
		*at cost price	

A firm's balance sheet shows where the capital used in a business has come from, and what it has been spent on. It shows the financial position of the company at any particular moment in time. It is basically two lists, one showing all sorts of property the company owns (*assets*) and one which shows who the company is responsible to for various sums of money (*liabilities*). The assets are placed in order of 'liquidity', the most liquid (easiest or quickest turns into cash) being at the bottom. From the lists we can classify the capital used by the firm in various ways.

Cash flow

The flow of money in and out of a business is called *cash flow*. It is the difference between the receipts from sales and the amount spent on expenses such as raw materials, wages, interest paid on loans, dividends

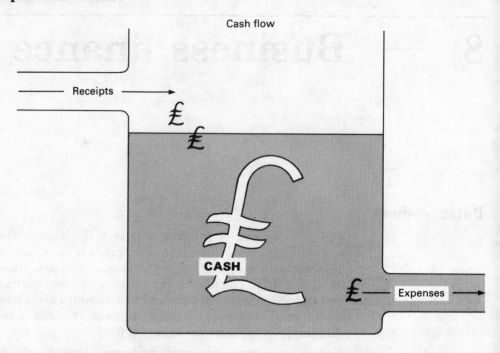

paid to shareholders, etc. A trading surplus adds to the reserves whereas a deficit reduces reserves.

From the diagram it will be obvious that if income from sales is equal to expenditure the firm will not have a cash flow problem. Where expenses exceed income the business may have to obtain additional capital in order to continue operating and avoid bankruptcy.

To achieve even cash flow is no simple matter. It is important to recognise that payments for goods or services will often not be received until some time after supply. This will mean that the business must budget with this possibility in mind. If the company budgeting is unsound the firm will have to request extended credit from its own suppliers, seek financial support from a bank or some other financial institution, or obtain further capital from another source.

Capital

SOURCE OF CAPITAL

Capital is money, or the assets bought with money, used to run the business. There are three main sources of capital used in a business.

1 *Share capital* (equity) – money subscribed to the company by shareholders in return for a share of the company's profits ('dividend'). Share capital is not repayable.
2 *Loan capital* (loan, debt or debenture) – usually a long-term loan which must be repaid at some time.
3 *Reserves* (retained earnings, undistributed profits, reinvestment) – percentage of gross profits ploughed back into business.

CATEGORIES OF CAPITAL

Capital can be usefully divided into groups and used in calculations as a means of analysis, and further interpretation of the balance sheet.

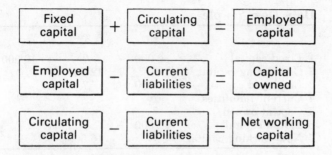

Fixed capital/assets

Durable (long-term) assets of a business which are used over a long period of time and are tied up in permanent use. Examples: land, buildings, machinery, furniture, vehicles, etc.

Circulating capital/current assets (working capital)

Capital which is continually changing in quantity, total value or nature. Examples: stocks, cash, bank balance, and the amount of money owed to a firm by its customers (debtors).

Employed capital

This is obtained by adding together the fixed and current assets of the firm. In other words, it is the total of all the assets being used by the business.

Current liabilities

Debts which will have to be repaid in the near future. Examples: bank overdraft, debts owed to suppliers (creditors), taxes payable to the government, etc.

Capital owned

Net value of the assets owned by a business. In other words, it is employed capital minus current liabilities.

Liquid capital

That part of the current assets which are cash or are easily changeable into cash without delay, for example, bank balance, cash in tills and debts owed by others (debtors). It is important because it is used to pay creditors immediately and, therefore, should always be above the current liabilities figure.

Net working capital

Current assets minus the current liabilities. Net working capital is particularly important because it takes into account the possibility of all the creditors to the business calling for payment. Therefore, it is important for a business to have sufficient working capital to exist as far as possible without borrowing from a bank.

Daly Designs plc

	£		£		£	£	£
1 Fixed capital	80 000	+	?	+	10 000		= 110 000
2 Circulating capital	?	+	12 000	+	?	+600	= ?
3 Employed capital	110 000	+	?				= ?
4 Current liabilities	?		?		?		= 16 000
5 Capital owned	?	−	?				= 144 000
6 Liquid capital	12 000	+	?	+	?		= 18 000
7 Net working capital	?	−	16 000				= ?

Refer to the balance sheet on p. 83 and complete the above analysis of the trading figures of Daly Designs plc

Turnover

This refers to the gross income or sales of an organisation over the previous year. Turnover can indicate how 'active' the firm has been in a given period. Generally speaking, the greater the turnover the more business the firm is doing, although this is not always the case.

NET TURNOVER

This is calculated by taking the total sales of the business minus the value of goods returned or credit notes issued.

RATE OF TURNOVER/RATE OF STOCK TURN

Rate of turnover is the number of times the average stock of a business has been sold in the year. There are two methods of calculating the rate of stock turnover depending whether the stock is looked at in terms of cost price or selling price.

$$(1)\ \text{Rate of turnover} = \frac{\text{Cost of stock sold}}{\text{Average stock at cost price}}$$

$$(2)\ \text{Rate of turnover} = \frac{\text{Net turnover}}{\text{Average stock at selling price}}$$

Average stock is worked out by taking the stock value at the beginning and at the end of the trading period, adding them, and dividing by two.

Example

		£
Jan 1	Stock	4 000
Dec 31	Stock	6 000 +
		£10 000

$$\text{Average stock} \quad \frac{£10\,000}{2} = £5\,000$$

Application Daly Designs plc has a net turnover of £50 000 and average stock at cost price is £5 000

$$\frac{50\,000}{5\,000} = 10 = \text{Rate of stock turnover}$$

IMPORTANCE OF RATE OF TURNOVER

Rate of turnover is important because it indicates how 'busy' the firm is. The figure can be used to make comparisons with previous years of trading or with the rate of other firms engaged in the same type of business.

COMPARISONS OF RATES OF TURNOVER

- A low rate of turnover is associated with sellers of highly valued goods or consumer durables.

Example

	Normal rate of turnover
Jewellers	3
Electrical shops	6
Furniture shops	6
Confectioners	12

- A high rate of turnover is associated with businesses selling perishable goods.

Example

	Normal rate of turnover
Butchers	78
Dairies	67
Greengrocers	53
Bakers	42

- An increasing rate of turnover indicates that the firm is doing more business in real terms, assuming all other things remain unchanged. It is selling more products, so profits should also be increasing.

Profits

Profit is the reward the business person receives for taking the risk involved in business and for being able to combine all the factors required to produce and sell goods or services.

The profitability of a business can be looked at from the point of view of gross profit or net profit.

GROSS PROFIT

The gross profit of a firm is the net sales minus the cost of the goods sold. Gross profit can be expressed as a percentage of the cost or selling price.

Example

	£
Selling price	1.00
Cost price	0.75
Gross profit	0.25

Mark-up (on cost price) = $\dfrac{25}{75} \times 100 = 33\frac{1}{3}\%$

Profit margin (on selling price) = $\dfrac{25}{100} \times 100 = 25\%$

Gross profit takes no account of the overheads the business has to pay, for example, wages, advertising, heating, etc.

As a percentage figure gross profit can be used to compare with previous trading periods, and with the gross profit of other firms. The method for calculating the gross profit percentage is as follows:

$$\text{Gross profit percentage} = \frac{\text{Gross profit}}{\text{Turnover}} \times 100$$

Example

	£
Turnover	80 000
Cost of goods	60 000
Gross profit	£20 000

As a percentage $\dfrac{20\,000}{80\,000} \times 100 = 25\%$

Falling gross profit

Most businesses require a gross profit of between 20 per cent and 40 per cent to ensure they are covering their overheads (expenses) easily. Over the years, gross profit percentage should stay relatively stable. If it starts to drop there is cause for concern. If it drops too much the busi-

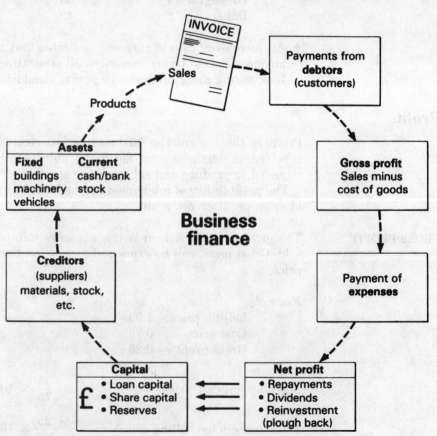

ness may fail to cover its overheads, and start to make an overall loss. There are a number of reasons for a falling gross profit percentage:

- staff stealing stock or takings
- stock being damaged or allowed to perish
- rising cost of stock not being passed on to customers
- too many staff employed (overmanning)
- rising expenses, for example, wages, heating, lighting, etc.

NET PROFITS
This is the residue of gross profit after allowing for expenses incurred in carrying on the business such as wages, rent, rates, advertising and bills of all kinds.

Net profit = Gross profit − Expenses

If expressed as a percentage, net profit can be used to make comparisons.

Method

$$\text{Net profit percentage} = \frac{\text{Net profit}}{\text{Turnover}} \times 100$$

Financial projections

DECIDING A PRICE
One of the tricky questions the entrepreneur has to answer is
- What should the selling price be?

Initially this looks a simple question to answer. It might be suggested that all the costs involved are added up, i.e. the entrepreneur adds on a bit extra as profit and makes sure that the eventual selling price remains competitive with other firms. Unfortunately the answer to the question is a lot more complex than it appears at first sight. For example, not all costs have the same characteristics. *Fixed costs* (e.g. rent and rates) are relatively constant figures up to the point where the business has to be expanded. On the other hand, the cost of the products sold by the business is dependent on the volume of sales and, therefore, these costs are *variable*.

For this reason it is not practicable to add up these two costs until a decision has been made about how much the firm plans to sell.

Example
A firm sells only one product and has only two relatively fixed costs, i.e. rent and rates. The variable costs are £20 per article.

Rent and rates	£10 000
Cost of producing 1000 units	20 000
Total costs	£30 000

The cost per article is £30 000 divided by 1000, which is £30 per article.
So long as the firm sells at a price above £30 per article it will always

be profitable. But what happens if all the 1000 items are not sold? If a selling price of £35 were decided and all 1000 items are sold, a profit of £5000 will be achieved (£35 × 1000 = £35 000 *less* £30 000 costs, profit = £5000). But if only 500 items were sold, the revenue drops to £17 500, which means that the business makes a £12 500 loss. This loss could be even greater if the 500 unsold items were perishable and could not be stored for later sale. Conversely, the greater number of articles produced the lower will be the cost per article, because the fixed costs are spread over a greater number of articles.

BREAKING EVEN

You can see from the above that there is a need to keep several factors in focus at the same time, e.g. costs, sales, volume, selling price and profit margin. The manner of doing this lies in a sales volume/price equation applied over a given period of time. This equation is shown in graphical form below.

In the graph the vertical axis shows the value of sales and costs in £000s and the horizontal axis shows units of sales volume in thousands. In this case the volume is 60 000 units.

The lower horizontal line represents the fixed costs. These do not change as the volume of sales increases. The graph shows an example of fixed costs of £3000. The next horizontal line shows the firm's profit objective (what it is aiming to achieve). In this case it is £2000. To obtain this profit sales of 60 000 units for a total of £8000 will have to be reached.

The top angled line represents the variable costs. These costs vary directly with output and include items such as raw materials; every extra unit produced adds to variable costs.

The lower angled line shows how much sales revenue is needed to cover fixed costs and variable costs (to *break-even*). In this hypothetical case it is necessary to sell 33 000 units to break-even.

From this illustration it can be seen that 'break even' is the point where income from sales equals costs. In other words, it is the point

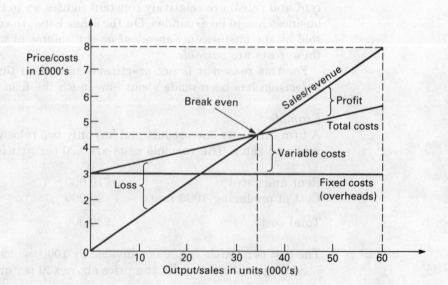

which sales must exceed in order for a profit to be achieved. Conversely, if sales do not reach break-even point the business will make a loss.

Return on capital invested

This figure is the most important to the businessman because it shows how much profit has been made as a percentage of the capital originally put into the business. The return on investment must be sufficient to make it worthwhile for the owners of the business to face the risks of business. If the return on the investment is not sufficient the owner(s) may be tempted to place their money in other less risky forms of investment.

$$\text{Return on capital invested} = \frac{\text{Net profit}}{\text{Capital at start of year}} \times 100$$

MAKE A NOTE OF IT

1 What is the main aim of a business?
2 What is the purpose of a balance sheet? What kind of information is contained in a balance sheet?
3 Explain the main difference between assets and liabilities.
4 What steps must a firm take in order to avoid creating a cash flow problem?
5 What is business capital and from where is it obtained?
6 Briefly describe each of the categories that capital can be divided into. Why is it useful to categorise capital in this way?
7 Why is it important that liquid capital should not fall below current liabilities?
8 A firm has fixed capital of £60 000, circulating capital of £6 000 and £7 000 current liabilities. What is its capital owned and its net working capital?
9 Define turnover. Explain the difference between gross turnover and net turnover.
10 What is 'rate of turnover' and why is this important to a firm?
11 The following figures relate to Akela Ltd:

Jan 1   Stock   £ 6 000
Dec 31   Stock   £ 9 000
Net turnover   £60 000

   Calculate the rate of stock turnover and estimate whether the rate would be good for a butcher's shop. Give reasons for your answers.
12 Explain the relevance of 'high', 'low', and 'increasing' rates of turnover to the businessperson.
13 Define profit and explain the difference between gross profit and net profit.
14 Give three examples of 'overheads'.
15 State at least four reasons that might account for a falling gross profit.
16 What do you understand by the term 'breaking even'?
17 Why is the 'return on capital invested' probably the most important figure to the owners of a business?

9 The Stock Exchange

Functions and control

When a company invites the public to invest in it the managers then put the money invested to permanent use. They will buy the buildings, machinery, stock and other assets that the business needs to operate. The money cannot be returned to the investor because it has been used. The only way that the shareholders can get their money back is by selling their shares to someone else. The Stock Exchange provides a market place where they can do this.

The Stock Exchange is a market place for the buyers and sellers of all kinds of existing securities. It is a 'free' market, that is, one where the prices of securities are allowed to fluctuate in response to supply and demand. The market price of shares is particularly influenced by the past performance and profitability of a company. General market trends can provide an indicator or barometer of the future outlook for industry and the economy as a whole.

The fact that the Stock Exchange enables people to dispose quickly of any listed shares they hold is particularly useful for individuals but also for institutional investors (those who collect and invest the savings of many others) such as insurance companies, pension and union funds and investment and unit trusts. These organisations need to obtain a good return on the capital invested for their members, but at the same time the securities must be easily turned into cash.

The Stock Exchange is often referred to as if there were only one exchange, the London exchange. However, there are in fact a number of other Stock Exchange trading floors in important provincial centres. They all work closely together following the same rules and standards. The stock market business is worldwide, and there are exchanges situated in many other countries.

The Stock Exchange is controlled by The Stock Exchange Council which is elected by the members of the Stock Exchange. The Council has the following functions:

- it controls the admission of new Members;
- it disciplines Members who are guilty of misconduct;
- it formulates the Stock Exchange rules;
- it settles disputes between Members;
- it provides settlement and information services to Members.

New shares

Although new issues of shares are made outside the Stock Exchange on the part of the capital market known as the 'new issue market', application is usually made for the shares of public companies to be listed (quoted) on the Exchange. This encourages investors to buy a new issue because they know that the shares can easily be resold. New shares are sold by one of the following methods.

OFFER FOR SALE

Issuing houses acting as agents on behalf of the company will sell the shares direct to the general public. This may be done by publishing a prospectus giving details of the company and its aims. If all the shares offered are not taken up by the general public, the issuing house will guarantee to buy all shares that are left and then dispose of them as best as they can. This ensures that the company raises the full amount of capital it requires.

PLACING

All the shares are 'placed' in blocks with large buyers such as institutional investors, for example, pension or union funds.

RIGHTS ISSUE

These are shares offered only to existing shareholders of the company at lower than current market prices and in proportion to their shareholding. This method is used to raise additional capital for a firm.

Membership

Only Member Firms of the Stock Exchange are allowed to take part in dealing on the Exchange floor and outsiders must carry out their buying and selling through them. The Member Firms are called Broker/Dealers (Brokers) and some of these specialise as what are known as Market Makers. These Member Firms include many organisations from outside the Stock Exchange such as banks and other financial organisations from the UK and overseas.

BROKER/DEALERS (BROKERS)

These are Stock Exchange Member Firms which buy or sell shares as agents for public investors, or as principals for their own account with other Member Firms or outside investors, or they can act in a dual capacity as both agent and principal. Some Broker/Dealers specialise as Market Makers.

MARKET MAKERS

Market Makers can operate on the Stock Exchange floor, off-floor, or both on and off floor. They make a market in shares by being prepared to buy or sell shares at all times to and from Broker/Dealers. They may deal direct with the Broker/Dealers on the Exchange floor, or indirect through the Stock Exchange Automated Quotation System (SEAQ-described later). They are required to maintain a two-way price on SEAQ, whereas Broker/Dealers are not permitted to operate in this way.

Bargains are often carried out by private negotiation and sealed by verbal agreement. These agreements are honoured thus upholding the principle of the Stock Exchange motto 'Dictum Meum Pactum' – My Word is My Bond.

Market Makers tend to specialise in a particular range of securities. For example, there are specialists in shares related to shipping, aircraft, oils, property, mining and industry.

The Stock Exchange operates a computer system (SEAQ) which details competing Market Makers' quotes to Broker/Dealers by VDUs. A Market Maker will quote a double (two-way) price verbally and also on SEAQ, for example, 420 to 428 – indicating that he is willing to buy a certain share at 420p and sell at 428p. A Broker/Dealer interested in buying or selling the shares in question can compare the quotes of all the Market Makers via SEAQ and choose the 'best' deal for themselves or their clients.

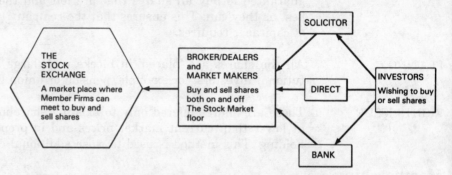

CLERKS

The staff of Broker/Dealers consists of two groups: those who are engaged in work outside the Stock Exchange, and those who are involved with work inside the Exchange. The latter group can be subdivided into 'authorised' and 'unauthorised' clerks.

- *Authorised clerks* have the authority to act on behalf of their principals and to enter into transactions on their behalf.
- *Unauthorised clerks* are permitted to enter the House but do not have the authority to enter into transactions.

Share transfer procedure

THE BROKER

It is through the broker that the outside investor contacts the central market to buy or sell shares. The broker may decide to carry out the deal with the client on their own account, or they may deal with a market maker.

CONTRACT NOTE

The contract note is a document which provides evidence that the broker has carried out his client's instructions. It tells the client:

- the number of shares bought or sold;
- the unit price
- the commission to be paid by the client;
- government taxes – contract stamp, VAT and transfer duty;
- total payment due to the broker;
- settlement date.

Stock Exchange dealing room – by permission of the Stock Photobank

BOUGHT	BY ORDER OF	BARGAIN NUMBER 23(W)	BARGAIN DATE & TAX PT 24th Nov. 19x2

A. N. BROKER & CO
99 THROGMORTON STREET – LONDON EC2X ABC
LONDON – CHICAGO – SYDNEY – HONG KONG

TELEPHONE:	TELEX:	V.A.T. REGISTRATION
01–588 2355 (20 lines)	44259	NUMBER: 242 0024

Miss A. BUYER
38 High Street
ANYTOWN   AN6 5QT

A Public Company Ltd. £1 Ordinary Shares

PARTNERS

T. H. WOOD	S. G. CORK
A. B. JONES	S. H. THUMB
C. D. SMITH	A. K. WOOD
K. A. WIER	B. G. OAK
T. D. CHILD	R. N. SWEEPER

CONSULTANT
T. C. BOOTH

AMOUNT	PRICE	CONSIDERATION
500	£1.28	£640.00

1.65% on £640.00	TRANSFER STAMP	13.00	N
	CONTRACT STAMP	0.30	N
	COMMISSION	10.50	T
	V.A.T. 15%	1.58	

A. N. BROKER & CO.

CONTRACT
STAMP
£0.30

MEMBERS OF THE STOCK EXCHANGE

Subject to the rules and regulations including temporary regulations of The
Stock Exchange. For Capital Gains and V.A.T. purposes this contract note
should be retained. An asterisk means commission is shared with
yourselves a member of the staff or an agent

V.A.T. Symbols;   T = Taxable;   E = Exempt;   N = Outside the scope

E & O E	FOR SETTLEMENT	6TH December 19X2	TOTAL £	665.44

SETTLEMENT DATE The contract note shows a date on which the transaction is due for settlement and on that date the outstanding amount should be paid to the broker by the client.

If the buyer wishes to postpone payment until a later date, an additional fee called 'contango' has to be paid.

If the seller has contracted to sell some stock and finds it inconvenient to deliver at the settlement, a fee called 'backwardation' has to be paid to 'borrow' the stock from another dealer.

SHARE
CERTIFICATE

The broker sends the registrar of the company whose shares have been sold details of the new owner of the company's shares. The registrar records the details of the new owner and sends them a share certificate through the broker. The new owner of the shares will eventually receive dividends direct from the company whose shares are now held.

Types of security

'Security' is the collective name given to the wide range of investments with which the Stock Exchange is concerned. Securities fall into two categories, 'fixed interest' and 'equities'.

With fixed interest stocks the investor knows in advance the amount of interest he is due to receive. Usually, the rate of interest is truly 'fixed' and is stated prior to investment, in a few cases the stock may receive a 'variable rate' of interest, for example, in the case of index-linked stocks. Here the actual interest received can vary, but the amount payable is governed by a set formula, linked to some well-known index.

Equities are so called because they represent an equal share of the capital of the business, and an equal division of the profits. Nothing is 'fixed' in respect of equities – if the company does well, so does the shareholder, if the company does badly, the shareholder may receive no return on his investment.

GOVERNMENT STOCKS OR BONDS (GILT-EDGED SECURITIES)	Often referred to as 'gilts' these securities are used to raise money to finance government projects. They represent a very safe form of investment because they are backed by government resources. They are issued for a fixed period of time and receive a fixed rate of interest. If the rate of inflation exceeds the rate of interest the value of the stock is eroded.

GOVERNMENT STOCKS OR BONDS (GILT-EDGED SECURITIES)

Often referred to as 'gilts' these securities are used to raise money to finance government projects. They represent a very safe form of investment because they are backed by government resources. They are issued for a fixed period of time and receive a fixed rate of interest. If the rate of inflation exceeds the rate of interest the value of the stock is eroded.

LOCAL AUTHORITY BONDS

These are issued by local authorities and the money invested represents a loan to the authority. They are initially placed with institutions, but can be bought by the public through the Stock Exchange. They are a secure form of investment paying a fixed rate of interest and having a fixed date for repayment.

DEBENTURES

Debentures are in effect a loan to a company and are often referred to as 'stocks'. They receive a fixed rate of interest which must be paid even if the company does not make a profit. Debenture holders have no involvement in the management of the company.

Debentures may be secured against specific assets or by a general charge on all the assets of the company, and are backed by an agreement similar to a mortgage. They may be bought and sold on the Stock Exchange and are redeemable at a fixed date or before.

PREFERENCE SHARES

Ordinary preference shares

Preference shareholders have a priority call on the profits of the company after debenture holders. Preference shares pay a fixed rate of dividend, but only if sufficient profits are available to make a payment. Usually preference shares carry no voting rights.

Cumulative preference shares

If cumulative preference shareholders do not receive their full dividend in one year, the balance is carried forward and must be met from profits earned in subsequent years, and until these have been paid no payment can be made to ordinary shareholders.

Participating preference shares

Because of the relatively safe nature of preference shares, and the fact that they pay a fixed rate of dividend, the preference shareholder does not reap any additional reward when the company does well and makes good profits.

Sometimes companies will create participating preference shares in which preference shareholders can take dividends at a fixed rate and, if there is still any profit left after payment of other dividends, the participating preference shareholder may receive a further dividend additional to the fixed rate already paid.

ORDINARY SHARES (EQUITIES)

Ordinary shares or 'equities' represent a share in the ownership of a company. Each share is entitled to an equal proportion (dividend) of the company's profits. The amount of dividend to be paid is decided by the directors of the company and is dependent upon the profitability of the firm and, therefore, ordinary shares are somewhat speculative.

In return for accepting the speculative risk involved, the ordinary shareholder usually stands to receive a relatively high return on the investment. The shareholder may gain not only through his share of the company's profits, but also from an improvement in the current market price of the shares. In addition, the ordinary shareholder has some power (through voting rights) in the running of the company.

Ordinary shareholders are generally the last in line for distribution of profits, and, therefore, they are the most risky form of shareholding. However, they can give the highest rate of return when the company is successful.

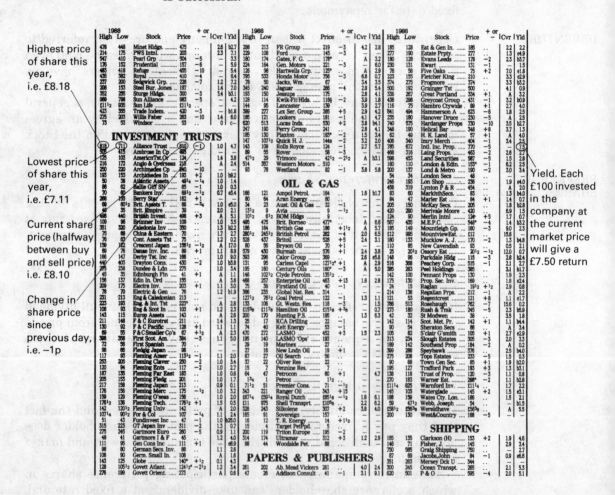

Highest price of share this year, i.e. £8.18

Lowest price of share this year, i.e. £7.11

Current share price (halfway between buy and sell price) i.e. £8.10

Change in share price since previous day, i.e. −1p

Yield. Each £100 invested in the company at the current market price will give a £7.50 return

Share prices

1 (a) Which three shares have the highest price shown?
(b) Which three shares have the highest yield?
2 Why is the yield figure important when deciding whether to buy a particular share?
3 Why do you think that there is such a wide variation in share prices?

The money paid for a share when it is first issued is used by the company and cannot be returned to the investor. However, ownership of ordinary shares can be bought or sold second-hand on the Stock Exchange. Ordinary shares with the highest status as investment are known as 'blue chips'.

UNIT TRUSTS

A method of minimising the risk of holding ordinary shares is for the investor to spread his investment between a variety of different holdings. Unit trusts also work on this basis.

Trust managers offer 'units' of the funds for sale direct to the public. The expert knowledge of the trust managers is used to invest the funds wisely in a wide range of company and government stocks to enable a profitable investment to be made with the risk of loss minimised.

AUTHORISED UNIT TRUSTS

	Init Chrge	Canc. Price	Bid Price	Offer + or Price -	Yield Gr's
Abbey Unit Tst Mngrs (1000)H					
80 Holdenhurst Rd, Bournemouth				0345 717373	
High Income					
American Income	6	44.99	45.46	48.36 +0.19	5.67
Gilts & Fixed Int	6	112.3	112.3xd	119.1 +0.2	8.40
High Inc Equity	6	116.6	119.2xd	126.8 +0.8	4.69
Worldwide Bond	6	191.9	191.9	203.4 +0.2	4.77
Capital Growth					
American Growth	6	153.5	155.6	165.5 +0.5	0.98
Asian Pacific	6	67.46	67.46	72.15 +0.37	1.50
Assets & Earnings	6	137.1	141.8	150.8 +0.6	1.21
Capital Reserve Acc	0	81.28	81.28	81.58 +0.1	3.68
Comdty & Energy	6	89.15	89.15xd	95.35 +0.5	0.00
European Capital	6	73.05	73.50	78.19 +0.27	0.96
General	6	158.6	161.6	171.9 +1.1	2.62
Japan	6	86.00	86.00	91.98 -1.12	0.00
Mastertrust	6	71.91	71.91xd	76.91 -0.82	2.12
UK Growth Acc	6	173.6	181.8	193.4 +0.5	1.18
UK Growth Dist	6	116.4	122.0	129.7 +0.3	1.77
US Emerging Cos	6	44.08	45.55	48.45	0.00
Income & Growth	6	260.1	265.5	282.4 +2.2	3.36
Ethical Growth	6	42.95	43.95	46.75 +0.19	2.67
Abtrust Management Ltd (1000)H					
10 Queens Terrace, Aberdeen AB9 1QJ				0224 633070	
30 Finsbury Circus, London, EC2M 7QQ				01-374 6801	
Dealing (Freephone)				0800 833580	
American	5¼	41.82	41.82	44.49 +0.03	2.02
Australian	5¼	22.41	22.62xd	24.07 +0.10	1.43
European	5¼	45.91	45.91	48.66 +0.15	—
Extra Income	5	38.01	38.01xd	40.35 +0.42	5.14
Fund Inv Tst	5	96.99	96.99	103.10 -0.20	1.00
Do Accum	5	146.90	146.90	156.10 -0.50	1.00
Gilt & Fixed Int	5¼	22.51	22.51xd	23.94	-9.97
Global Income	5¼	35.27	35.27xd	37.53 +0.05	5.15
Income & Growth	5¼	64.93	65.76xd	69.95 +0.53	4.29
Japan	5¼	157.20	157.20	167.20 -2.20	0.01
Nth Amer Inc (z)	5	26.18	26.18xd	27.79 +0.09	3.84
Special Situations	5¼	63.34	63.34xd	67.38 +0.54	1.30
UK Growth	5	31.58	31.58xd	33.52 +0.47	2.76
World Gwth	5	38.94	38.94	41.33 -0.05	1.16
Aegis Unit Tst Mngmt Ltd (1400)F					
94 Whiteladies Rd, Bristol, BS8 1QX				0272 237593	
CAMco Intl Recovery	5	46.47	47.96	50.49 -0.04	1.50
St Nicholas St Gth Inc	5	44.28	44.28	47.15 +0.24	4.58
St Nicholas St Gth Acc	5	44.96	44.96	47.88 +0.25	4.58
Blackstone Franks UK	5	43.62	44.50	47.35 +0.07	2.50
Blackstone Franks Int	5	45.93	47.06	50.07 +0.11	0.10

	Init Chrge	Canc. Price	Bid Price	Offer + or Price -	Yield Gr's
Asset Unit Trust Mngrs Ltd (0900)F					
Pl"n"tn Hse, Fenchurch St, London EC3				01-220 7231	
Growth Sept 23	5	101.96	101.96	108.33	1.61
Income Set 23	5	103.67	105.73	112.78	5.13
Baillie Gifford & Co Ltd (1430)H					
3 Glenfinlas St, Edinburgh				031-226 6066	
Japan Expt Sep 23	2	504.8	504.8	522.3	—
UK Exempt Oct 3	5	361.2	371.5	395.2	0.39
Mngd Expt Oct 3	5	98.19	99.36xd	105.7	2.88
BG Japan	5	210.3	210.3xd	223.7 -1.8	—
BG America	5	120.6	120.6xd	128.2 +0.6	0.60
BG Technology	5	186.0	186.0	197.8 +0.4	—
BG Energy	5	200.3	200.3	213.0 +1.2	1.64
BG Income Gwth	5	242.8	242.8xd	259.6 +1.7	5.47
BG Europe	5	101.1	101.1	107.5 +0.4	1.70
BG Conv & Gen	5	62.62	64.24	68.33 +0.16	7.81
BG British Gwth	5	38.74	38.74	41.21 +0.15	0.70
Bank of Ireland Fund Mgrs Ltd (1200)F					
36 Queen St, London, EC4R 1BN				01-236 4210	
Brit & O'seas	5	129.2	134.2	142.1 +2.00	1.71
Income Plus	5	65.66	70.94	75.07	3.23
Inv Trusts	5	72.14	78.88	83.48	1.24
Capital Gwth	5	63.55	68.01	71.97	3.35
W'wide Opps	5	68.54	73.01	77.26	2.59
Barclays Unicorn Ltd (1000)H					
Unicorn Hse, 252 Romford Rd, E7				01-534 5544	
Unicorn America	5¼	77.24	77.42	82.58 +0.11	2.00
Do Aust Acc	5¼	183.5	384.9	197.2 +1.0	2.03
Do Aust Inc	5¼	127.9	128.8	137.4 +0.6	2.03
Do Capital	5¼	78.95	78.95	84.21 +0.83	3.37
Do Euro Gwth Acc	5¼	66.75	67.17	71.65 +0.67	1.11
Do Euro Gwth Inc	5¼	65.20	65.61xd	69.98 +0.65	1.11
Do Exempt	5	58.92	59.17	63.11 +0.48	4.57
Do Extra Income	5¼	93.24	94.50	100.8 +0.97	4.97
Do Financial	5¼	65.45	66.69	71.14 +0.66	3.14
Do 500	5¼	343.0	351.0xd	374.4 +2.7	2.71
Do General	5¼	162.7	164.3xd	175.2 +1.4	3.45
Do Gilt & Fxd Int	3¼	52.90	53.18xd	54.82 +0.14	9.51
Do Growth Acc	5	198.9	202.6	216.1 +1.0	2.58
Do Income	5¼	396.2	401.3	428.0 +3.9	4.05
Do Intl Income	5¼	48.28	48.46	51.69 +0.18	4.29
Do Jpn & Gen Acc	5¼	208.5	209.8	223.8 -2.8	0.00
Do Jpn & Gen Inc	5¼	206.2	207.4	221.2 -2.8	0.00
Do Jpn Spec Sits	5¼	47.07	47.46	50.62 -0.77	0.00
Do Leisure (z)	5¼	101.4	103.2	110.1 +0.5	0.91
Do Recovery	5¼	273.3	277.6	296.1 +2.0	2.53
Do Smllr Cos Acc	5¼	37.52	38.87	41.46 +0.17	1.42
Do Smllr Cos Inc	5¼	36.96	38.29	40.84 +0.16	1.42
Do Special Sits	5¼	170.9	176.1	187.8 +1.3	1.93
Do Trustee	5¼	128.3	129.6	138.2 +1.1	3.61
Do Univ Tech Acc	5¼	53.03	53.68	57.26 +0.18	0.39
Do Univ Tech Inc	5¼	52.27	52.92	56.45 +0.18	0.39
Do Worldwide	5¼	128.7	129.6	138.2	1.20
B'tst Inv Fd Acc	2	399.9	399.9	418.7 +4.9	3.60
B'tst Inv Fd Inc	2	246.6	246.6	258.2 +3.0	3.60

Unit trust prices from the Financial Times

Speculation

There is an important distinction between an investor and a speculator. An investor buys shares in order to receive a share of the company's profits (a dividend). A speculator on the other hand hopes to make a quick profit by anticipating changes in share prices. There are three types of speculator and they are known by the colourful names of 'bulls', 'bears', and 'stags'.

- *Bulls* – buy or hold shares anticipating a price rise and make a profit by selling at a higher price. In a 'bullish' market prices are generally rising.
- *Bears* – sell shares anticipating a fall in market prices, perhaps buying them back later at a lower price, for example, if they need to fulfil a contract to supply the shares. In a 'bearish' market prices are generally falling.
- *Stags* – buy new issues of shares expecting to resell them at a profit when second-hand dealing starts on the Stock Exchange.

It should be noted that when referring to bulls, bears and stags, we are talking about the way someone is behaving, and not three different people. An individual may be a bull at one time or bear at another. The terms may be used to describe someone even if he is not a member of the Stock Exchange.

Return on shares

A dividend is a payment from a company's profits to its shareholders. It is the 'reward' paid to the investor. The dividend is usually calculated as a percentage of the nominal, or par value of the share, for example, as a percentage of the issue price or the price the share was originally sold for (normally 25p or £1). If the dividend is declared to be 9p, then investors will receive 9p for each share they hold e.g. in the case of shares with a par value of £1 = 9%.

However, the owner of the shares may well have bought them at a price above (or below) their par value. In this case the investor is interested in the 'real' return of his investment, taking into account the current market price. This is called the yield.

The yield on a share is calculated as follows:

$$\frac{\text{Dividend}}{\text{Market value}} = \text{yield}$$

The 'market value' refers to the price paid for a share on The Stock Exchange. If a shareholder had paid £2 for a share with a par value of £1 and a dividend of 9p is declared, the yield would be 4.5%.

$$\frac{9p}{£2} = 4.5\% \text{ yield}$$

Factors affecting share prices

Obviously, if speculators could accurately predict share price movement they could guarantee that they would make a fortune several times in one week. However, investment in shares remains speculative because there are numerous factors that influence rise or fall in share prices.

Some of these factors can be summarised as follows:

- supply and demand for the shares
- recent performance of the company: good or poor profits
- political changes affecting the company, for example, change of government
- changes in interest rates or taxation
- popularity or otherwise of the company's products
- changes in market trends
- take-over or merger being considered
- general national prosperity
- industrial disputes, or settlements.

Importance of the Stock Exchange

Many large businesses need to appeal to the public for the vast sums of money they require to finance the purchase of new premises, new machinery, or to expand the business. People are not willing to invest money to finance this sort of development unless they can be sure that they can get the money back again. But, as we have observed earlier in this chapter, the business uses the money invested with it and it cannot be returned.

When an investor needs his money back, he does not need to go to the company with whom it was originally invested. Instead, the investor sells his shares to some other investor through the Stock Exchange. In other words, although the Stock Exchange does not directly raise new capital for business, it encourages people to invest in companies because it provides facilities for the sale of second-hand securities.

The government also needs to borrow money from the public to help finance the many industries and services it provides through central or local government. These require a continuous supply of new capital to fund new equipment and development research. Local and central government and the nationalised industries rely on the Stock Exchange to help raise the capital they need.

All stock exchanges have an international importance because they provide a market for the shares of foreign countries. For example, more than half of the value of the shares quoted on the London Stock Exchange is made up of the shares of overseas countries.

> **MAKE A NOTE OF IT**

1 List the functions of the Stock Exchange.
2 What is the function of the Stock Exchange Council?
3 Why is it usual for public companies to apply for new issues of their shares to be 'quoted' on the Stock Exchange?
4 Briefly describe the main methods involved in selling new shares.
5 What is the function of a stockbroker? How do they ensure that they obtain the best price for their clients?
6 'All Market Makers are broker/dealers, but not all broker/dealers are Market Makers'. Explain this statement.

7 Briefly explain the difference between an 'authorised' and an 'unauthorised' clerk.

8 What are market makers?

9 Describe the process of share transfer.

10 Explain the difference between fixed interest securities and equities.

11 What are gilt-edged securities? Give one example.

12 Why is the return on debentures invariably poorer than the return on equities?

13 How do preference shares differ from ordinary shares?

14 'Ordinary shares are the most risky form of investment, but they can also be the most rewarding.' Discuss this statement.

15 In what way do unit trusts spread the risks involved in investment?

16 Clearly describe the activities of stock market speculators including use of the terms 'bulls', 'bears' and 'stags'.

17 What is meant by the 'par value' of a share?

18 Explain the difference between the dividend and the yield of a share.

19 How is share yield calculated?

20 List at least six factors that influence the market value of shares.

10 Insurance

Importance of insurance

All individuals and organisations face a wide variety of risks, but only some of them actually suffer a loss during the course of a year. To offset the possible effect of a loss, all those at risk can contribute a small sum of money (called a 'premium') to a fund operated by an insurance company. These many small sums contribute to form a large pool of money. Managed efficiently the fund will be sufficient to compensate ('indemnify') those who suffer a loss.

The result of co-operating with others in this way is that risks are 'spread' or 'shared' between the many people and organisations that have contributed to the insurance pool. Hence, insurance is sometimes said to be the 'pooling of risks'.

Insurance is vital to individuals, all forms of business and to the economy. If as individuals we had to face all the risks of life ourselves there are many things that we would not do, and we would hesitate at times even to leave our homes. Similarly, many businesses would not be formed if those doing so had to face all the risks of enterprise themselves. Insurance relieves business people from some of the risks they face, and they are, therefore, encouraged to take part in enterprises which result in increased economic activity.

Much of the money collected by insurance companies in premiums is invested in industry and councils, thus giving resources and encouragement to economic activity as well as to technological developments.

British insurance is the country's largest single source of 'invisible earnings' (see Chapter 14). British insurance companies insure the industries, buildings, ships, etc. of other countries. In addition, insurance companies of other countries seek to be insured by British insurance companies, thus spreading the risk of cover they have offered in their own countries. This process is known as 'reinsurance', that is, accepting an insurance risk and then transferring it (or part of it), elsewhere.

When Britain receives payment from other countries for insurance, the effect is of bringing foreign money into the country, thereby assisting our balance of payment figures.

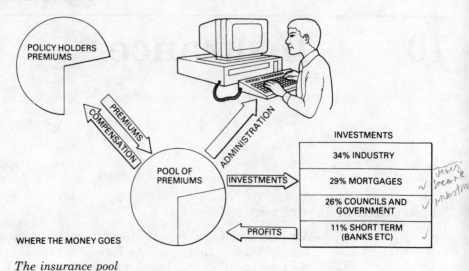

POLICY HOLDERS PREMIUMS

PREMIUMS

COMPENSATION

POOL OF PREMIUMS

ADMINISTRATION

INVESTMENTS

PROFITS

WHERE THE MONEY GOES

INVESTMENTS

| 34% INDUSTRY |
| 29% MORTGAGES |
| 26% COUNCILS AND GOVERNMENT |
| 11% SHORT TERM (BANKS ETC) |

The insurance pool

Uninsurable risks

The success of insurance is based on statistical analysis. Underwriters have to judge correctly how much they should charge to cover a particular risk if they are to have sufficient money in the pool to pay out against claims, and also meet running costs. From statistical records of claims underwriters can calculate the probability of a loss occurring, and fix the appropriate premium. Generally, insurance companies are willing to consider giving cover on all types of risks where they can calculate the probability of loss involved. But it is not possible to insure against happenings that are inevitable. The following are typical examples of uninsurable risks:

- When the probability of loss is inevitable (an exception is life assurance).
- Where there is insufficient past experience to assess the premium.

Not all risks can be insured

- If the proposer does not have insurable interest.
- Against fair wear and tear such as rust and corrosion.
- That a business enterprise will be successful.

Principles of insurance

For insurance to work effectively and fairly all those involved are expected to honour *four* legal principles.

1 *Insurable interest*
    (a) Only the person who stands to suffer financial loss or liability can insure against a particular risk.
    (b) To have insurable interest the insured must own, or be responsible for, the article to be insured.
2 *Utmost good faith*
    (a) This insurance principle requires the parties to an insurance contract to be truthful.
        - The insured must disclose all relevant facts to the insurer.
        - The insurers must honour all the promises in their policy.
    (b) Intentional withholding of information invalidates the contract.
3 *Indemnity*
    (a) This is the insurance principle by which a policyholder is compensated for the loss incurred.
    (b) The insured should not profit if the event insured takes place.
    (c) If the insured overinsures an item, in the event of a loss he will only be compensated for the true value.
    (d) If a loss occurs where the item is underinsured, the policyholder will only receive a proportion of the loss.
        e.g.   House value   £50 000
                Insured for   £40 000
                Damage by fire £10 000 (i.e. one-fifth)
                Compensation
                (one-fifth)   £8 000
    (e) *Contribution.* This aspect of indemnity applies when more than one insurer is liable for a loss. In this case, each contributes a proportionate amount to the compensation. For example, a camera lost on holiday could be the subject of both a house contents policy and also holiday insurance.
    (f) *Subrogation.* This word means 'to take the place of'. Having received compensation from the insurer the insured has no further rights over the item insured. The right of ownership (e.g. for scrap value) passes to the insurer after the insured has accepted claim compensation. The compensation has taken the place of the item insured.
4 *Proximate cause*
    This insurance principle states that the insurer is *not* only liable for a loss caused directly by a risk insured against. An insurance claim would be valid not only for damage caused by fire, but also for repairs to doors damaged by firemen breaking in to tackle the blaze. This damage is not caused by the fire, but it is directly related to it.

Types of insurance

There are four broad categories of insurance: fire, life, accident and marine. These categories can be remembered by memorising FLAM which is a combination of the initial letter of each word.

FIRE

Fire insurance, as the name suggests, primarily covers fire risk. But many policies combine cover with other risks such as theft, storm, flood and lightning, etc.

This form of insurance can include cover for loss of earnings (e.g. by business) or rental of alternative property while a building damaged by fire is being repaired.

Fire policies exclude certain special conditions such as fire resulting from earthquake or riots. In addition, items of high value (e.g. paintings, jewellery, antiques, etc.) must be insured separately.

LIFE ASSURANCE

This type of cover is referred to as 'assurance' rather than insurance. In the case of insurance, cover is given against a risk that *may* happen. Life assurance covers an event that *will* happen – death. There are two main types of life assurance, whole life and endowment.

1 *Whole life* policies provide for a payment after the death of the insured with the idea of providing for the dependants of the deceased.
2 *Endowment* policies provide for the payment of a basic sum at a certain age or on death of the insured, whichever occurs first. This provides not only for dependants, but a useful sum of money for the insured if he survives the period. A variation of this type of policy is one 'with profits' which, for a higher premium, entitles the insured to a share in the company's profits.

ACCIDENT

This type of insurance covers a wide range of policies. The following are the main examples.

Motor

Any vehicle taken on public roads is required to have a certain minimum level (third party) of insurance to ensure that drivers can meet their liability for injury to others. The two commonest types of motor insurance are:

1 *Third party, fire and theft* – the motorist insures the liability for damage to other people and their property, plus the loss or damage to his own car through fire or theft.
2 *Comprehensive* – policies not only give the above third party cover but also provide compensation for accidental damage to the vehicle of the insured.

Personal accident and sickness

These are policies which can be taken out against death or disability in special circumstances, for example, holidays, flights, etc.

Liability

This type of policy covers the risk of liability for the injury or death of someone else. There are two main forms:

1 *Employer's liability* – covers the employer's legal liability for the safety of each employee.
2 *Public liability* – covers the liability of individuals and businesses for members of the public visiting their premises.

Property

Covers a wide variety of items from goods in transit or in store to buildings or contents. Applies to both the businessman and the private householder.

Credit

Covers against losses resulting from bad debts, for example, the failure of customers to pay for goods obtained on credit.

Fidelity

Used particularly by businesses to protect against loss by fraud and stealing by employees.

Insurance for business

- Employer's liability
- Public liability

- Damage to premises
- Stock damage
- Consequential loss (earnings)
- Theft, burglary
- Motor fleet
- Bad debts
- Product liability

Business interruption (or consequential loss)

Loss from fire in a business premises may not only result in physical damage. Business may have to be suspended for a time resulting in loss of earnings for both the owners of the firm and the employees. Insurance cover is available for such losses and the cover can include loss of wages, rent and the cost of temporary alternative accommodation.

MARINE

Marine insurance in Britain mainly centres around Lloyd's of London, which plays a major role in this worldwide market. This insurance is applied to ships and their cargoes. There are four broad categories of marine insurance.

1 *Hull insurance* – covers damage to the vessel itself and all its machinery and fixtures.
2 *Cargo insurance* – covers the cargo the ship is carrying.
3 *Freight insurance* – it is customary for an insurance policy to be taken out to cover the possibility that for some reason the shipper does not pay the transport (freight) charges to the shipowner.
4 *Shipowner's liability* – the owner of a vessel has to insure himself against a wide variety of events, for example, collision with other vessels or dock, injury to crew members or passengers, pollution of beaches, etc.

The insurance contract

Insurance is provided by insurance companies, friendly societies, Lloyd's underwriters and the government (national insurance). Non-government insurance may be taken out through agents working for a particular company or brokers selling insurance for a number of companies. Whichever approach is used a basic procedure is followed.

PROPOSAL

This form is provided by the insurer to be completed by the person seeking insurance cover (the proposer). The form consists of a number of questions which the proposer must answer truthfully (in 'utmost good faith'). When completed and signed by the proposer it represents a proposition from the proposer to the insurer.

PREMIUM

If the insurer is willing to provide cover on the terms of the proposal he will quote a premium, which is the amount the proposer must pay into the pool to effect cover.

POLICY

Once the contract is completed the insurer issues a policy which states the details of the contract between the insured and the insurer. The following documents may also be insured in association with the insurance policy.

- *Certificate of insurance* – for employer's liability and motor insurance, the law requires evidence of cover to be provided by this certificate.
- *Cover note* – this is a temporary document provided whilst the certificate of insurance is being prepared.
- *Endorsement* – a notice of an amendment to a policy, usually by the insurer. The endorsement is attached to the policy and thereafter becomes part of the contract.
- *Renewal notice* – issued by the insurer prior to expiry date, invites the insured to renew the cover and advises the renewal premium and the date on which it is due.

CLAIM

If the risk insured against takes place the insured completes a claim form and submits this to the insurer for consideration. Loss adjusters are frequently engaged by insurers to ensure that claims are settled fairly from the point of view of both the insured and the insurer.

The insurance market

INSURANCE COMPANIES

Insurance companies have branches spread throughout the country to issue policies and deal with claims. 'Friendly' societies specialise in life and sickness assurance. Those wishing to take out insurance cover can approach insurance companies directly or through insurance agents or insurance brokers.

Insurance *agents* work for an insurance company or a friendly society selling only the policies of that company.

Insurance *brokers* work independently of insurance companies and, therefore, are able to give unbiased advice as to which is the best policy to buy.

Whether it is decided to buy insurance direct from the insurance company, their agents, or brokers, the cost of the insurance cover is the same because the agent or broker is paid by the company which actually provides the insurance policy.

LLOYD'S OF LONDON

Lloyd's of London is a corporation that provides market facilities for members engaged in selling insurance. There are two classes of membership of Lloyd's, Lloyd's brokers and underwriters.

Underwriters are the only people allowed to accept insurance at Lloyd's. Underwriters are backed by their own personal wealth and have unlimited liability to indemnify insurance claims made against them. Underwriters frequently form into groups called *syndicates* who work together to accept larger shares of risk than a single individual could manage.

Lloyd's brokers are the source of contact with Lloyd's insurance market. The function of Lloyd's brokers is to get the best deal they can for their clients, who may be insurance companies or large organisations such as businesses and local government.

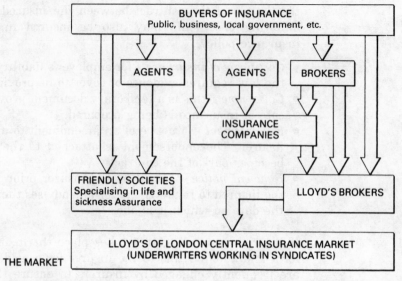

The insurance market

The Lloyd's broker approaches underwriters who specialise in the risk to be covered. The premiums offered by several underwriters are compared, and the best offer is accepted. Sometimes the risk may be divided between several underwriters. Should a claim occur under the latter circumstances, each of the underwriters contributes to the compensation in proportion to the amount of the risk they have accepted.

Glossary of insurance terminology

Actuary: statistician who calculates premium based on degree of risk.

Adjuster: an independent professional who assesses loss.

Agent: employed by one insurer to sell insurance, on commission.

Assessor: a person who negotiates the amount to be paid out against a claim.

Broker: independent professional who sells insurance for a number of insurers.

Claim: a request by a policyholder for compensation under the policy.

Cover note: issued to give temporary cover against risks while a policy is being prepared.

Friendly societies: companies specialising in life assurance or sickness benefit schemes.

Insured: the person who is covered by insurance.

Insurer: the party who gives insurance cover.

Knock for knock: arrangement where each insurer pays for damage to its policyholder's vehicle irrespective of who was to blame.

No claim discount: a reduction in the renewal premium of motor insurance when there has been no claim during the previous year.

Policy: written evidence of the contract between the insurer and the policyholder.

Premium: the payment made by the policyholder for the insurance cover given.

Proposal: application by a person or company (proposer) requesting insurance.

Reinsurance: a system whereby an insurer sacrifices part of the premium to share part of the risk with another insurer.

Renewal notice: sent to insured to advise premium and renewal date for next year of cover.

Underwriter: the person who accepts risk and promises to pay compensation if a loss occurs.

MAKE A NOTE OF IT

1 How does insurance spread risks?
2 Explain how insurance encourages business activity.
3 In what way does insurance contribute to the balance of payments?
4 What is reinsurance?
5 Why are some risks uninsurable? Give four examples.
6 In what way can insurance be said to have a statistical basis?
7 Give a brief description of what happens to money contributed to an insurance pool.
8 Explain, giving an example, the meaning of insurable interest.
9 Name the insurance principle which requires the parties to an insurance contract to be truthful.
10 Insurance is said to be a contract of indemnity. What does this mean?
11 What do the terms contribution and subrogation mean in relation to insurance?
12 Give an example, and explain the insurance principle of proximate cause.
13 Name the four main types of insurance.
14 Explain the difference between insurance and assurance.
15 In relation to life assurance, explain the terms whole life, endowment, with profits.
16 Briefly explain the differences between third party, third party fire and theft and comprehensive motor insurance.
17 Why would a shop owner be likely to take out both employer's liability and public liability insurance?
18 Briefly describe the four broad categories of marine insurance.
19 Describe the process of putting an insurance contract into effect including mention of the documents and payment involved.

20 Why is the certificate of insurance particularly important to both employers and motor vehicle drivers?
21 Explain the purpose of a renewal notice.
22 What is the function of a loss adjuster?
23 Briefly describe the difference between an insurance agent and an insurance broker.
24 What is Lloyd's of London?
25 Describe the work of underwriters and Lloyd's brokers in the insurance market.

Part 2

MONEY, CAPITAL AND FINANCE

1 This question is related to the bank cash dispenser system.

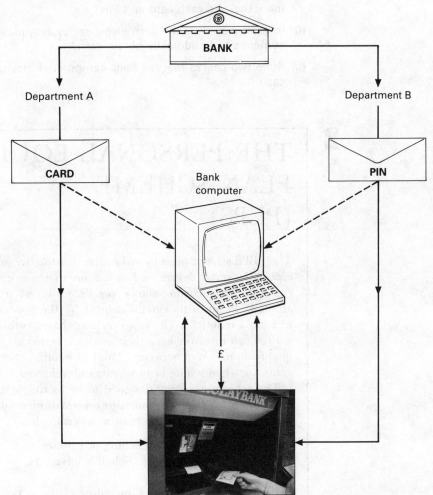

CASH DISPENSER

The cash dispenser system. Different departments of the bank are involved in the issue of a cash card. One department sends out the card which shows a number that can be 'read' by a cash dispenser. Another part of the bank issues a personal identity number (PIN) to the account holder. Both of these are filed in the bank computer. The account holder puts the cash card into the cash dispenser and keys in their PIN. Both numbers are passed to the bank computer, and if they pair up correctly the machine will issue cash up to the permitted daily amount, so long as enough funds are available. The customer's account is debited immediately. Should some unauthorised person try to use the card after the person has made a few unsuccessful attempts at obtaining money and guess the PIN, the machine will confiscate the card.

(a) Why is the machine referred to here called a 'cash dispenser'? (1)

(b) What do the letters PIN stand for? (1)

(c) Explain the words 'permitted daily amount' included in this explanation. (2)

(d) The first question the bank will ask a customer who reports their cash dispenser card as stolen is usually, 'Has the PIN been revealed?' Why do you think this question is asked? (3)

(e) Why do you think that different parts of the bank are involved in the issue of a cash card and PIN? (3)

(f) In what way does the cash dispenser system make it difficult for someone to fraudulently obtain cash? (4)

(g) State two checks that the bank computer carries out before issuing cash. (6)

2

THE PERSONAL EQUITY PLAN SCHEME (PEPS)

The PEPS scheme aims to make it more attractive and simple for people, especially small savers and first-time share-buyers, to invest in UK equities. The scheme allows people to invest a monthly or yearly amount, within a maximum defined by the government (currently up to £200 a month, or £2400 a year), in shares entirely free of tax.

Provided investors keep their money invested in their plans for a short qualifying period of between 12 and 14 months, they will not pay capital gains tax when selling or income tax on reinvested dividends or interest.

The scheme has been designed to be as simple as possible for investors, and is particularly suited to the small investor.

Plans are administered by plan managers, who:

- arrange the buying and selling of equities;
- hold share certificates on behalf of investors;
- keep records;
- deal with tax authorities, including claiming tax relief on dividends.

(a) What do the letters PEPS stand for? (1)

(b) What are 'equities'? (2)

(c) Why are PEPS likely to appeal to the small investor? (3)

(d) Explain the difference between an investor and a speculator. (4)

(e) In what way does this scheme try to ensure that it encourages genuine investors rather than speculators? (4)

(f) How does the return and the risk of equity investment differ from that of a building society or bank account? (6)

3

TYPE OF ASSURANCE

Certain "TYPES OF ASSURANCE" appearing in the schedule are defined below.

WHOLE LIFE

The benefit is payable on the death of the life assured.

ENDOWMENT

The benefit is payable on the termination date or previous death of the life assured.

TEMPORARY

The benefit is payable on the death of the life assured on or before the termination date.

FAMILY INCOME

The benefit is payable only if the life assured dies on or before the termination date and consists of annual instalments of a capital sum commencing on the date of death with subsequent instalments on each anniversary of that date. The last instalment shall fall due on the anniversary prior to the termination date and shall be proportionate to the remaining period.

ADDITIONAL INFORMATION

REFERENCES TO THE DEATH OF THE LIFE ASSURED SHALL MEAN THE FIRST OF THE LIVES ASSURED TO DIE.

THE POLICY SHALL BE SUBJECT TO THE SPECIAL OPTIONS ATTACHED HERETO.
IF DEATH OCCURS WITHIN 3 YEARS PRIOR TO THE TERMINATION DATE THREE ANNUAL INSTALMENTS OF FAMILY INCOME SHALL BE PAYABLE.

LIFE POLICY SCHEDULE

THE ASSURED	POLICY NUMBER: CR 2931812
DAVID H. LETCHFORD AND CHRISTINE A. MOODY	COMMENCING: 16. 6.1978

THE LIFE ASSURED	DATE OF BIRTH
DAVID H. LETCHFORD	12. 4.1954
CHRISTINE A. MOODY	10. 3.1954

TYPE OF ASSURANCE	BENEFIT	TERMINATION DATE
MORTGAGE ENDOWMENT	£11,000 DECREASING AS IN SCALE BELOW WITH PROFITS ON £1,100 PLUS	16. 6.2003
FAMILY INCOME	£1,100 PER ANNUM WITHOUT PROFITS	16. 6.2003

PREMIUM (ceasing on death of the life assured)	FIRST PAYMENT DUE	FREQUENCY	LAST PAYMENT DUE
£8.51	16. 6.1978	MONTHLY	16. 5.2003

WHERE PAYABLE	SURRENDER VALUE
LIVERPOOL	AFTER FOUR YEARS' PREMIUMS PAID

ADDITIONAL INFORMATION

THE MORTGAGE ENDOWMENT BENEFIT AS IN SCALE BELOW IS PAYABLE ON DEATH IN YEAR ENDING ON DATE SHOWN OR £1,100 PAYABLE ON SURVIVAL TO THE TERMINATION DATE, WITH PROFITS IN EITHER EVENT ON £1,100

16.6.79 £11,000	16.6.88 £9,911	16.6.97 £6,644
16.6.80 £10,934	16.6.89 £9,702	16.6.98 £6,006
16.6.81 £10,857	16.6.90 £9,460	16.6.99 £5,280
16.6.82 £10,769	16.6.91 £9,196	16.6.00 £4,466
16.6.83 £10,659	16.6.92 £8,888	16.6.01 £3,553
16.6.84 £10,549	16.6.93 £8,536	16.6.02 £2,508
16.6.85 £10,417	16.6.94 £8,151	16.6.03 £1,331
16.6.86 £10,274	16.6.95 £7,711	
16.6.87 £10,109	16.6.96 £7,205	

(a) What is the premium payable under the policy shown? (1)

(b) What is the maximum time the premium is payable for? (1)

(c) Calculate the amount that C Moody would receive from the family income part of the policy if D H Letchford died on 2.4.2002 (2)

(d) Explain why D H Letchford and C Moody may have taken out this policy. (3)

(e) The premiums for this policy could be paid by standing order or direct debit through a commercial bank. Explain how each of these facilities operate and say, with a reason, which you feel would be most appropriate in this case. (5)

(f) Compare an endowment policy to any National Savings scheme as a method of saving. (8)

4

Sources of capital funds (£m) for industrial and commercial companies 1979–1984						
	1979	1980	1981	1982	1983	1984
Retained profit	24 328	18 618	20 569	18 236	26 771	33 019
Bank borrowing	3 981	6 340	5 847	6 568	1 552	7 967
Ordinary shares	879	900	1 660	1 033	1 872	1 127
Debentures and preference shares	−22	523	738	245	608	249
Other	3 167	2 590	3 069	3 175	3 733	1 350
Total	32 333	28 971	32 621	29 257	34 536	43 712

Source: CSO, Financial Statistics, August 1984 and August 1985

(a) How much capital was raised by the sale of ordinary shares in 1988?   (1)

(b) Calculate the % of the total capital (to the nearest 5%) that the most popular source represented in 1984.   (2)

(c) What explanations can you suggest for the low investment through bank borrowing in 1983?   (2)

(d) State three factors that a bank would take into account before granting a business a loan.   (3)

(e) If you own a large number of shares in a company which needed £1/4 million to finance expansion, would you prefer the capital to come from (i) retained profits, (ii) the issue of new shares or (iii) through a bank loan. Give reasons for your choice.   (4)

(f) What role is played by (i) merchant banks and (ii) the Stock Exchange in the raising of new capital for industry?   (8)

5

Look at the bill on the opposite page.

(a) With which bank do the Essex Water Company hold their account?   (1)

(b) (i) Calculate the total standing charge on this bill.   (1)

  (ii) Why are standing charges levied?   (2)

(c) If Mr. Leicester paid this bill by cheque through the post, on the cheque who would be:
(i) The payee
(ii) The drawer
(iii) The drawee   (3)

(d) In the interest of security such a cheque should be crossed. What could Mr. Leicester write between the lines of the crossing to make the cheque safer?   (1)

(e) How is this particular bill going to be paid?   (2)

(f) State two advantages of using this method of payment from the point of view of:
(i) Mr. Leicester
(ii) The Essex Water Company   (4)

(g) Describe two ways in which this bill could be paid with the aid of National Girobank.   (6)

Principal Office: Hall Street,
Chelmsford, Essex CM2 0HH
Revenue Office: P.O. Box 700,
Chelmsford, Essex CM2 0DP

If you have a query about this
bill please telephone

**CHELMSFORD
(0245) 491011**

WATER SERVICES BILL

For all other queries please telephone
Chelmsford (0245) 491234

Customer Reference Number	Owner No.	Supply size in millimetres Water Sewerage	Year Commencing
433 852 00301 6		15	1ST APR 1988

MR W LEICESTER
42 GREEN LANE
CHELMSFORD
CM23 9HQ

433   S T A T E M E N T
852   - - - - - - - - - -
00301 FOR INFORMATION ONLY

RE:

Rateable Value £	Yearly Rate p in £	Rate Based Charge £	Standing Charge £	Amount £	Total £
WATER SUPPLY CHARGES FOR ESSEX WATER COMPANY					
302	12.000	36.24	14.00	50.24	50.24
SEWERAGE-ENVIRONMENTAL CHARGE FOR ANGLIAN W.A.					
302	28.490	86.04	23.40	109.44	109.44

YOU MAY SETTLE THIS ACCOUNT BY A SINGLE PAYMENT OF   X X X X X X X X   REACHING THE COMPANY

ANNUAL AMOUNT DUE
£   159.68

PAYMENT WILL BE AUTOMATICALLY DEDUCTED
FROM YOUR ACCOUNT — SEE DETAILS BELOW

ALTERNATIVE INSTALMENTS AND VARIOUS WAYS TO PAY ARE EXPLAINED ON THE BACK OF THIS BILL

Girobank NATIONAL *Trans cash*
Bootle Merseyside GIR 0AA

PAYMENT SLIP

Bank Giro Credit

135 205	Customer reference number	Credit account number	Amount due	By transfer from Girobank a/c No.
	433 852 00301 6	357 0959	£	

Standard fee payable at PO counter

Cashier's Stamp   ITEMS

Signature ....   Date ....

FEE

57-09-59

National Westminster
H.O. Collection Account
Essex Water Company

Total Cash
Cheques etc.
£

Name of Customer   Year Commencing

MR   1ST APR .88

Please do not write or mark below this line

IN ACCORDANCE WITH YOUR SIGNED MANDATE YOUR VISA CARD
ACCOUNT WILL BE DEBITED FOR £79.84 ON 28/04/88 AND
FOR £79.84 ON 28/10/88

V7003570959 91   X

6

Wealth: its creation and distribution by a company

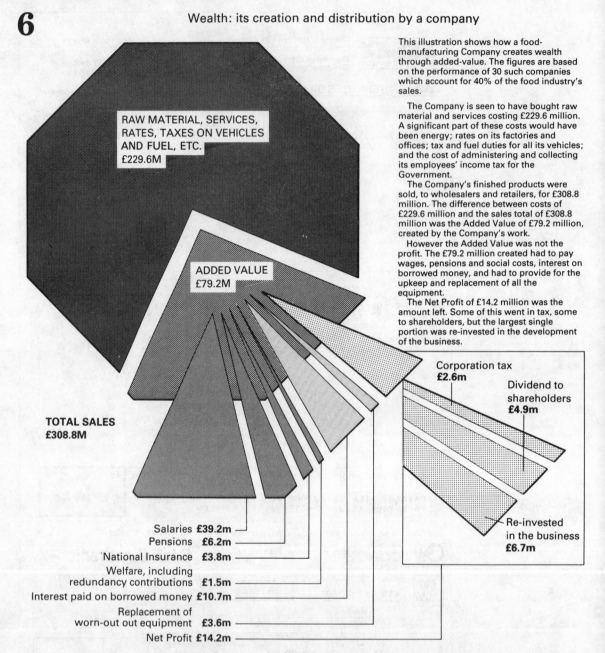

RAW MATERIAL, SERVICES, RATES, TAXES ON VEHICLES AND FUEL, ETC. £229.6M

ADDED VALUE £79.2M

TOTAL SALES £308.8M

This illustration shows how a food-manufacturing Company creates wealth through added-value. The figures are based on the performance of 30 such companies which account for 40% of the food industry's sales.

The Company is seen to have bought raw material and services costing £229.6 million. A significant part of these costs would have been energy; rates on its factories and offices; tax and fuel duties for all its vehicles; and the cost of administering and collecting its employees' income tax for the Government.

The Company's finished products were sold, to wholesalers and retailers, for £308.8 million. The difference between costs of £229.6 million and the sales total of £308.8 million was the Added Value of £79.2 million, created by the Company's work.

However the Added Value was not the profit. The £79.2 million created had to pay wages, pensions and social costs, interest on borrowed money, and had to provide for the upkeep and replacement of all the equipment.

The Net Profit of £14.2 million was the amount left. Some of this went in tax, some to shareholders, but the largest single portion was re-invested in the development of the business.

Corporation tax £2.6m

Dividend to shareholders £4.9m

Re-invested in the business £6.7m

Salaries £39.2m
Pensions £6.2m
National Insurance £3.8m
Welfare, including redundancy contributions £1.5m
Interest paid on borrowed money £10.7m
Replacement of worn-out out equipment £3.6m
Net Profit £14.2m

Industry in Perspective is a publication issued for use in schools and is sponsored by a group of major companies and the Department of Trade and Industry.

Refer to the data about wealth creation and answer these questions:

(a) How much money has the firm put back into the business this year?

(1)

(b) If the firm spent £229.6m on raw materials, etc., and achieved sales of £308.8m., why is it not possible to say that the firm made £79.2m profit? (2)

(c) Part of the added value was used to pay 'social costs'. Give two examples of social costs included in the data. (2)

(d) Define the term 'overheads' and give two examples of overheads this firm has to meet. (2)

(e) How does net profit differ from gross profit and how much gross profit did this company make? (3)

(f) Explain the words corporation tax and dividend used in the data. (4)

(g) In what ways does the data shown demonstrate that this firm is generating wealth as well as profit for its owners. (6)

| Coursework and Assignments | Part 2 |

MONEY, CAPITAL AND FINANCE

1 Choose ten different shares and monitor the movement of their market price over a period of six months. Present your record in diagrammatic form and explain the reason for the changes you observe.

2 Make a comparison between the final accounts of two firms of similar size and comment upon the differences observed in them.

3 To what extent do we now have a 'cashless society'?

4 Make a comparison between a commercial bank and National Girobank as a means of money transfer from the point of view of a large business organisation.

5 Choose any large firm selling consumer durables and describe the various methods of payment it allows customers to use. State which of the methods you would personally prefer, giving reasons for your choice.

6 Ivor is the director of a small but successful landscape gardening business in a town about 20 miles from where you live. He wants to raise £100 000 to expand his business and set up a new site in your locality.
(a) Examine the ways in which he might raise the £100 000 he needs.
(b) Present a report recommending a local site for consideration by Ivor.

7 Choose three contrasting methods of saving and investment and record their profitability over a six-month period. Give reasons for any differences in rate of return you identify.

8 Congratulations! You have inherited £60 000. Invest this money in three contrasting ways and record the progress of each £20 000 over a six-month period. Give reasons for any differences in the return achieved.

Part 3
MARKETING

11 Markets

Market functions

There are many stages of sale and purchase between the raising of raw materials and the eventual sale to the consumer. The main function of a market is to provide facilities where buyers and sellers of goods or services can trade. A market need not be a physical place but can be any situation or organisation where purchases can be negotiated. Markets take a variety of forms from a simple street market to highly complex finance markets.

Types of market

COMMODITY
MARKETS

London is the main world centre for commodity markets. These markets provide facilities where large numbers of buyers and sellers of raw materials can get together and prices are fixed. The London commodity markets include cotton, wool, sugar, tea, coffee, cocoa, copra, vegetable oils, grains, furs, diamonds and many others. The London metal exchanges deal in silver, aluminium, lead, copper, zinc, tin and nickel. Commodity markets are examined in more detail in Chapter 13.

FINANCIAL
MARKETS

Money market

This is not a market in the physical sense but refers to a number of institutions which provide short-term loans in the widest sense. The market includes the following:

(a) *Commercial banks*: provide loans and extend overdrafts to businesses and individuals.
(b) *Discount houses*: buy dated bills of exchange, Treasury bills, etc. before they are payable thus allowing the businessperson to obtain cash immediately rather than at a later date.
(c) *Merchant banks*: extend short-terms loans to British as well as foreign firms.
(d) *Hire-purchase companies*: allow individuals and businesses to borrow and pay back later in instalments while the goods purchased with the money are used as security against the loan.
(e) *Finance companies*: offer loans repayable by instalments, but in this case it is not necessarily the purchased goods that are used as security.

Capital market

This also is not a physical market but a number of institutions providing long-term loans almost entirely to business and industry. This market includes:

(a) *Insurance companies*: loan out some of the money they collect as premiums in the form of long-term loans (Lloyd's of London is the central insurance market).

(b) *Building societies*: apart from loaning out money for house purchase, building societies invest some of the money deposited with them by providing loans for the capital market.

(c) *Investment trusts*: buy shares of other companies using the money they get from the sale of shares in their own company.

(d) *Unit trusts*: invite the public to buy 'units'. The money received from selling the units is then used to buy shares in many different companies.

(e) *Pension funds*: collect regular contributions from members and provide them with pensions when they retire. The contributions are made to work by investing in low-risk securities.

(f) *Issuing houses*: arrange long-term capital for businesses by selling shares of the company concerned to the public.

(g) *The Stock Exchange*: provides a market place for the buyers and sellers of second-hand securities (the stock market).

CONSUMER MARKET

The consumer market is one in which everyone participates. We have wants and needs for a variety of products and services. Generally, when people purchase goods we say they are *customers* and when they receive a service or advice they are referred to as *clients*.

Many of the wants and needs of consumers are satisfied through the commercial activities of the channels of distribution such as retail, wholesale and foreign trade which are examined in the next few chapters. Other social needs for specialist help or advice are satisfied by government services such as health, welfare and education. In addition to the social services provided by the government, there are many private sector organisations such as those engaged in banking and insurance which also provide services to meet consumer requirements. Some of these organisations are examined in other places in this book.

Channels of distribution

During the process of marketing and distribution, merchandise usually passes through the hands of one or more intermediaries between the producer and the consumer. Commerce provides the important links between the producer and consumer.

Commerce can be divided into two broad areas, trade and services to trade. Trade is the branch of commerce directly engaged in the change of ownership of goods and consists of the retailers, wholesalers and exporters and importers who are examined in the next chapters. The services (aids) to trade are those businesses and organisations that assist trade in carrying out its functions, and these are examined in various places throughout this book.

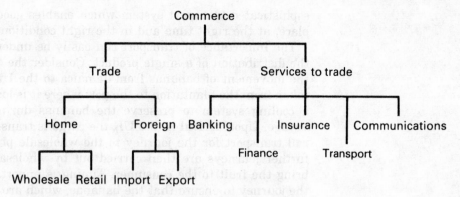

Trade (home and foreign)

(a) *Wholesaler*: intermediary between producer and retailer. Sometimes sells direct to consumer.

(b) *Retailer*: buys commodities from a wholesaler or direct from producer. Sells in small quantities to consumers.

(c) *Importer*: brings commodities into country.

(d) *Exporter*: sends commodities to another country.

Services (aids) to trade

(a) *Banking*: provides short-term finance and facilities for easy payment transfer.

(b) *Finance*: various institutions (e.g. the Stock Exchange) providing long-term finance for industry, commerce and consumer credit.

(c) *Insurance*: spreads the risks faced by industrial and commercial businesses.

(d) *Transport*: engaged in the movement of commodities from one place to another.

COMMUNICATIONS

(a) *Postal*: transfer of written communications through mail services.

(b) *Telecommunications*: immediate distance transfer of written, verbal or data communications by electronic devices.

(c) *Advertising*: provides potential customers with information about goods and services available.

Direct services

This is the general name given to the many occupations that are not of a productive or commercial nature but which are important to the well-being of the population. Examples are doctors, nurses, teachers, policemen, entertainers and athletes.

Importance of transport to marketing

Transport plays an important part in the marketing of goods because without transport raw materials would not reach the producer, and the finished article would not be distributed.

For marketing to be effectively carried out there is a need for a sophisticated transport system which enables goods to reach the right place, at the right time and in the right condition.

The importance of transport can easily be understood if we examine the distribution of a single product. Consider the transport involved in the movement of bananas from Jamaica to the UK. The fruit must be taken from the plantation to the port where it is loaded onto a ship with a cooling system to preserve the bananas during the long Atlantic voyage. Upon arrival in the UK the cargo is trans-shipped onto road or rail transport for the journey to the wholesale produce market. Many further journeys are then carried out by wholesalers and retailers to bring the fruit to the consumer. Timing is important at every stage of the journey to ensure that the bananas, which are harvested in a green condition, reach the consumer before the ripening process is complete.

MAKE A NOTE OF IT

1 What is the main function of a market?
2 State three forms a market might take.
3 What is a commodity market?
4 List five of the institutions which make up the money market.
5 Describe three different ways in which businesses might use the money market as a source of finance.
6 List the institutions which form the capital market.
7 In what way do insurance companies, building societies and pension funds help to finance business and industry?
8 Describe two ways in which you personally participate in the consumer market.
9 Explain the difference between the use of the terms 'client' and 'customer' in respect of marketing.
10 Define trade.
11 Name the four elements into which trade can be divided.
12 List the forms of enterprise that aid trade.
13 Why is advertising recognised as a part of the communication process in marketing?
14 What is 'direct' about the services given by doctors and teachers?
15 Why is transport important to marketing?
16 Describe the transport needs for the manufacture and marketing of wooden furniture from the provision of raw materials overseas to delivery to the consumer.

12 Retail trade

Functions of retail trade

Today we live in a society in which specialisation plays a major part. Most of us concentrate on carrying out our particular specialism and rely on others to satisfy most of our needs. For each of us to be able to specialise in this way requires an intricate pattern of distribution between producers and consumers. This involves a whole range of intermediaries such as banking, insurance, transport, advertising and the many other aspects of commercial activities that were mentioned in the previous chapter. Here we shall concentrate on retail trade which is the final and important link between producers and consumers.

The retailer is the last stage in the passage of goods from the producer to the consumer. In this position the retailer performs a number of important functions:

1 *Outlet* – the retailer performs a valuable service to the producer by providing him with an outlet for his products, thus saving the producer from the need to market his own goods.
2 *Stocks* – the retailer holds stocks which the consumer can purchase locally in small, convenient quantities.
3 *Choice* – the consumer is able to choose from the variety of products of different producers offered by the retailer.
4 *Information and advice* – the retailers' expert knowledge and experience enable them to advise and inform customers on quality and suitability of products.
5 *Feedback* – the retailer provides a feedback of consumer responses to wholesalers and producers. This helps the producer to become aware of what the consumer market wants, and also helps to ensure that consumers' requirements are satisfied.

Types of retailer

DOOR TO DOOR

Traders involved in this form of selling generally deal in sales of minor items of goods or services.

(a) *Pedlars*: carry goods from door to door on foot.
(b) *Hawkers*: use some method of transport.
(c) *Mobile shops*: a vehicle adapted to serve as a travelling shop.

MARKET TRADERS

These operate from stalls in open or covered areas, sometimes in streets or areas specially kept for markets. They are often able to keep prices very low because they avoid expenses ('overheads') such as heating, high rent, shop fittings, etc.

Street markets often operate in areas closed off from traffic.

Market traders can offer good value for money because their overheads are low.

INDEPENDENT SHOPS (SOLE TRADERS: CORNER SHOP; UNIT SHOP)

This type of shop is owned by a sole trader or small partnership and is typical of the small shop sited away from town centres. This type of retailer often specialises in offering a single commodity or service, for example, baker, butcher confectionery, wool, etc.

Advantages

- Gives personal attention to customers
- Saves customer from need to travel into town
- Owner has thorough knowledge of the business
- Sometimes allows customers credit.

Disadvantages

- Cannot buy in very large quantities
- Prices often higher than larger shops
- Carries a limited range of stock
- Difficulties in running shop if the owner is sick.

VOLUNTARY ASSOCIATIONS (VOLUNTARY RETAIL CO-OPERATIVES)

Mace, Wavy Line and Spar are typical examples of this sort of retailer. They are independently-owned shops that combine together under a single name to purchase in bulk in order to obtain lower prices.

MULTIPLES (CHAIN STORES)

Multiples are chains of shops trading under a single name of common ownership. They are generally controlled from a central headquarters and tend to be sited in town centres and shopping precincts. Examples are Bata (footwear), Boots (chemists), Tesco (supermarkets), Woolworths (variety).

The multiple shop enjoys many advantages over smaller retailers:

- Their large size enables them to by-pass wholesalers and buy in large quantities direct from the producer.
- A single national advertisement can cover all branches nationwide.
- They have the resources to rent or buy stores in prime central sites with large car parking space.
- They can afford to attract customers with 'loss leaders' (goods sold at below cost price).

SELF-SERVICE STORES AND SUPERMARKETS

A self-service store is considered to be a supermarket when it has more than 2 000 square feet of shopping area and three or more checkout points. Such stores are often organised as multiples.

These shops deal particularly in prepacked, priced products. Loss leaders are frequently used to attract custom, and customers serve themselves. The provision of shopping trolleys reduces the customers' awareness of the weight of their purchases and encourages impulse buying (unplanned purchases).

Because supermarkets are often organised in multiples they usually enjoy the advantages mentioned earlier. They also benefit from economies of scale, for example, being able to employ specialist staff such as butchers, bakers and fishmongers. In addition, they save in staff because the customers do much of the work by serving themselves.

Although this type of shop has many advantages over other retailers it faces some disadvantages:

- Large premises in prime areas are expensive.
- Pilferage (stealing) levels are high.

- Customers receive little personal contact.
- Shopping trolleys are stolen.

DEPARTMENT STORES

This type of shop is sometimes called a 'shop of shops' because it is divided into commodity departments. Each department is operated like a single shop responsible for its own profitability.

Department stores tend to be comfortably equipped with carpets, lifts and a restaurant. Merchandise is attractively displayed, and credit facilities (sometimes interest free) are given to suitable customers. Some have introduced their own charge cards.

Advantages

- Customers can shop in comfort.
- Wide variety of goods available under one roof.
- Shop assistants give personal service.
- Sited in towns and convenient to transport and car parks.

Disadvantages

- Large central sites are expensive.
- Cannot compete with prices of multiples.
- Comfortable surroundings can be a drain on profits.
- Labour-intensive compared with some retailers.

CO-OPERATIVE RETAIL SOCIETIES

The co-operative retail movement was started in 1844 by twenty-eight weavers who were known as the 'Rochdale Pioneers'.

Today membership is open to anyone buying at least one £1 share. The shares are not transferable but are redeemed by the society on demand. Members share in the profits of the society in one or more ways:

- A fixed rate of interest paid on shares.

- Dividend stamps issued with purchases exchangeable for cash or goods.
- Reduced prices through ploughing profits back into the business.

Co-operative retail societies are controlled by a management committee appointed by members. Each member has only one vote irrespective of the number of shares they hold. Their operations extend to factories, farms, plantations and their own wholesalers (Co-operative Wholesale Society – CWS).

HYPERMARKETS

These are a very large form of supermarket with a shopping area in excess of 50 000 square feet. They offer a very wide range of goods in many specialist departments similar to the divisions in a department store, or parts of the hypermarket complex may be rented out to other approved traders.

Hypermarkets are usually one of many in a chain. They are frequently sited on the outskirts of towns where sites are cheaper. Good parking facilities are provided and some late night trading.

MAIL ORDER

Products are sold in a variety of ways through the mail order method:
- Advertising in the press, radio or on television, inviting potential customers to buy by post.
- Direct selling with customers choosing articles from a catalogue at home.
- Part-time agents selling to friends from catalogues in return for a commission.

Advantages

- Interest free credit often given
- Buying in comfort of home
- Goods chosen at leisure.

Disadvantages

- Prices often dearer than shops
- Difficult to assess quality from a catalogue
- Can be inconvenient to return unsuitable goods.

VENDING MACHINES

These retail outlets are open twenty-four hours a day and provide a wide variety of products such as hot and cold snacks, confectionery, drinks, petrol, etc. Vending machines are sited in busy public places and they sometimes suffer as a result of vandalism.

Patterns in retailing

SHOPPING PRECINCTS

Sometimes called malls or shopping centres, these are shopping areas shut off from traffic, well served by public transport, road links, car parks and an information centre.

LOSS LEADERS

A popular product being sold at below market price to encourage customers to enter the shop.

Brent Cross shopping centre (by courtesy of Hammerson Group Developments)

BRANDED GOODS	Producers use a distinctive trade or brand name to allow easy identification of their goods (Fairy Liquid, Smarties, PG Tips). Sometimes traders have all their goods 'branded', for example, Marks and Spencer (St Michael), Woolworth (Winfield).
FREE GIFTS	Items such as tumblers, ashtrays and pens are often given away free with purchases.
TRADING STAMPS	Stamps are given away with purchases and can be exchanged for cash, goods, or gifts. These were very popular in the 1960s but their use has declined in recent years.
CREDIT FACILITIES	Many retailers offer suitable customers credit facilities, sometimes without charging interest. Some of the larger retailers have introduced their own charge cards which allow customers to buy and pay later in instalments.
FRANCHISE SHOPS	A franchise agreement is made between an entrepreneur (business person) and a franchise house. The agreement allows the entrepreneur to use the name of a well-known company (e.g. Wimpy) and the exclusive right to market their products within a specified area. This form of business is particularly evident in the fast food ('takeaway') trade.
LOGOS	Many large firms now use logos (symbols) with the company title and on their products to assist easy recognition.

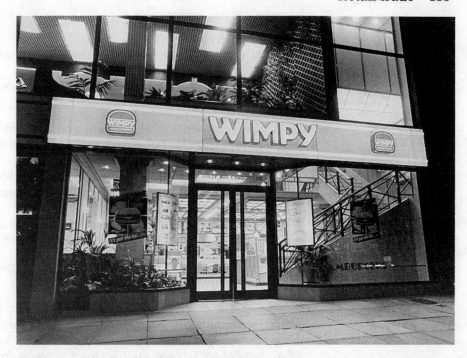

COMPETITION AND
LOTTERIES

Some traders give lucky numbers or competition tokens with each purchase.

Selling on credit

Selling on credit means allowing a buyer the use of goods while paying for them later, perhaps over a period of time by regular instalments. There are a variety of forms that selling on credit may take.

TRADE CREDIT

Trade credit occurs where the seller allows the buyer to have goods and pay for them after an agreed period of time. For example, a producer or wholesaler may allow the retailer to have supplies and pay for them at the end of the month. This allows the seller the opportunity to resell the goods before he has even paid for them, thus increasing the scope of his business.

HIRE PURCHASE
AGREEMENT (HP)

This is a contract for hiring goods for a fixed period with an option to purchase them for a nominal sum (e.g. £1) at the end of the period.

An initial deposit is paid, which consists of a percentage of the purchase price, and a number of equal weekly or monthly instalments are repaid over a given period. Interest is charged for the credit given.

The goods purchased do not become the property of the buyer until the last instalment has been paid. The item purchased must not be sold until the last repayment has been made because the seller or finance company remains the rightful owner until the last instalment has been paid.

The seller can repossess the item if the buyer defaults on repayments.

But there are some restrictions on repossession laid down in the Consumer Credit Act, 1974.
- If the buyer has paid one-third of the value of the item a court order is needed to repossess the item.
- The item cannot be repossessed at all once two-thirds of the value has been paid.

CREDIT SALE AGREEMENT

This is also a deposit and instalment and interest system similar to a HP agreement, but the buyer becomes the owner of the goods immediately the agreement has been made.

In the case of a credit sale agreement, if the buyer defaults on the repayments the seller or finance company does not repossess the goods but can sue for repayment of the debt.

Note: Most retailers do not finance HP and credit sales agreements themselves but use companies that specialise in this kind of finance.

INTEREST-FREE CREDIT

The buyer is allowed to pay for purchases by regular instalments but is not charged any interest.

CREDIT CARDS

The holder of a credit card can use it to make purchases up to a set amount (e.g. £200) without paying cash. The trader claims the money due for the purchases from the company that has issued the credit card.

The card holder is presented with an account from the issuer of the credit card. Payment of the outstanding amount can be made at once in full, or at some later time. Interest is charged on the outstanding balance.

Examples of credit cards are Access, American Express, Diners Club, Barclaycard.

CHARGE CARDS

Some retailers have introduced their own form of credit card for use in their stores e.g. Next, Marks and Spencer. These allow approved customers to make purchases and charge these to their personal account which will be repaid later. The system is frequently linked to an instalment system operated by the firm, sometimes providing interest-free credit.

ANNUAL PERCENTAGE RATE (APR)

APR is just a way of comparing the cost of credit deals – it is the 'price' of credit. It is difficult for a customer to work out which credit deal is best for them, but APR makes it easier. It is a percentage figure that takes into account all of the charges and costs involved. Generally, the lower the APR, the better the deal.

Mark-up and profit margin

Both of these terms refer to ways of looking at the differences between a trader's cost price and his selling price.

- *Mark-up* refers to the percentage profit which is added to the cost price by a trader to establish his selling price. For example, if an article has a cost price of 80p and it is to be sold for £1, the mark-up is:

$$\frac{20}{80} \times 100 = 25\%$$

● *Profit margin* is the percentage of the selling price which is the seller's profit. For example, on an article with a cost price of 80p which is sold for £1, the profit margin is:

$$\frac{20}{100} \times 100 = 20\%$$

Setting up a retail business

The following factors need to be taken into account when setting up a retail business:

HOW WILL THE CAPITAL REQUIRED BE RAISED?

● Savings of owner
● Borrowing from a bank or other institution
● Contributions from partners
● Selling shares privately or publicly.

WHAT TYPE OF BUSINESS IS TO BE ESTABLISHED?

● *Sole trader* – one owner running the business with or without employees to assist.
● *Partnership* – with one or more partners which enables responsibilities to be shared, but also means ownership and profits are shared.
● *Limited company* (private or public) – shareholders providing capital in return for a share of the profits and some say in the operation of the business.

DO THE OWNERS OR ASSISTANTS HAVE THE NECESSARY SKILLS?

● A thorough knowledge of the products to be sold.
● The ability to manage a business – accounts, stock records, cash flow, profit margins, VAT, wages, advertising, etc.
● The personality and temperament necessary to deal with employees and customers.

WHERE WILL THE SHOP BE SITED?

Site costs vary considerably. A central or busy site may be good for trade, but will also be expensive. The entrepreneur needs to be sure that there is sufficient demand (or not too much competition) to support the shop in a chosen position.

WHAT SAFEGUARDS MUST BE OBSERVED?

● *Health and Safety At Work Act 1974* – this Act sets out employers' responsibilities concerning the health, safety and welfare of all employees.
● *Insurance* – public liability, employers' liability, fire, theft, plate glass, vehicles, fidelity bonds, bad debts, business interruption.

MAKE A NOTE OF IT

1 Describe the functions of the retail trade.
2 Explain the difference between a pedlar and a hawker.
3 What are 'overheads'?
4 List the advantages and disadvantages of being a sole trader.
5 What advantage would a sole trader gain from becoming a member of a voluntary association?
6 What are chain stores and how are they generally controlled?
7 Name four examples of multiples.
8 List the advantages the multiple store enjoys over smaller retailers.

9 'All supermarkets are self-service stores, but not all self-service stores are supermarkets.' Explain this statement.

10 Give three examples of the economies of scale gained by operating as a multiple shop.

11 What are the main disadvantages faced by supermarkets?

12 Why is a department store sometimes called a 'shop of shops'?

13 List the advantages and disadvantages of department stores.

14 State three ways in which a co-operative retail society differs from other forms of retail organisation.

15 List three methods of mail order selling.

16 What are the advantages and disadvantages of buying by mail order from the point of view of the customer?

17 Make a list of ten items you can think of that are sold through vending machines.

18 Briefly describe the features of a shopping precinct.

19 What are 'branded' goods?

20 Describe two techniques used by shops to encourage people to enter their premises.

21 What are franchise shops?

22 How does trade credit benefit the retailer?

23 Explain the difference between a hire purchase agreement and a credit sale agreement.

24 What is the advantage to a customer of buying on interest-free credit?

25 Briefly describe the use of the credit card system in retail trade.

26 Give three examples of credit cards.

27 Explain the terms 'mark-up' and 'profit margin'.

28 Describe three factors it is necessary to take into account when setting up a retail business.

29 Why is the siting of a shop very important?

30 Describe two legal requirements that need to be observed by the shop owner.

13 Wholesale trade

Producers need to sell their products in large quantities to enable them to carry out mass production and enjoy economies of scale. But many retailers cannot buy in the large quantities that manufacturers want to sell. Wholesalers bridge the gap between producers and retailers by buying in large quantities and selling in smaller, more convenient lots to the retailer.

The wholesaler's premises are usually a large warehouse divided into sections dealing with specific commodities, and operating on organisational lines similar to a large supermarket.

Retailers may visit the wholesaler to choose their purchases, or orders may be telephoned in or passed to the wholesaler's representative on periodic visits to retailers.

Functions of wholesalers

ACTING AS AN INTERMEDIARY

The wholesaler is positioned between the producer and the retailer.

Producer ——▶ Wholesaler ——▶ Retailer ——▶ Consumer

But there are exceptions where the producer will sell direct to the retailer, or even straight to the consumer, by-passing both the wholesaler and the retailer.

BREAKING OF BULK

Buying in large quantities from the producer and selling in smaller lots, usually to the retailer.

TAKING ON RISKS

Predicting market trends and buying ahead of demand.

WAREHOUSING

By storing goods the wholesaler saves space for both the producer and the retailer.

OFFERING CREDIT

The wholesaler may supply goods and allow the retailer to pay at some later date (trade credit). This gives the retailer the opportunity to possibly sell the goods before he has paid for them.

Services provided by the wholesaler

FOR THE
PRODUCER

- *Reduces transport costs.*
- *Advises producer* of current market trends.
- *Finishes goods* by grading, packing and branding.
- *Makes mass production possible* by ordering in large quantities and therefore reducing production costs.

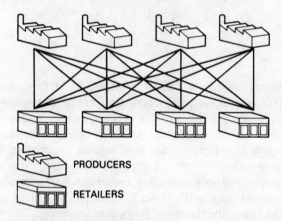

PRODUCERS

RETAILERS

(a) **Without wholesaler**   *We can see how the wholesaler saves in transport costs if we take a simple example of four different producers each supplying their produce to four retailers without the use of a wholesaler. Each producer would need to make four journeys to supply each retailer.*

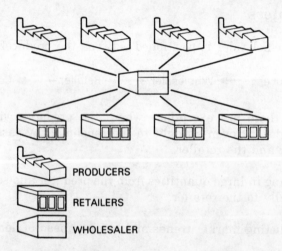

PRODUCERS

RETAILERS

WHOLESALER

(b) **With wholesaler**   *If we now introduce a wholesaler between the producers and the retailers each producer now only makes one journey to the wholesaler and the wholesaler makes one journey to each retailer.*

FOR THE RETAILER

- *Offers choice* of products from many producers.
- *Supplies small quantities* to suit retailers' needs.
- *Locally situated* providing quick access to goods and open until late in the evening.
- *Advises* latest trends and 'best buys'.

- *Pre-packs goods* ready for the retailers' shelves (graded, labelled, priced, weighed).

Importance of the wholesaler

Wholesalers are sometimes referred to as 'leeches' because they increase the price of goods *but*

- Their functions still have to be carried out by others if they are eliminated.
- They help smaller retailers to exist and therefore encourage competition.
- They make mass production possible and so reduce overall costs.

However, there are many ways in which the wholesaler is being eliminated.

Elimination of the wholesaler

Sometimes the producer will by-pass the wholesaler and sell direct to the retailer such as in the following circumstances:

- If the retailer is part of a large multiple chain, it can buy in large quantities and deal direct with the producer.

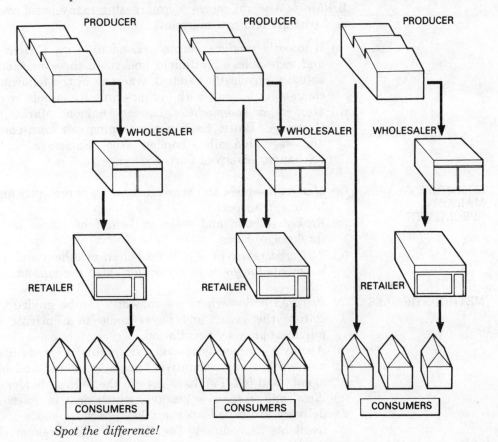

Spot the difference!

- Where after-sales service is particularly important, for example, washing machines, televisions, cookers.

The producer sometimes omits both the wholesaler and the retailer:

- Products made to specific requirements, for example, fitted furniture.
- Mail order firms selling direct by catalogue, agents, advertisements.
- Very large, expensive items such as machinery for industry.

Types of wholesaler

There are three basic forms of wholesaler:

(a) *General* wholesalers operate from large warehouses sited for convenient access from many local towns. They will allow retailers credit and will also deliver goods to their shops.

(b) *Cash and carry* wholesalers do not allow credit and do not deliver goods. Retailers come to warehouses, select goods, pay for them and provide their own transport.

(c) *Co-operative Wholesale Society* (CWS) supplies its own retail outlets, often obtaining goods from its own factories, farms and plantations.

Commodity markets

Britain is a world centre for marketing many basic commodities such as foodstuffs and raw materials.

(a) *Wholesale produce markets* (London). New Covent Garden (fruit and vegetables), Smithfield (meat). In these markets products are actually physically handled, whereas in the following markets the commodity is dealt with perhaps only by sample or description.

(b) *Markets for commodities*. London Diamond Market, London Metal Exchange, Baltic Exchange (shipping, air transport, grain, seeds and vegetable oils), London Wool Exchange, Liverpool Cotton Exchange, Liverpool Corn Exchange.

COMMODITY
MARKET
SPECIALISTS

(a) *Merchant* – buys on his own behalf, pays promptly and may provide his own transport.

(b) *Broker* – buys and sells on behalf of others on a commission (brokerage) basis.

(c) *'Del credere' agent* – sells on behalf of others and also guarantees payments for goods in return for extra commission.

METHODS OF SALE

(a) *Private treaty* – where a commodity can be graded (e.g. wheat and cotton) the seller and buyer come to a private agreement on purchase price by negotiation.

(b) *Auctions* – where goods vary in quality or grade (e.g. tea, tobacco and wool) a representative sample is offered and buyers or their agents will bid. Purchase goes to the highest bidder.

(c) *'Spot' and 'futures'* – markets which deal in goods for immediate delivery are called 'spot' markets, because goods and payment are available immediately ('on the spot'). 'Futures' markets are those

Part of a wholesale warehouse

where goods are being sold for delivery and payment at some time in the future. It is only possible to sell as a 'future' if the commodity can be graded.

<table>
<tr><td>

MAKE A NOTE OF IT

</td><td>

1 List the functions of wholesalers.
2 Why is the wholesaler sometimes referred to as an intermediary?
3 In what way can the wholesaler be said to 'break bulk?
4 Why is trade credit useful to the retailer?
5 List the services that the wholesaler provides
  (a) for the producer,
  (b) for the retailer.
6 How does the wholesaler reduce transport costs?

</td></tr>
</table>

7 In what way does the wholesaler help to make mass production possible?

8 Why is the wholesaler sometimes called a 'leech'?

9 Give three reasons why wholesalers are important even if they do cause an increase in distribution costs.

10 Give an example of a product that the wholesaler might grade or pack on behalf of the retailer.

11 Describe two circumstances in which the producer might sell direct to the retailer.

12 Give three examples where the producer might by-pass both the retailer and the wholesaler.

13 What are the main ways in which general wholesalers and cash and carry wholesalers differ?

14 What do the initials CWS stand for?

15 Who receives supplies from the CWS?

16 Name three London wholesale produce markets.

17 State the main way in which a wholesale produce market differs from other commodity markets.

18 List five major commodity markets.

19 Briefly describe the functions of three commodity market specialists.

20 Briefly describe the main methods of sale used in the wholesale marketing of commodities.

14   Foreign trade

What is foreign trade?

Foreign trade is the buying and selling of goods and services between different countries of the world.

- *Imports* are bought from other countries and result in outflow of funds.
- *Exports* are sold to other countries and result in inflow of funds.
- *Visible trade* refers to import and export of goods (e.g. food, machinery, vehicles).
- *Invisible trade* is the importing and exporting of services (e.g. tourism, transport, insurance and banking).

Importance of international trade

Differences between countries in the form of climate or natural resources mean that they have to trade in order to obtain goods which they cannot produce themselves, or do not find it economic to produce. One country may have natural deposits of oil or gas while another may have metal deposits not found in many other countries. By each country concentrating on production of those goods for which it has the comparative advantage, greater output is achieved more cheaply, which is in the best interest of all people. This is an extension of specialisation or division of labour that economists refer to as following the principle of comparative costs.

Acquired differences between countries can also be seen to contribute to international trade. A country may have developed the expertise to produce a particular commodity that other countries require, for example, microelectronic components. Countries will participate in international trade in order to obtain the benefit of the specialism of others.

By specialising and trading in this way, countries are able to obtain a wider variety of goods than they would have had without international trade. Thus, by participating in foreign trade each country enhances the way of life of its people.

International trade is a two-way process. Countries import to obtain the variety of things they need, and they need to export in order to pay for imports.

In what ways does Britain's trade with other countries contribute to the food you eat?

The UK needs to import because:

- We are not self-sufficient in foods.
- We do not have a climate suitable for producing all our needs.
- We need raw materials, some of which are only found overseas.
- We enjoy the benefits to be gained from international specialisation.

The UK needs to export (mainly manufactured goods) in order to obtain the foreign currencies required to pay for imports, and also to satisfy our desire for foreign produce. Imagine how boring our diet would be without tea, coffee, oranges and the many other products the UK buys from other countries.

Balance of trade

In the same way that every family has to budget to ensure it spends only what it can afford, so every country must also keep its spending within the limits of its income.

The family may keep a record of its income and expenditure, and countries will also record the difference in value between its imports and exports. The difference between the value of goods a country imports and exports is recorded in the *balance of trade*. Because goods can be seen they are collectively called 'visibles'.

When exports exceed imports the balance, or 'trade gap', is said to be *favourable* because a *surplus* has been created which has resulted in a net flow of funds into the country.

When imports exceed exports the balance is said to be *adverse* (unfavourable). A *deficit* (loss) has been created which has resulted in a net outflow of funds. The UK frequently has an adverse balance of trade.

Balance of trade figures (£ million)

1 Visible exports	+ 48 440	
Visible imports	− 47 322	
Balance of trade	+ 1 118	surplus
2 Visible exports	+ 47 322	
Visible imports	− 48 440	
Balance of trade	− 1 118	deficit

Balance of payments

In our trade with other countries the UK buys and sells a number of services. Because these services cannot be seen in the same way as goods they are collectively called 'invisibles'. More than one-third of the money the UK earns abroad comes from 'invisible' trade, and this is frequently sufficient to make up for the balance of trade deficit mentioned in the previous section.

The balance of payments is a statement of the difference in total value of all payments made to other countries and the total payment received from them. This balance includes both visible and invisible trade, and it shows whether the country is making a profit or a loss in its dealings with other countries.

- A *favourable* balance of payments is when there is net inflow of capital. The country has earned more than it has spent.
- An *adverse* balance is when there is a net currency outflow. The country has spent more than it has earned.

Balance of payments figures (£ million)

1 Visible exports	+ 48 440		
Visible imports	− 47 322		
Balance of trade		+ 1 118	surplus
Invisible exports	+ 25 650		
Invisible imports	− 23 120		
		+ 2 530	surplus
Balance of payments on current account		+ 3 648	surplus
2 Visible exports	+ 47 322		
Visible imports	− 48 440		
Balance of trade		−1 118	deficit
Invisible exports	+ 25 650		
Invisible imports	− 23 120		
		+ 2 530	surplus
Balance of payments on current account		+ 1 412	surplus
3 Visible exports	+ 48 440		
Visible imports	− 47 322		
Balance of trade		+ 1 118	surplus
Invisible exports	+ 23 120		
Invisible imports	− 25 650		
		− 2 530	deficit
Balance of payments on current account		− 1 412	deficit

Methods of selling abroad

The channels for selling abroad can be grouped into two broad categories: (a) selling from the UK, and (b) selling from an overseas base.

SELLING FROM
THE UK

There are several ways in which an exporter can sell abroad without going overseas. Advertising in foreign journals or circulating catalogues, brochures and other sales literature can be effective, although some items are not easy to describe and more direct contact is necessary. This can be achieved through contact with the agents of overseas buyers visiting the UK.

Where a firm is not large enough to operate its own export department it may use an *export house* which is a firm that specialises in securing orders from abroad. The export house may act as a merchant or an agent:

- *Merchant* – the export house actually buys the goods from the producer and then markets the goods overseas, accepting the risk of loss.
- *Agent* – the export house may market the goods on behalf of the seller from whom it receives a commission.

SELLING FROM AN
OVERSEAS BASE

The firm may send its own representatives overseas to make direct contact with potential customers. Alternatively, the exporter might employ an agent already based overseas and willing to seek contracts for sales in return for a commission.

Whichever of the foregoing approaches is employed, the representative or agent will be helped by trade fairs and exhibitions which provide a useful meeting place for buyers and sellers involved in international trade.

Problems faced by exporters

We have already recognised that it is important for a country to export in order to pay for its imports, but companies that engage in foreign trade face a number of difficulties. Some of these are also experienced in home trade, others are particularly evident in overseas trade. The main problems can be summarised as follows:

- *Language* – the exporter needs to be conversant with the language of the country to which he intends to export.
- *Differences in measurements*, weights and sizes also have to be taken into account by the exporter.
- *Suitability* of products, regulations, safety standards, etc., may differ in some foreign countries.
- *Import regulations* – the exporter must observe and be familiar with the import regulations of other countries.
- *Damage* to goods during their long journey to the customer.
- *Packaging* may need to be stronger than that used for home trade.
- *Transport* will be more difficult to organise and that chosen must be efficient and economic.
- *Documentation* and payment arrangements can be complicated in overseas trading.
- *Agent* – it may be necessary to find a suitable agent to act on behalf of the exporter to make contracts for the sale of goods.

- *Payment defaults* by overseas customers are more difficult to sort out than those in home trade.
- *Exchange rate* fluctuations can adversely affect market price of exports.
  (a) A *rise* in the value of the pound results in a fall in the cost of imports, and a rise in the price of exports.
  (b) A *fall* in the value of the pound results in a fall in the cost of exports and a rise in the price of imports.

Aids to exporters

DEPARTMENT OF TRADE

This is a branch of the Department of Trade and Industry. It operates a number of divisions and sub-departments and publishes journals aimed at informing, helping and encouraging exporters. Help given includes:

- Assessment of potential overseas markets for products.
- Providing details of current import regulations abroad (e.g. tariffs and quotas, etc.).
- Advice on financial standing of potential overseas customers.
- Introductions to prospective customers.
- Issue of UK export licences when necessary.
- Organisation of and/or assistance with international trade exhibitions or fairs.
- ECGD (*see* below).

EXPORT CREDITS GUARANTEE DEPARTMENT

This part of the Department of Trade plays an important part in helping exporters by providing the following on a non-profit basis:

1 *Insurance* against non-payment of debts by foreign importers due to:
  (a) importer being unable to pay
  (b) Export restrictions by UK government
  (c) Political restraints (e.g. war or diplomatic relations) on payment.
2 *Grants* or low-interest loans to assist exporters in meeting initial expense of exporting.

CONSULAR OFFICIALS

UK government officials who are based overseas collect information useful to exporters, and give local help to traders while they are abroad. Foreign officials based in the UK are also a source of advice and information.

BANKS

Provide help for exporters with:

- Short and long-term loans
- Financial advice
- Arranging documentary credit.

Free trade restrictions

If every country specialised in the things it does best, and then its products were freely traded anywhere in the world, all countries would gain maximum benefit. In fact, free trade between countries is difficult to organise. Countries sometimes use a variety of techniques in order to restrict free trade between countries. The following are the methods most frequently used.

SUBSIDIES   A government may give finance towards the cost of the home-produced product to enable it to be sold at a lower price abroad.

TARIFFS   These are a tax or custom duty imposed on imported goods to raise the price of foreign goods to the home consumer and thus protect the home market. There are two methods of imposing tariffs, which are collected by HM Customs and Excise Department:

(a) *Specific duties* are a set price for each item imported.
(b) *Ad valorem duties* are calculated as a percentage of the value of the imports.

Note: The importer can place goods in a *bonded warehouse* under Customs supervision until they are able to pay the duty due, or until the goods are re-exported.

QUOTAS   A quota is a limit on the quantity of a product allowed to enter the country during a year. An import licence must be obtained before goods subject to quota restrictions can be imported.

EXCHANGE   Sometimes a country will restrict the availability of foreign currency
CONTROLS   to importers, thus restricting their ability to pay for imports.

EMBARGO   This is a straightforward government ban on trading between one country and another.

Reasons for introduction of trade restrictions

There are four main reasons why a country may decide to impose trade restrictions.

(a) *To protect home producers* Infant (newly formed) industries may need protection until they have become sufficiently established to be able to compete fairly. Other industries may require protection because they are important to future national security.
(b) *To resist 'dumping'* 'Dumping' means selling goods at a loss abroad. Some countries will dump goods abroad either to reduce supplies at home or to increase their share of the market overseas. This kind of action can be very damaging to some industries in the country where the goods are being dumped.
(c) *To safeguard jobs* Even when goods are brought into a country fairly and competitively it may threaten a particular industry. Under such circumstances the importing country may feel it necessary to introduce trade restrictions.
(d) *To correct a balance of payments deficit* A continuous balance of payments deficit cannot be ignored. One way in which a deficit can be rectified is by reducing imports by imposition of import control.

Free trade

Free trade exists when no tariffs, quotas or other restrictions to trade exist between countries. Free trade is important because it encourages countries to specialise in producing the goods and services they are best at supplying, and where they have a 'comparative advantage'. Specialisation between countries, each exporting the goods and services in which it has a comparative advantage, raises the standard of living in every country. The result of this is that all countries simultaneously benefit.

There have been varied attempts by some groups of countries to reduce restrictions to free trade. The following describe some of these.

GENERAL AGREEMENT ON TARIFFS AND TRADE (GATT)

GATT became operational in 1948 and it seeks to encourage reduction of trade barriers between countries and to promote free trade. Countries which are members (including the UK) meet in Geneva to try and reach agreements leading to a reduction of trade barriers. Customs unions have been set up by members, aimed at removing tariffs between members. The European Free Trade Association and the European Economic Community are examples of customs unions.

EUROPEAN FREE TRADE ASSOCIATION (EFTA)

EFTA was formed in 1957. Common tariffs are charged between member countries, but members are allowed to impose whatever restrictions they wish on non-members.

Members: Austria, Iceland, Norway, Portugal, Sweden, Switzerland.

Britain was at one time a member of EFTA but left to become a member of the EEC in 1973.

EUROPEAN ECONOMIC COMMUNITY (EEC – 'COMMON MARKET')

The EEC was formed by the Treaty of Rome in 1957 by six countries: France, Luxembourg, Belgium, the Netherlands, Italy and West Germany. Later, Denmark, Ireland, Greece and the United Kingdom became members. More recently Portugal and Spain have joined to bring membership to twelve countries.

Aims of the EEC

- To raise the living standards of people in member countries.
- To promote freedom of movement of labour, capital and services between member countries.
- To encourage close co-operation between members in matters of commerce, farming, finance, social services and legal systems.
- Reduction of trade restrictions between members, and establishment of a common tariff policy to non-members.

Organisation of the EEC

(a) *The Commission* – the European civil service. Headquarters in Brussels (Belgium). Members appointed by governments of member countries to carry out daily administrative tasks.

(b) *European Parliament* – meets in Strasbourg (France) six times a year. Each member country has seats in proportion to its population

THE EUROPEAN COMMUNITY

WHO? WHAT? WHY? HOW?
Where does Britain fit in?

THE EUROPEAN COMMUNITY
Total population — 320 million
Total Gross Domestic Product — £1639bn
Total Exports from Community — £396390m
Total Imports to Community — £417413m

FRANCE
Population — 54 million
Gross Domestic Product — £339bn
Exports
(inside EEC) £29770m
(outside EEC) £30794m
Imports
(inside EEC) £36943m
(outside EEC) £32768m

UNITED KINGDOM
Population — 56 million
Gross Domestic Product — £296bn
Exports
(inside EEC) £26885m
(outside EEC) £34772m
Imports
(inside EEC) £29010m
(outside EEC) £38349m

ITALY Population — 57 million
Gross Domestic Product — £236bn
Exports
(inside EEC) £22317m
(outside EEC) £26008m
Imports
(inside EEC) £22803m
(outside EEC) £30535m

GERMANY
Population — 62 million
Gross Domestic Product — £431bn
Exports
(inside EEC) £53990m
(outside EEC) £58339m
Imports
(inside EEC) £51035m
(outside EEC) £50357m

NETHERLANDS
Population — 14 million
Gross Domestic Product — £87bn
Exports
(inside EEC) £31341m
(outside EEC) £12073m
Imports
(inside EEC) £21756m
(outside EEC) £18999m

IRELAND
Population — 3 million
Gross Domestic Product — £11bn
Exports
(inside EEC) £3950m
(outside EEC) £1774m
Imports
(inside EEC) £4382m
(outside EEC) £1699m

BELGIUM
Population — 10 million
Gross Domestic Product — £53bn
Exports
(inside EEC) £24087m
(outside EEC) £10405m
Imports
(inside EEC) £23694m
(outside EEC) £13166m
(includes figures for Luxembourg)

SPAIN
Population — 38 million
Gross Domestic Product — £109bn
Exports
(inside EEC) £5760m
(outside EEC) £7357m
Imports
(inside EEC) £5669m
(outside EEC) £13630m

GREECE
Population — 10 million
Gross Domestic Product — £23bn
Exports
(inside EEC) £1557m
(outside EEC) £1410m
Imports
(inside EEC) £3075m
(outside EEC) £3334m

LUXEMBOURG
Population — 0.5 million
Gross Domestic Product — £2.0bn
Exports and Imports
included with Belgian
figures

PORTUGAL
Population — 10 million
Gross Domestic Product — £14bn
Exports
(inside EEC) £1617m
(outside EEC) £1400m
Imports
(inside EEC) £1903m
(outside EEC) £3391m

DENMARK
Population — 5 million
Gross Domestic Product — £38bn
Exports
(inside EEC) £5207m
(outside EEC) £5577m
Imports
(inside EEC) £5315m
(outside EEC) £5600m

Aerial view of the Commission building in Brussels

The electorate of the EEC member countries elect European MPs to serve in the
European Parliament. The functions of the European Parliament are:
(a) to advise the Council of Ministers on Commission proposals
(b) with the Council of Ministers, to determine the Budget for the community
(c) to exert some political control over the Council and the Commission

The European Court of Justice hears cases involving Community laws from all member countries. For example, firms can be prosecuted in the European Court for operating restrictive trade practices. The Court has judges from each community country.

size. Representatives directly elected by the electorates of member states.

(c) *Council of Ministers* – The ultimate decision-making body. It consists of one minister from each country. Meets periodically. Important decisions must be unanimous.

(d) *European Court of Justice* – safeguards the principles and laws of the community. Considers complaints and cases from member countries, private and public industries and individuals.

<table>
<tr><td>

**MAKE A
NOTE
OF IT**

</td></tr>
</table>

1 Define the terms 'imports' and 'exports'.
2 Explain the term 'principle of comparative costs'.
3 Give one result of following the above principle.
4 Give two examples why international trade is important to all countries.
5 Why does Britain in particular need to import?
6 Define 'balance of trade'.
7 What are 'visibles'? Give three examples.
8 Explain each of the following terms:
   (a) trade gap
   (b) surplus
   (c) deficit.
9 What are 'invisibles'? Give three examples.
10 Explain the following statement. 'Balance of trade is related to visible trade, but balance of payments includes both visible and invisible trade.'

11 Why is it important to have a favourable balance of payments?
12 Briefly describe ways in which an exporter can sell abroad without going overseas.
13 Explain the difference between the work of merchants and agents.
14 List eight problems, other than fluctuation in exchange rates, that are faced by exporters. Describe four of these problems in detail.
15 Clearly explain how fluctuation in exchange rates can affect the price of both imports and exports.
16 List the aid given by the Department of Trade to exporters.
17 How does the ECGD help exporters?
18 List the main ways in which banks assist exporters.
19 What are tariffs? Describe the two ways that tariffs are collected.
20 What is the function of a bonded warehouse?
21 What is a quota?
22 Why might a government subsidise home produced goods?
23 What is an embargo?
24 Describe the four main reasons countries impose trade restrictions.
25 What is the main aim of GATT?
26 Name the countries which are members of EFTA.
27 State one way in which EFTA differs from the EEC.
28 List the member countries of the EEC.
29 What are the aims of the EEC?
30 Briefly describe the ways in which the UK and other countries have a say in the operation of the EEC.

15 Business documents

Purpose of business documents

The complete process of supplying goods and services from ordering to payment is called a *transaction*. A variety of documents are raised at various stages in the process and most of these pass between the buyer and the seller. Most of these documents are trading documents, i.e. those that are directly involved in the change of ownership. Others are sometimes used supplementary to trading documents in order to assist the trading process. These supplementary documents are particularly evident in foreign trade.

Businesses need documents to:

- Ensure that there is no confusion about what has taken place between the buyer and seller.
- Provide a record or proof of that activity at a later date.

Trading documents

ENQUIRY

The enquiry may be a letter or a standard form that is sent by the buyer to one or several firms seeking information about products or services available. Alternatively, the buyer may invite any number of suppliers to *tender*, or make an offer to supply. Based on the information received in response to the enquiry the buyer will decide who to purchase from.

QUOTATION

The quotation may take the form of a letter or a standard printed form, a catalogue or price list. It is an offer by the seller to supply at a *quoted* price. The quotation may also contain:

Delivery period

How long before delivery (or despatch) can be executed.

Discount offered

- *Cash discount* ('terms') – offered by seller to encourage prompt payment by buyer.
- *Trade discount* – given to people in the same trade as the seller to enable them to make a profit on resale of goods purchased.

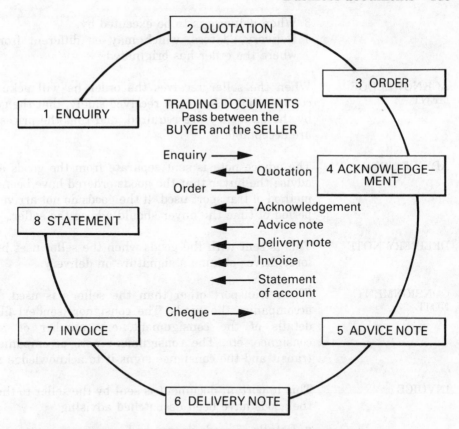

TRADING DOCUMENTS
Pass between the
BUYER and the SELLER

2 QUOTATION

3 ORDER

1 ENQUIRY

4 ACKNOWLEDGE-MENT

8 STATEMENT

7 INVOICE

5 ADVICE NOTE

6 DELIVERY NOTE

Enquiry ⟶
⟵ Quotation
Order ⟶
⟵ Acknowledgement
⟵ Advice note
⟵ Delivery note
⟵ Invoice
⟵ Statement of account
Cheque ⟶

(a) Name the first and the last document in the chain shown.
(b) What is the name given to this complete chain?
(c) At what point in this chain would the customer be asked to pay their outstanding account?
(d) Where in the chain shown would a credit note be most likely to appear?
(e) Give two reasons why a credit note might be issued.
(f) Under what circumstances would this diagram show the words consignment note and where would the words appear in the diagram?
(g) State three items of information likely to be included in a quotation.
(h) Briefly describe each of the following trading documents including an explanation of the function of each; order; acknowledgement; advice note.

Carriage arrangements

Carriage paid – price includes transport costs.
Carriage forward/ex-works – price does not include transport costs.
Promotional material – catalogue, price list, samples, etc.
Estimated cost – where it is not possible to give a precise price, the seller may give an estimated or expected cost.

ORDER   If the prospective customer finds the quotation of interest he will send the seller an official order. This may take the form of a letter, but more often it will be a standard form. The order will convey four pieces of information in particular.

1 Number and description of items required.
2 Price the buyer is expecting to pay.

3 When delivery is to be executed by.

4 Delivery address, which may be different from the address from where the order has originated.

ACKNOWLEDGE-
MENT

When the seller receives the order he will acknowledge receipt and confirm that it has been received safely, that the goods can be supplied by the date they are required, and that the prices stated on the order are acceptable.

ADVICE NOTE

The advice note is sent separate from the goods and its purpose is to advise the buyer that the goods ordered have been despatched, and the method of transport used. If the goods do not arrive within a reasonable period of time the buyer should advise the seller.

DELIVERY NOTE

This is sent with the goods when the seller uses his own vehicles. The lorry driver obtains a signature on delivery.

CONSIGNMENT
NOTE

When transport other than the seller's is used, a consignment note accompanies the goods. The consignor (sender) fills in the form with details of the consignment, e.g. number of packages, details of consignee, etc. The consignment note accompanies the goods during transit and the consignee signs it to acknowledge receipt.

INVOICE

This important document is sent by the seller to the buyer immediately the goods have been despatched advising:

- Details of goods despatched
- Cost per item
- Total cost, including VAT where applicable
- Discounts offered, for example, trade or cash discount

Many trading documents, and particularly those concerned with charging for goods or services supplied, show the letters E & OE somewhere. These letters stand for 'errors and omissions excepted'. The seller puts this on documents to advise the buyer that if a mistake has been made, the right to correct the error at a later date has been reserved.

PRO-FORMA
INVOICE

The pro-forma invoice is frequently used by the seller to charge a customer for goods in advance of despatch, but it can also be used when goods are sent on 'approval' or on a 'sale-or-return' basis.

STATEMENT OF
ACCOUNT

The statement of account is sent by the seller to the buyer at the end of each month to summarise the trading position since the previous statement was issued, and to request payment of the outstanding balance. It shows all the following:

- The amount outstanding from the previous month's statement.
- The date, value and document number of each subsequent transaction.
- The cumulative balance.
- Payments received since the last statement was issued.

- Current balance outstanding.
- Discounts offered for prompt payment.

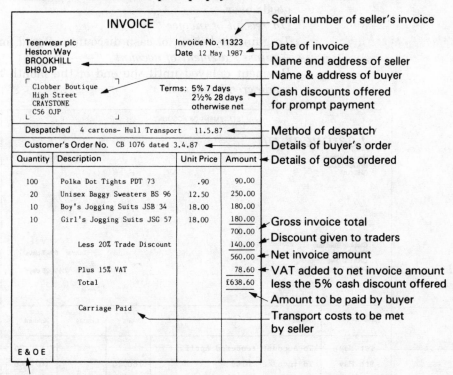

INVOICE

Teenwear plc — Invoice No. 11323 ← Serial number of seller's invoice
Heston Way — Date 12 May 1987 ← Date of invoice
BROOKHILL ← Name and address of seller
BH9 0JP

Clobber Boutique — Terms: 5% 7 days ← Name & address of buyer
High Street — 2½% 28 days ← Cash discounts offered
CRAYSTONE — otherwise net — for prompt payment
C56 0JP

Despatched 4 cartons- Hull Transport 11.5.87 ← Method of despatch
Customer's Order No. CB 1076 dated 3.4.87 ← Details of buyer's order
← Details of goods ordered

Quantity	Description	Unit Price	Amount
100	Polka Dot Tights PDT 73	.90	90.00
20	Unisex Baggy Sweaters BS 96	12.50	250.00
10	Boy's Jogging Suits JSB 34	18.00	180.00
10	Girl's Jogging Suits JSG 57	18.00	180.00
			700.00
	Less 20% Trade Discount		140.00
			560.00
	Plus 15% VAT		78.60
	Total		£638.60
	Carriage Paid		

Gross invoice total
Discount given to traders
Net invoice amount
VAT added to net invoice amount less the 5% cash discount offered
Amount to be paid by buyer
Transport costs to be met by seller

E & O E

E & O E Errors & Omissions Excepted – seller reserves right to correct any mistakes at a later date

Look at the invoice above and answer the following questions.
(a) This invoice has a number (11323). What is the purpose of including this number at the top of the document?
(b) Name the seller and the buyer involved in this transaction.
(c) What is the significance of the numbers and letters at the end of each of the addresses shown?
(d) Explain the meaning of the words 'carriage paid' on this invoice.
(e) Why are there three different dates shown on this document?
(f) How does the function of an invoice differ from that of a statement of account?
(g) Explain the method of applying VAT to an invoice using simple figures (but not those shown in the example) to illustrate your answer.
(h) What would be the net value of this invoice if there was no VAT applicable and the trade discount read 25% instead of 20%?
(i) Explain the meaning and the purpose of the section shown as 'Terms' on this document.
(j) Explain the purpose of the 'unit price' and 'amount' columns.

PAYMENT FOR GOODS AND SERVICES

There are a variety of arrangements that may be made between the seller and the buyer for payment of goods or services supplied, and these will be influenced by how well the seller knows the buyer. The buyer may pay:

1 *In advance*
   (a) Cash with order (CWO)
   (b) In response to a pro-forma invoice.

2 *Cash on delivery (COD)*
The carrier will be expected to collect payment before handing the goods over.

3 *On receipt of invoice*
To gain the benefit of cash discounts offered for prompt payment.

4 *Against statement of account*
Payment delayed until the end of the month to take full benefit of trade credit allowed.

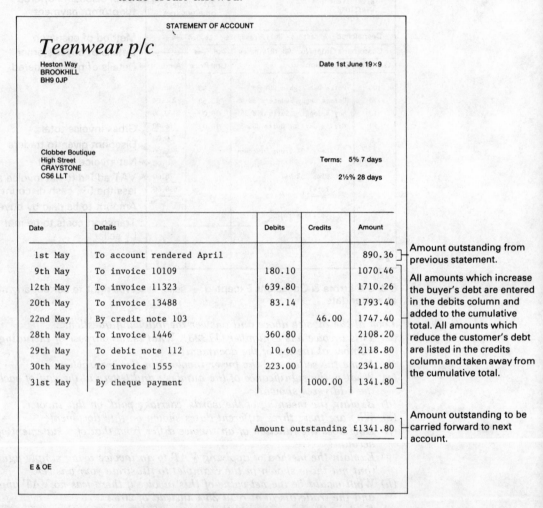

STATEMENT OF ACCOUNT

Teenwear p/c

Heston Way
BROOKHILL
BH9 0JP

Date 1st June 19×9

Clobber Boutique
High Street
CRAYSTONE
CS6 LLT

Terms: 5% 7 days

2½% 28 days

Date	Details	Debits	Credits	Amount
1st May	To account rendered April			890.36
9th May	To invoice 10109	180.10		1070.46
12th May	To invoice 11323	639.80		1710.26
20th May	To invoice 13488	83.14		1793.40
22nd May	By credit note 103		46.00	1747.40
28th May	To invoice 1446	360.80		2108.20
29th May	To debit note 112	10.60		2118.80
30th May	To invoice 1555	223.00		2341.80
31st May	By cheque payment		1000.00	1341.80

Amount outstanding from previous statement.

All amounts which increase the buyer's debt are entered in the debits column and added to the cumulative total. All amounts which reduce the customer's debt are listed in the credits column and taken away from the cumulative total.

Amount outstanding £1341.80

Amount outstanding to be carried forward to next account.

E & OE

(a) *How frequently are statements of this sort usually sent out?*
(b) *Why does this document show three months, April, May and June?*
(c) *What purpose does this document serve?*
(d) *Name the buyer and the seller on this document.*
(e) *What is the meaning of the words 'to account rendered'?*
(f) *What will be the amount shown as 'To account rendered' for the month following this statement?*
(g) *Give three possible reasons for the entry dated 22nd May.*
(h) *What was the total amount spent by the customer during the period covered by the statement?*
(i) *The figure in the amount column is sometimes called a cumulative balance. Why is it referred to in this way, and how are these figures calculated?*

The most common method of payment of debts today is by *cheque* which is used to pay for all or part of the balance of a statement. Where the buyer sends a cheque covering only some of the invoices listed on the statement a *remittance advice note* may also be sent listing the invoices which the cheque is intended to pay.

CORRECTING
MISTAKES

Two documents are used to effect changes in invoice values, the credit note (usually printed in red) and the debit note (printed in black).

Credit note

This is sent by the seller to the buyer to correct an overcharge or to give a refund. It has the effect of reducing the charge made.

Reasons for issue:

- An invoicing error has resulted in the customer being overcharged.
- Some of the goods have been returned as faulty.
- Too few goods were delivered.
- Refund on returned packing material.

Debit note

Sent by the seller to the buyer to correct an undercharge. The debit note has the effect of increasing the charge made.

Reasons for issue:

- An invoicing error has resulted in the customer being undercharged.
- Too many goods were sent and the buyer has agreed to keep them.

VALUE ADDED TAX
(VAT)

This is a tax levied on some goods and services. It is collected by traders by adding to the purchase price and this addition is passed to the government. VAT is levied as a percentage added to the purchase price after deduction of discounts.

Documents in foreign trade

We have seen in the previous chapter the important part foreign trade plays in providing a country with many of the wants and needs that it cannot economically produce. Similar to other forms of trading examined in earlier chapters, documentation is raised at various stages in the marketing and distribution of products. The following are the main documents used in foreign trade.

BILL OF LADING

The bill of lading is used in shipping of goods and it represents the title to ownership of goods. On it are shown details of the goods, their destination and the terms under which the shipping company agrees to carry the goods. Three copies of the bill of lading are raised.

(a) One is retained by the exporter.
(b) One is given to the ship's captain.
(c) One is given to the importer who has to produce his copy to take possession of the goods on arrival.

CANADA MARITIME LIMITED

BILL OF LADING

SHIPPER		CARRIER CODE NO 9385	VES. VOY. SHIPMENT No. GRP.		TT

PITMAN PUBLISHING LTD

SOUTHPORT

E.C.I.

A/C No.   AGENTS A/C No.   CM AGENT   REV.

CANADA MARITIME

CONSIGNEE	DANGEROUS GOODS CLASSIFICATION

ERA BOOK CO LTD
10-16 PORTLAND ST
KOWLOON
HONG KONG

A/C No.

TEMPERATURE CONTROL IN CENTIGRADE   TO

INSTRUCTIONS

NOTIFY ADDRESS (WITHOUT LIABILITY TO CARRIER)

A/C No.

PRE-CARRIAGE BY	PLACE OF RECEIPT	EXPORTERS REF. 243 607	AGENTS REF.
OCEAN VESSEL SEVEN SEAS	PORT OF LOADING FELIXSTOWE	ORIGIN OF SHIPMENT	FOR CM USE ONLY
PORT OF DISCHARGE HONG KONG	PLACE OF DELIVERY	FREIGHT PAYABLE AT MANCHESTER	

MARKS & NUMBERS	CONTAINER No.	No. OF PKGS., DESCRIPTION OF GOODS	WEIGHT	MEASURE
ERA. B.C. P.L. 206 HONG KONG		1 PAL BOX PRINTED EDUC. BOOKS	500 KG	1.030 cm

NO. OF PKGS. IN WORDS:—

Inchbrook Printers Limited

NON-NEGOTIABLE EXPRESS BILL OF LADING
(SEE CLAUSE 26 OVER FOR CONDITIONS)
CFDS 31 REV 09/84

AIR WAYBILL

This is used in connection with air transport and it serves as a receipt for goods by an aircraft captain to the sender of a consignment. The air waybill shows details of goods, departure and destination points, and consignor and consignee.

MANIFEST

A summary of all the bills of lading and cargo a ship is carrying.

					HOUSE AIRBILL NUMBER
Mitchell Cotts Airfreight	CRN				7443773

HOUSE AIR WAYBILL
NOT NEGOTIABLE

VAT REGISTRATION No. 321 2294 00	M.A.W.B. No. 13228305	CONSOLIDATION REF No.	Airport of DESTINATION HONIARA	% NO	CODE

CONSIGNED TO: SOLOMON ISLANDS — COLLEGE OF HIGHER EDUCATION
KUKUM CAMPUS   P.O. BOX 923   HONIARA , SOLOMON ISLES

ALSO NOTIFY:

No. OF PACKAGES	METHOD OF PACKING	NATURE AND QUANTITY OF GOODS	MARKS AND NUMBERS	DIMENSIONS OR VOLUME	GROSS WEIGHT SPECIFY KGS. OR LBS.
1	EXPORT CARTONS	PRINTED EDUC. BOOKS	COMPUTER LABELS	19 X 13 X 10 .040 cm	20 KG

CONSIGNEE'S ORDER NUMBER: 43642   SHIPPERS REFERENCE NUMBER: 43642

DOCUMENTS TO ACCOMPANY SHIPMENT: – INVOICES **3** CON. INV. [ ] C. of O. [ ] T.Doc/M.Cert. [ ]

SHIPPERS DECLARED VALUE (Specify Currency)
FOR CUSTOMS   FOR CARRIAGE •
£230.00

METHOD OF ROUTING AND CHARGES   Agreed stopping places are those places (other than the places of departure and destination) shown under Air Carriage, and/or those places shown in carrier's timetables as scheduled stopping places for the route. SEE CONDITIONS ON THE REVERSE HEREOF.

INTERNATIONAL AIR CARRIAGE DEPARTURE (ADDRESS OF (Airport of) FIRST CARRIER)	CHARGEABLE WEIGHT KGS.	RATE CLASSIFICATION	RATES	CODE	PREPAID	CHARGEABLE TO CONSIGNEE zero rated for VAT
TO FIRST CARRIER	20 KG		1.40	01	YES	
TO CARRIER				01		
CLEARANCE AND HANDLING			02	7 50		
CARTAGE			03	2 50		
E.E.C. DOCUMENTS			04			
CONSULAR / CERTS. OF ORIGIN			05			
PACKING			07	1 50		
INSURANCE VALUE PREMIUM			08	N/R		
FREE DOMICILE FEE			10	N/R		
SHIPPERS C.O.D.			11	—		
SHIPPER'S C.O.D. IN WORDS						
C.O.D. FEE			12			
AGENTS DISBURSEMENT			14			
			16			
INCLUSIVE PROCESSING CHARGE			→			

PAYABLE BY CONSIGNEE

NAME and Address of SHIPPER   PITMAN PUBLISHING LTD   SOUTHPORT

TOTAL DUE 99

CERTIFICATION
We hereby declare that the goods mentioned herein were despatched as shown below and a copy of this House Waybill was forwarded to the consignee on the same aircraft.

The shipper certifies that the particulars on the face hereof are correct and agrees to the CONDITIONS ON THE REVERSE OF THE SHIPPERS/CONSIGNEES COPY.

Carrier certifies above described goods were received for carriage SUBJECT TO THE CONDITIONS ON THE REVERSE OF THE SHIPPERS/CONSIGNEES COPY, the goods then being in apparent good order and condition except as noted herein.

_____ AT _____
(date and tax point)   (place)
ISSUING AIR FORWARDER

_____ SIGNATURE OF ISSUING AIR FORWARDER

Mitchell Cotts Airfreight (U.K.) Limited,
Galleymead Road, Colnbrook, Slough, Berkshire, England SL3 0EL
Telephone: Slough (0753) 684555
Telex: 847552 Mcair
Telegrams: Mcair Slough

Registered Office. Cotts House. Camomile Street, London EC3A 7BJ
Registration No. 710872 England

1
ORIGINAL – Shipper
THIS IS NOT A TAX INVOICE FOR VAT PURPOSES

We draw your attention to our TRADING CONDITIONS overleaf.

Air waybill

FREIGHT NOTE

The bill or charge for shipping goods, it is sent to the exporter by the shipping company.

CERTIFICATE OF ORIGIN

This is a document certifying the country of origin of goods. This document is sometimes required by the importing country if it has been agreed that the goods of a particular country will be allowed to enter the country at a more favourable tariff rate.

Pandair Freight Limited

PANDAIR
INTERNATIONAL AIRFREIGHT

SHIPPERS AIR FREIGHT INSTRUCTIONS

WE HAVE DESPATCHED TO YOU TODAY VIA:-

☐ YOUR COLLECTION SERVICE ☑ OUR TRANSPORT ☐ PARCEL POST

☐ PASSENGER TRAIN TO .... STATION (T.B.C.F/TO BE DELIVERED)

FOR AIRFREIGHT TO ➤

DESTINATION AIRPORT: MALTA

CONSIGN GOODS TO:	ALSO NOTIFY
MCE Bookshop	PITMAN PUBLISHING LTD
MALTA COLLEGE	SLAIDBURN CRESCENT
MCAST MFIDA	SOUTHPORT
MALTA	
Telex .... Telephone	Telephone ....
Consignees Order No: 26307	Shippers Order No: 26307

SPECIAL INSTRUCTIONS (e.g. LETTER OF CREDIT/CONSULAR REQUIREMENTS/H.M. CUSTOMS)

CONSOLIDATION SERVICE REQUIRED
CARGOSPEED ☐
CARGOSAVER ☐
CARGOTHRIFT ☐

For Goods destined for the EUROPEAN ECONOMIC COMMUNITY:-
We Hereby Certify that these goods are in free circulation within the EEC and Authorise PANDAIR FREIGHT LIMITED to issue T2L on our behalf
Signed ....

I.A.T.A. RESTRICTED ARTICLES REGULATIONS—SEE "RESTRICTED AND PROHIBITED CARGO (AIR)" OVERLEAF.

NO. OF PACKAGES	METHOD OF PACKING	NATURE AND QUANTITY OF GOODS	MARKS AND NUMBERS	MEASUREMENTS (Specify cms or ins)	GROSS WEIGHT (Specify Kilos or lbs)
1	EXPORT CARTONS	PRINTED EDUC. BOOKS	M.C.E. BOOKSHOP	19 X 13 X 10 .040 CM	20 KG
		RESTRICTED/NON RESTRICTED CARGO (Delete Accordingly)			

DECLARED VALUE FOR CUSTOMS ..... NIL

DECLARED VALUE FOR CARRIAGE £ NIL
(NOT ACCEPTABLE IN CONSOLIDATION) (IF REQUIRED)

INSURE FOR .... (IN WORDS) £ .... (IN FIGURES)

AMOUNT OF C.O.D. .... (IN WORDS) £ .... (IN FIGURES)

CHARGES	PAYABLE BY	
	SHIPPER	CONSIGNEE
AIR FREIGHT		49.50
FOB (Processing)		N/R
INSURANCE		N/R
AT DESTINATION		

DOCUMENTS ATTACHED (Please Indicate)	
COMMERCIAL INVOICES	3
CERTIFICATE OF ORIGIN/CONSULAR INVOICE	N/R
EEC DOCUMENTS (State Type)	N/R
RESTRICTED ARTICLES CERTIFICATE (In Duplicate)	
OTHERS	

SHIPPERS NAME AND ADDRESS

....
....
....

Telephone Number ....

J168 (Revised August 1983)

The Shipper hereby declares that the above particulars are correct and that he is aware of and accepts the Conditions of Trading referred to on the reverse side of this form.

Signed on behalf of Shipper

By ....

Dated ....

IMPORT LICENCE	Issued by the importing government giving permission to bring certain commodities into the country. It can be used to enforce quotas.
EXPORT LICENCE	An export licence is sometimes needed before certain goods are allowed to leave a country (e.g. firearms, works of art, etc.).
BILL OF EXCHANGE	The bill of exchange is widely used in the settlement of international debt. It is a document made out by the seller of goods (exporter – creditor) requiring the buyer (importer – debtor) to pay a named sum of money on demand, or on an agreed future date (usually three months).

The bill is signed first by the seller, and then by the buyer and returned to the seller. When the buyer has signed the bill it is said to have been 'accepted'.

The use of a bill of exchange enables the importer to obtain credit for a period of time. It also helps the seller because instead of waiting for payment he can:

- Sell the bill at a *discount*.
- Or negotiate it by using it to pay off his own debts, or use it as collateral against a bank loan.

Note: A bill of exchange is drawn up by the seller (creditor) whereas a cheque is drawn up by the buyer (debtor).

1 A seller in the U.K. will draw up a Bill of Exchange, sign it, and send it to the buyer.

Bill of Exchange

No. .... Exchange for £ .... London....................

At .... after day pay this Second of Exchange.

First unpaid, to the Order of ....

payable at the current rate of exchange for sight drafts on London with Bank Commission, Colonial Stamp, Postages and all Charges Value received.

To ....

For and on behalf of
Pitman Publishing
Credit Controller.

U.S.A.

U.K.

2 The buyer accepts the Bill and signs it and returns it to the seller.

MAKE A NOTE OF IT

1 What is a transaction?
2 Name the main parties involved in a transaction.
3 Why do businesses need documents?
4 What is the purpose of an enquiry?
5 State three forms a quotation may take.
6 What is an estimate?
7 Explain the difference between a trade discount and a cash discount.
8 Give three examples of promotional material.
9 Explain the difference between carriage paid and carriage forward.
10 State four items of information likely to be found on an order.
11 What is the function of an advice note?

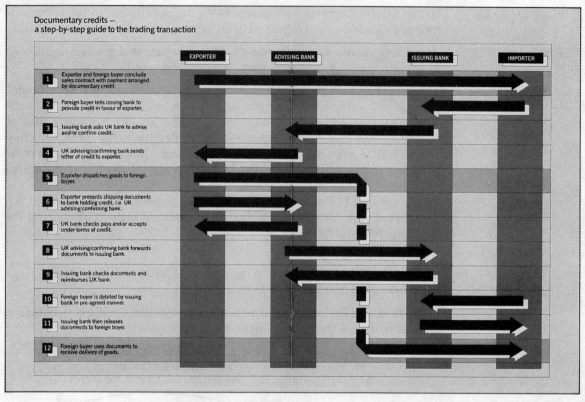

Documentary credits —
a step-by-step guide to the trading transaction

| EXPORTER | ADVISING BANK | ISSUING BANK | IMPORTER |

1 Exporter and foreign buyer conclude sales contract with payment arranged by documentary credit.

2 Foreign buyer tells issuing bank to provide credit in favour of exporter.

3 Issuing bank asks UK bank to advise and/or confirm credit.

4 UK advising/confirming bank sends letter of credit to exporter.

5 Exporter dispatches goods to foreign buyer.

6 Exporter presents shipping documents to bank holding credit, i.e. UK advising/confirming bank.

7 UK bank checks pays and/or accepts under terms of credit.

8 UK advising/confirming bank forwards documents to issuing bank.

9 Issuing bank checks documents and reimburses UK bank.

10 Foreign buyer is debited by issuing bank in pre-agreed manner.

11 Issuing bank then releases documents to foreign buyer.

12 Foreign buyer uses documents to receive delivery of goods.

12 Explain the difference between a delivery note and a consignment note.

13 State four items of information found on an invoice.

14 What is the purpose of putting the letters E & OE on a trading document?

15 Give two possible reasons for the issue of a pro-forma invoice.

16 What do the letters CWO and COD stand for?

17 Name the most common method of payment of debts.

18 What is the purpose of a remittance advice note?

19 Explain the difference in function between a credit note and a debit note.

20 What is value added tax?

21 A trader buys goods valued at £400. He is entitled to 25 per cent trade discount. How much will he actually pay for the goods?

22 An invoice value of £200 is subject to an addition of 15 per cent VAT. How much will the buyer actually pay?

23 What is the purpose of a bill of lading?

24 How are the three main copies of a bill of lading distributed?

25 State one way in which an air waybill differs from a bill of lading.

26 Name the document that states where imported goods were made.

27 Explain the difference between an import licence and an export licence.

28 Give a detailed explanation of the function of a bill of exchange.

29 Explain the difference between a 'discounted' and a 'negotiated' bill of exchange.

16 The marketing department

What is marketing?

Marketing refers to the process of selling products or services. It begins with an examination of what people want from a product or service (*market research*). This is followed by an assessment of how to produce the product or service (*product development*) that will satisfy that requirement, and at the same time make a profit in the process. The next stage is to develop a *marketing strategy* that will get the product to the appropriate market at a competitive price. This will involve creating an advertising campaign that is backed by selling and distribution procedures.

The following flow chart shows the way that the marketing process is developed.

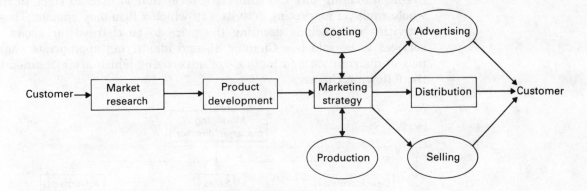

Functions of a marketing department

The marketing department will be controlled by the Marketing Director or a senior manager. This position entails carrying out sales policies decided by the board of directors, and supervising the work of all people employed in the department including the company's sales representatives whose job is to visit potential customers and obtain orders.

All documentation related to sales of the firm's products will be dealt with either directly or indirectly by the marketing department. This will include sending out mail shots (sales leaflets), dealing with customers' enquiries and orders, arranging for despatch of goods, and sending out invoices and statements of account (refer to Chapter 15).

A major part of the work of the marketing department is to choose the method of sales to be employed. This will vary according to the product or service being marketed. For example, the method of marketing a new chocolate bar will differ from that used to sell a valuable antique.

The marketing department will obviously be involved in advertising the firm's products. Where the firm is large it may have a separate advertising department. This department will carry out the instructions of the marketing department, and will also offer advice on marketing strategies, including market research. These aspects of marketing are covered in the next chapter.

The marketing mix

A firm's marketing department is concerned with selling its products or services. This can mean disposing of products the firm has produced, but more often it is a case of identifying what customers want and then arranging to meet the need that exists, hopefully making a profit in the process.

There are many ways to organise a marketing department and its structure will be influenced by the size of the firm. In a large company it would be possible to split the department into several sub-divisions, each with a specific marketing function. In a small organisation a few members of staff may have to incorporate several of these functions into their duties.

The *marketing mix* is a collective term that is used to refer to the whole range of marketing activities in which a firm may engage. These activities will include deciding the price to be charged for goods or services to be sold (*see* Chapter 8), and identifying appropriate channels of distribution and methods of advertising which are examined in the following chapters.

Typical structure of a marketing department of a large company

Product life cycle

In addition to deciding marketing mix a firm must consider how sales might develop. All products move through identifiable stages which are referred to as the *product life cycle*. Understanding this 'cycle' assists the preparation of a sound marketing plan.

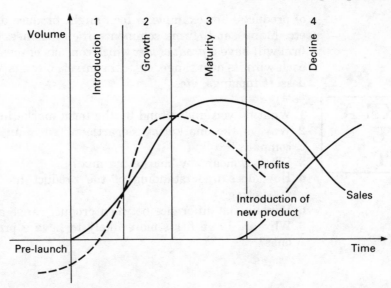

Product life cycle

PRE-LAUNCH	This stage consists of all the developmental work undertaken before the product is put on the market. During this time the decision has to be taken whether it is worthwhile to pursue the new development. Once it has been decided to proceed a considerable amount of capital is consumed with no income.
INTRODUCTION	In the early stages of marketing sales tend to be low but large amounts of capital continue to be consumed. It is some time before break-even (*see* Chapter 8) stage is reached and the product begins to show a profit.
GROWTH	If all goes well, sales and profits are steadily rising. Marketing becomes more economically viable as an increasing volume of cash comes in from customers. This is a time for vigorous advertising to promote maximum demand for the product.
MATURITY	During this crucial period the rate of sales growth begins to slow down. The advent of this is often signalled by prior falling off of profits. The product reaches its ceiling and begins to decline. This is a crucial period for the business because it is important to recognise the signal to improve the product or find a new one.
DECLINE	This is the period when sales volume shows a marked fall. It reveals that the product has lost its appeal or competitive edge. If steps have not already been taken to improve the product it will probably now have to be withdrawn in order to avoid making a loss.

Product range and product mix

Most products are not marketed on their own but are part of a range of products. For example, a firm might produce a *range* of cake mixes, etc. Many small firms commence their business in this way. A large firm will have a *product mix* which consists of several different products, each with its own range, e.g. cake mixes, biscuits, crisps, instant sauces, dessert toppings, etc.

MAKE A NOTE OF IT

1 What do you understand by the term marketing?
2 Why is the marketing department such an important part of a company?
3 What is meant by 'marketing mix'?
4 How does understanding of the product life cycle assist planned marketing?
5 Explain the difference between product range and product mix.
6 Why are large firms more likely to have a product mix than small ones?

17 Advertising and market research

Purpose of advertising

Advertising plays a major role in the marketing of goods and services. It is the commercial activity that brings the commodities of producers and traders to the notice of the consumer. An advertisement is a message that uses words, pictures or sound to:

- *Inform* potential buyers of availability of goods and services.
- *Persuade* people to buy or behave in a particular way.

Informative advertising

This form of advertising gives detailed information about the goods or services available and leaves consumers to decide without persuasion if they wish to purchase. An informative advertisement will contain useful details such as colour, specification, sizes and material. This type of approach can also be employed in public relations and image creation.

Examples of informative advertising

Persuasive advertising

Much of advertising today seeks to go further than just conveying information. Persuasive advertising uses a variety of techniques in an attempt to persuade people to buy irrespective of whether they need the commodity or service. The following are just some of the techniques some advertisements employ in order to keep products in the public eye and create demand.

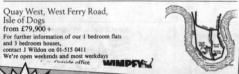

Look at these examples of persuasive advertisements. Notice how they attempt to try and convince the consumer that it is better than alternatives from other producers. Can you recognise any hidden persuaders?

HIDDEN
PERSUADERS

Hidden persuaders are a variety of techniques used by advertisers to arouse interest and promote demand.

- *Sex appeal* – product is claimed to make the user attractive to the opposite sex.
- *Ambition* – advertisement implies that those who use the product will be successful.
- *Personality appeal* – famous personalities are shown using the product to give it an acceptable image.
- *Social acceptability* – advertisement implies that by using the product the consumer becomes more acceptable to others.
- *Work simplification* – product is claimed to make a task easier to carry out.
- *Health* – advertisement suggests that use of the product contributes to good health.

Advertising media

There are many media through which advertising may take place, each of which has a varying degree of effectiveness and cost.

ADVERTISING
MEDIA TODAY

- *Television and radio* – very expensive but most effective method of reaching a large audience.
- *National press* – reaches a wide area, but is expensive and therefore mainly used by large companies.
- *Local newspapers* – offer cheaper advertising rates for cover of a limited area. 'Free' local newspapers rely on advertising to meet costs.
- *Magazines or journals* – have a more limited circulation but reach a 'selected' audience, offer greater scope for colour advertisements and have a longer life than newspapers.
- *Cinemas* – reach a relatively small audience but can be effective, particularly in advertising local shops, etc.
- *Posters and hoardings* – eye-catching, impact signs, sited in public places or on public transport.
- *Point-of-sale* – use eye-catching shop counter or window display to influence the consumer to buy on impulse.
- *Exhibitions* – such as the Ideal Home, the Boat Show, etc. attract large numbers of people who already have at least some interest in the product.
- *Circulation* – by leaflets ('mail shot') can be an effective media but is very labour-intensive.
- *Word-of-mouth* (by recommendation) – sometimes encouraged by firms carrying out a 'whispering' campaign by giving away free samples which they hope the users will talk about favourably.

FUTURE
ADVERTISING
MEDIA

Over the many years of its existence advertising has had to adapt as society has changed and marketing has become more competitive. In the future, advertising will undoubtedly continue to adapt to changes, especially those related to technology and its employment. Consider the

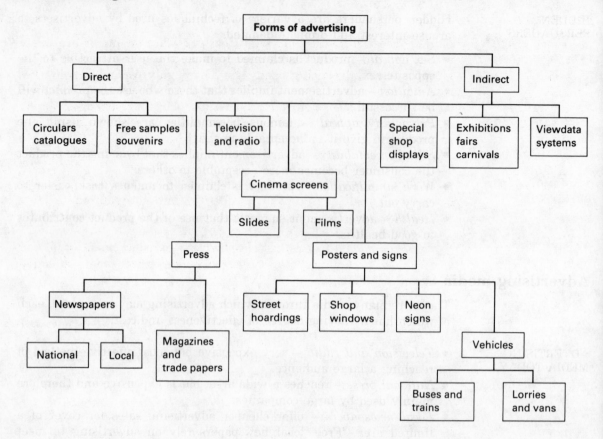

form that future advertising will take when every home has viewdata equipment enabling consumers to view goods, and purchase them, in their own home. One can only guess the form advertising will take in the future. What form do you think it will take?

Planning an advertising campaign

Some firms are large enough to have their own advertising department, others may decide it is preferable to employ an advertising agency to carry out an advertising campaign on their behalf. Whichever is the case, the advertiser or agency will have to take many factors into account. The following questions must certainly be answered if the campaign is to be effective.

- Which groups (target audience) of the public is the campaign intended to reach?
- How much money is available to be spent on the campaign?
- How extensive is the campaign intended to be – countywide, countrywide or worldwide?
- Which techniques will catch the attention of buyers?

Some of these questions, such as the amount of money to be put into the campaign, can only be answered by the advertiser. Others can be solved through market research.

Market research

Market research investigates what consumers are buying or are likely to buy in the future. The research is normally carried out before launching the advertising campaign. Thoroughly carried out, market research can help to direct advertisers to the most economic and effective way to run their campaign. Sometimes market research is carried out after the product is already well-established in order to assess and improve advertising and evaluate product performance.

AIMS OF MARKET RESEARCH

- *To find out what the public wants* so that the business does not waste resources producing goods or services that are not required.
- *To assess likely volume of demand* to ensure that overproducing does not occur.
- *To discover what will influence consumers* – product name, style and colour of packaging, best target audience, price range, effective hidden persuaders.

METHODS EMPLOYED IN RESEARCH

Those carrying out market research find out the information they seek by asking a cross-section of the public (from all age-groups and social backgrounds) a number of carefully designed questions. The questioning is carried out in a variety of places:

Please indicate your hobbies, sports and interests.

Hobbies and Interests

- ☐ 1 Cooking
- ☐ 2 Gourmet Foods
- ☐ 3 Gardening
- ☐ 4 Knitting
- ☐ 5 Photography
- ☐ 6 Dressmaking
- ☐ 7 Issues of Collectables/ Special Editions etc.
- ☐ 8 Home Computing
- ☐ 9 Listening to Music
- ☐ 10 Reading Books

How many magazines do you buy a month?
- ☐ 11 0
- ☐ 12 1 - 3
- ☐ 13 4 - 6
- ☐ 14 7+

Sports and Activities

- ☐ 15 Fishing
- ☐ 16 Tennis
- ☐ 17 Squash
- ☐ 18 Cycling
- ☐ 19 Horse Riding
- ☐ 20 Golf
- ☐ 21 Running/ Jogging
- ☐ 22 Shooting
- ☐ 23 Snow Skiing
- ☐ 24 Sailing
- ☐ 25 Water Skiing
- ☐ 26 Please tick if you normally include your sports and activities as part of your holidays.

Clothing & Fashion

- ☐ 27 Ladies Fashion
- ☐ 28 Mens Fashion
- ☐ 29 Winter/Thermal Underwear
- ☐ 30 Womens Clothes Size 16+
- ☐ 31 Please tick if you have ever bought anything for your Leisure via mail order.
- ☐ 32 Please tick if you were satisfied with the purchase.

What do you drink?
- ☐ 1 Beer
- ☐ 2 Wine
- ☐ 3 Spirits

Are you interested in buying?
- ☐ 4 Wine by mail order
- ☐ 5 Home Brewing Kits

Do you smoke?
- ☐ 6 Cigarettes/Cigars
- ☐ 7 A Pipe
- ☐ 8 Please tick if you would like to stop smoking

A market research questionnaire can be used to collect information about potential markets for goods and services.

In the street, shop or home

The researcher has a set of prepared questions. The answers to many of these questions can be quickly recorded by ticks in boxes marked Yes or No.

Questionnaires circulated in shops or homes

A carefully constructed questionnaire must be:

- Easy to understand
- Simple to answer, perhaps by ticks
- Capable of useful analysis (frequently by computer).

Sampling

- Members of the public may be invited to try the product, or compare one or more samples and make constructive observations.
- Test marketing may be carried out by selling the product in a small sample area in order to assess likely demand prior to commencing full-scale production.

Arguments for advertising

- It makes consumers aware of the range of choice available.
- Encourages healthy competition between suppliers.
- Promotes demand and makes mass production possible.
- Mass production provides employment and also keeps prices down.
- Helps to pay for sports events and concerts.
- Contributes towards the costs of newspapers and magazines.
- Brightens up town centres with colourful displays.

Criticisms of advertising

- The cost of advertising has to be incorporated into the price of goods or services.
- Most advertising aims to persuade people to buy whether they need the commodity or not.
- 'Hidden persuaders' appeal to emotions and prejudices.
- Some advertising encourages unsociable habits and behaviour.
- Some advertising misleads by making exaggerated claims.
- Encourages people to be wasteful and discard products for new ones.

Control of advertising

Advertising is a powerful and influential tool in the marketing process, and consumers must be safeguarded against the possibility of advertisers using this power unfairly. There are four main ways that consumers are protected.

1 *The Advertising Standards Authority (ASA)*
The ASA investigates complaints against advertisements.

It's easy to complain about an advertisement. Once you know how.

One of the ways we keep a check on the advertising that appears in the press, on posters and in the cinema is by responding to consumers' complaints.

Any complaint sent to us is considered carefully and, if there's a case to answer, a full investigation is made.

If you think you've got good reason to complain about an advertisement, send off for a copy of our free leaflet.

It will tell you all you need to know to help us process your complaint as quickly as possible.

The Advertising Standards Authority. ✔
If an advertisement is wrong, we're here to put it right.

ASA Ltd, Dept 1 Brook House, Torrington Place, London WC1E 7HN

This space is donated in the interests of high standards of advertising.

2 *Codes of advertising practice*
Administered by the ASA, these are a set of rules to which advertisers and advertisements must conform.

3 *Trades Description Act*
Imposes penalties on advertisers who falsely describe goods or services they sell.

4 *Media controls*
The advertising media are themselves concerned to ensure that advertising is not used to the detriment of the consumer. Television, newspapers and magazines will refuse to display advertisements from advertisers whose methods are found to be unacceptable. They will also investigate complaints against traders and advertisers on behalf of consumers.

MAKE A NOTE OF IT

1 What is advertising?
2 State one purpose of advertising.
3 Explain the difference between informative and persuasive advertising.
4 What are 'hidden persuaders' and in what way can they influence consumers?
5 Television and the national press are very effective forms of advertising, but they are inappropriate for publicising a jumble sale. Why is this so?
6 Who pays for 'free' newspapers?
7 Why do magazines generally have a longer life than newspapers?

In what way does this make magazines an attractive proposition as an advertising medium?

8 In relation to advertising, what is a hoarding?

9 How is a 'mail shot' used in advertising?

10 Describe two forms of 'point-of-sale' advertising with which you are familiar.

11 What is a 'whispering' campaign?

12 Describe one form that you think advertising could take in the future that does not exist today.

13 List the questions that must be taken into account when planning an advertising campaign.

14 What are the aims of market research?

15 Why is some market research sometimes carried out after the product is well established?

16 Describe three methods used in carrying out market research.

17 Give three questions that might be included in a typical market research questionnaire.

18 Compare the arguments for and against the use of advertising to sell goods and services.

19 What are codes of advertising practice?

20 In what way does the Trades Description Act help to control advertising?

18 Consumer protection

The need for consumer protection

All firms, people and even the government are consumers. We have seen in Chapter 2 of this book that the aim of production is to make things that can be used by consumers. In fact it has been said that, 'The sole end and purpose of all production is the consumer'. We have also seen in Chapter 17 that advertising aims not only to inform us about goods and services, but also to persuade us to buy them.

With the growth of large-scale production and increased spending power of people, the motivation for firms to obtain and maintain a larger share of the consumer market has risen considerably. This has been further encouraged by technological changes which have not only revolutionalised products and the way they are manufactured, but also the manner in which they are marketed.

At one time the attitude of the law in relation to the protection of the consumer was caveat emptor, or 'Let the buyer beware'. In other words, consumers were expected to protect themselves. This attitude has completely changed, and today consumers are protected in a variety of ways by laws, government agencies and independent organisations.

Traders cannot deprive consumers of their rights without facing the possibility of legal action. Obviously traders need to know their rights and responsibilities to their customers in order to ensure that they meet the requirements of their legal obligations. In addition, the trader has similar rights against his supplier as his customer has against him, so long as he has not agreed to give up those rights.

Consumer legislation

FOOD AND DRUGS
ACT 1955

(Enforced by public health inspectors)

- Forbids the sale of unfit food.
- States hygienic conditions for production and sale of food products.
- Regulates labelling and description of items.
- Provides minimum standards in food composition (e.g. meat content of sausages, pies, etc.).

WEIGHTS AND
MEASURES ACT
1963

- Requires quantity of pre-packed goods to be shown on the container.
- Makes short weight or false measurement an offence.
- Certain goods must be sold in 'prescribed quantities' (e.g. milk).

RESALE PRICES ACT 1964	<ul><li>Suppliers are not allowed to impose a minimum price at which their goods must be sold, but they can suggest a manufacturer's recommended price (MRP).</li><li>Suppliers cannot refuse supplies to a retailer who sells below the recommended price.</li><li>Books, maps and medicines are exempt from this Act.</li></ul>
TRADES DESCRIPTION ACT 1968	This Act makes it an offence punishable by fine or imprisonment to falsely describe goods or services offered for sale. The Act applies to verbal or written descriptions.
UNSOLICITED GOODS AND SERVICES ACT 1971	This Act makes it illegal to demand payment for goods or services that have not been ordered. Should unsolicited goods be delivered, the consumer has two clear courses of action: 1 They can write to the firm giving their name and address from where the goods can be collected. If the trader fails to collect the goods within thirty days they belong to the holder. 2 Alternatively, if unsolicited goods are not collected by the trader within six months they become the property of the holder.
FAIR TRADING ACT 1973	This Act established a permanent Office of Fair Trading which is a government body with the broad function to keep watch on trading matters in the United Kingdom and protect both consumers and business people against unfair practices.
PRICES ACTS 1974 AND 1975	These Acts gave the government the power to: <ul><li>Subsidise food.</li><li>Regulate food prices.</li><li>Require shopkeepers to display prices in a way that does not give a false impression.</li></ul>
CONSUMER CREDIT ACT 1974	The purpose of this Act is to control all forms of credit services. It includes regulation of credit and hire agreements, licensing of lenders, advertisements, breaches of agreements, extortionate charges and credit referencing. The Act protects the consumer in the following ways: <ul><li>All businesses involved with credit or hire agreements are required to obtain a licence from the Office of Fair Trading.</li><li>Consumers can ask a court to reduce unfair or 'extortionate' rates of interest.</li><li>Individuals can ask to see the contents of files referring to them held by credit reference agencies which supply information about the financial standing of people. The individual can ask for wrong information to be corrected.</li><li>All relevant information must be brought clearly to the notice of the borrower. Advertisements offering credit should not be misleading and must advise the consumer of the annual percentage rate (APR), i.e. the true annual rate of interest.</li><li>Compensation may be claimed for goods that are faulty.</li></ul>

Types of credit covered by the Act

- *Personal credit agreements* – bank loans, overdraft, personal loans, pawnbrokers, etc.
- *Credit token agreement* – credit card, charge card, cash dispenser card, etc.
- *Hire purchase (HP) agreement* – a contract for the hire of goods for a fixed period of time with an option to purchase for a nominal sum at the end of the period of repayment by regular instalments (refer also to Chapter 12).
- *Credit sales agreement* – similar to HP but goods become the property of the buyer immediately the deposit or initial payment has been made (refer also to Chapter 12).
- *Consumer hire agreement* – this relates to a true hire arrangement rather than a sale because the item rarely becomes the property of the person hiring the item.

RESTRICTIVE TRADE PRACTICES ACT 1976	This Act aims to safeguard the consumer against the practice of agreements between companies to limit production in order to keep prices artificially high, and to exploit a monopolistic position.
CONSUMER SAFETY ACT 1978	Regulates the sale of goods which may be potentially dangerous, for example, toys, electrical goods, cooking equipment, heaters, etc.
SALE OF GOODS ACT 1979	This Act covers all goods (including food) bought from a trader through a shop, doorstep seller, or sales by mail order. The seller has three main obligations. Goods must:

1 Be of 'merchantable quality'. This means that goods must be reasonably fit for their normal purpose, bearing in mind the price paid, the nature of the goods and how they were described. Thus a new item must not be damaged and it must work properly.
2 Be 'as described'. They must correspond with the description given by the seller, or in accordance with labels on the item or the packing.
3 Be 'fit for any particular purpose made known to the seller'. If you ask for plates that are 'dishwasher safe', and the seller assures you that they are, he has broken his contract with you if they are not.

Note: In the case of private sales only obligation 2 applies.

SUPPLY OF GOODS AND SERVICES ACT 1982	This Act applies the terms of the Sale of Goods Act to goods supplied as part of a service, e.g. faulty taps provided by a plumber, and where goods are hired or exchanged instead of actually being purchased. The Act also provides that a person providing a service must do so:

- With reasonable skill and care
- Within a reasonable time
- For a reasonable charge.

Although there is still a need for the 'buyer to beware' when making purchases, modern marketing methods and trends sometimes make it difficult for the consumer to fairly judge the quality and value of purchases. Pre-packed goods are difficult to examine before they reach home. And how can the purchaser (or even the retailer) of a complex computer or hi-fi system know if the equipment is sound?

It is for these reasons that the manufacturer as well as the retailer has responsibilities to the consumer under the Sale of Goods Act.

CONSUMER
PROTECTION ACT
1987

This Act makes it an offence to give a misleading price indication for any goods, services, accommodation or facilities. This also applies to 'special offers' which turn out to be false.

Government agencies providing consumer protection

DEPARTMENT OF
PRICES AND
CONSUMER
PROTECTION

This government department promotes legislation aimed at protection of consumers, and administers laws related to this. The department also encourages the formation of consumer advice centres and citizens advice bureaux.

OFFICE OF FAIR
TRADING

- Publishes consumer advice information.
- Encourages industries to form associations and codes of practice.
- Investigates and prosecutes traders who persistently commit offences.
- Checks on fitness of traders who provide credit or hire agreements.
- Make suggestions for changes in consumer law.

MINISTRY OF
AGRICULTURE,
FISHERIES AND
FOOD

Administers the law relating to milk production, fisheries, slaughter-houses and meat trade, and the composition and labelling of food.

DEPARTMENT OF
HEALTH AND
SOCIAL SECURITY

Concerned with the production and distribution of medicines and also hygiene.

LOCAL
AUTHORITIES

Trading standards (consumer protection) departments

Investigate local complaints about quality description, weights or measures of goods supplied.

Environmental health departments

Deal with complaints related to impure food and food production or selling premises.

Consumer advice centres

Set up by local authorities to deal with consumer problems.

Independent agencies providing consumer protection

CONSUMERS' ASSOCIATION
- A non-profit making association financed by members' subscriptions.
- Carries out comparative tests on goods and services.
- Publishes results in association magazine *'Which?'*.
- Publishes books on consumer-related matters.

CITIZENS ADVICE BUREAU
Gives confidential advice on legal and consumer matters, on a voluntary basis.

BRITISH STANDARDS INSTITUTION (BSI)
Publishes a series of standards intended to ensure products are fit for the purpose for which they are intended.
- The *kitemark* is awarded to products meeting the required standard.
- The *safety mark* is given to products which pass BSI safety standards.

DESIGN COUNCIL
Examines products of British manufacture and issues its own label to those which are judged to demonstrate a high standard in all aspects of design and performance.

PROFESSIONAL AND TRADE ASSOCIATIONS
Many trades and professions set up associations to form and administer codes of practice which include procedures for dealing with consumer complaints.

THE INSTITUTE OF
FINANCIAL ACCOUNTANTS

CODE OF ETHICS

This code is issued by the Council of the Institute and
applies to all Institute Members.

NATIONALISED INDUSTRIES CONSULTATIVE COUNCILS
Organisations, consultative councils and committees to protect the interests of consumers who deal with major domestic suppliers.

Examples
Post Office   – Post Office Users' National Council
Gas   – Regional Gas Consumers' Council
Electricity   – Electricity Consultative Council
British Rail   – Transport Users' Consultative Committee

MEDIA SUPPORT FOR CONSUMERS
Media such as television, radio and newspapers play a valuable part in consumer protection today by investigating complaints, comparing goods and services and evaluating and recommending 'best buys'.

MAKE A NOTE OF IT

1 Why is consumer protection so important today?

2 What does *'caveat emptor'* mean and why is this less relevant today?

3 List three aspects of consumer protection contained in the Food and Drugs Act.

4 In which way does the Weights and Measures Act aim to protect consumers?

5 What do the letters MRP stand for? What is the relevance of these letters to consumer law?

6 Briefly describe the purpose of the Trade Descriptions Act.

7 What are the two courses of action open to someone who has received unsolicited goods?

8 Name the important body established by the Fair Trading Act.

9 'The Consumer Credit Act is the main safeguard for those who buy on credit.' Explain this statement.

10 List and briefly describe the types of credit covered by the Consumer Credit Act.

11 Briefly explain the purpose of the two following consumer protection Acts:

(a) Restrictive Trade Practices Act

(b) Consumer Safety Act.

12 The Sale of Goods Act states that goods must be *'of merchantable quality'*, *'as described'*, and *'fit for the purpose'*. Explain these phrases.

13 Your friend has recently bought a pair of shoes that are now found to be faulty. Give three suggestions on how she should go about getting the matter put right.

14 State one function of the Office of Fair Trading.

15 Which government department is concerned with the production and distribution of medicines?

16 Briefly describe the work of three types of local authority departments which help to safeguard the interests of consumers.

17 Give a brief description of the contribution that the Consumers' Association makes to consumer protection.

18 The 'kitemark' and the 'safety mark' are both symbols that the consumer should look for. Why is this so?

19 In what way do professional and trade associations contribute to consumer protection?

20 In spite of the fact that many of the media rely on advertisers for much of their income, they still try to promote consumer awareness. Give two examples of how they do this.

DATA RESPONSE QUESTIONS

Part 3

MARKETING

1 Refer to the diagram of the possible structure of a marketing department shown on page 166 and answer the following questions.

    (a) Why is the diagram shown not likely to be typical of a small company? **(2)**

    (b) How do home sales differ from overseas sales? **(2)**

    (c) What work is carried out in the costing section of a marketing department? **(3)**

    (d) Why is market research an essential feature of marketing? **(3)**

    (e) In what way can the structure shown be said to be illustrative of 'marketing mix'? **(4)**

    (f) Explain how the development, sales, and marketing sections of this hypothetical marketing department are inter-related. **(6)**

2 The following questions are related to the chart of a product lifecycle shown on page 167.

    (a) Describe some of the work likely to be done during the 'pre-launch' stage of a product life cycle. **(2)**

    (b) Why does the 'pre-launch' stage show no profit being made? **(2)**

    (c) Why do large amounts of capital tend to be used during the early stages of marketing? **(3)**

    (d) Why is the 'growth' stage of the cycle the most profitable stage? **(3)**

    (e) What factors influence the introduction of a new product? **(4)**

    (f) How would the product life cycle of salt be likely to differ from that of pop records? You may use simple diagrams to illustrate your answer. **(6)**

3 Refer to the following data and the information in Chapter 15 related to bills of exchange and answer the questions that follow the data.

Daly Designs have received an order for £500 000 of the products that they manufacture. The order has come from the Koh Trading Company in India, whom Daly Designs have never traded with before.

    Daly Designs estimate that they will make £200 000 profit on the deal. It will take them four months to produce and deliver the goods, and they will give their usual '28 days to pay terms'. Consequently, Daly Designs cannot hope to obtain the £500 000 payment in less than five months from the receipt of the order. They cannot afford to operate on this basis.

(a) Clearly identify the buyer and the seller involved in the case referred to here. (1)

(b) How much are Daly Designs expecting that it is going to cost them to produce and deliver the order referred to here? (1)

(c) Briefly describe two difficulties Daly Designs face in trading with a firm in another country that they would not encounter in home trade. (4)

(d) Although the prospect of an order valued at £500 000 will obviously be attractive to Daly Designs, accepting it is clearly going to cause the company a cashflow problem. Explain this statement using information from the data given to illustrate your answer. (6)

(e) One way to overcome the cashflow problem would be for Daly Designs to raise a bill of exchange. Explain how this could solve the problem, including mention of the possibility of 'discounting' or 'negotiating' the bill. (8)

4

1992: Opening doors to Europe

December 31, 1992 should be a red-letter day for every business man and business woman. For on that day most existing trade barriers between the member countries of the European Economic Community should have been completely swept away. The 12 EEC countries have all signed the Single European Act which is committed to making Europe a unified market of some 322 million people by that date.

This internal market will not just happen overnight. Instead, in the years leading up to 1992, trade barriers will be gradually whittled away. By the time the internal market is complete, 300 individual pieces of legislation will have taken place. So far 75 have gone ahead.

Because of this continually changing situation, businesses throughout the Common Market need to be aware of what is happening and how it affects them. This is particularly the case in Britain, which tends to pay less attention to business opportunities within the EEC than the other members. France, for example, has invested a lot of money in making business aware of existing opportunities by running a massive television advertising campaign. Unfortunately, Britain does not yet feel European; an attitude which must be changed if British business is to benefit from the internal market.

European Commission

To ensure that Britain does not linger behind its counterparts, the Department of Trade and Industry launched an awareness campaign in March to alert businesses to the possibilities in Europe. However, it is generally the smaller businesses which have more difficulty obtaining information about European opportunities. Most small businesses simply do not have the resources to find out what is available.

Source: Employment News May 1988

(a) What do the letters EEC stand for? (1)

(b) What other name is the EEC known by? (1)

(c) What is the purpose of the Department of Trade and Industry's awareness campaign? (2)

(d) Name six countries, other than Britain, that are members of the EEC. (3)

(e) Why do you think that in the past Britain has paid 'less attention to business opportunities within the EEC than the other members'? (4)

(f) What does this article mean when it says that 'most existing trade barriers between the member countries of the EEC should have been swept away by 1992'? (4)

(g) In what way can the developments commented on in this article be seen to be a realisation of the original aims of the EEC? (5)

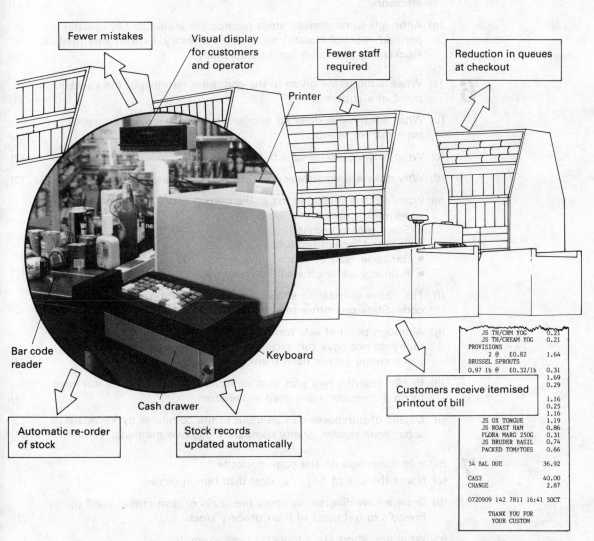

How a point of sale terminal improves supermarket efficiency. The above illustration shows a bar code reader being used. State one other method of reading a bar code.

5 Refer to the diagram on the previous page and answer these related questions:

(a) What is the name given to the series of lines that many shop products have on their labels? (1)

(b) Where would a point-of-sale terminal be found in a shop and why would it be placed in this position? (2)

(c) How does the use of point-of-sale terminals help to reduce queues in supermarkets? (3)

(d) How do computers help to reduce staffing levels in the retail trade? (3)

(e) In spite of their many advantages some shoppers are not happy about the introduction of point-of-sale terminals. Why do you think that it is the case? (3)

(f) Explain how point-of-sale terminals help shops to improve their efficiency. (4)

(g) Although computerised stock records are automatically updated, periodic manual stocktaking is also necessary. Explain why manual stocktaking has to be done occasionally. (4)

6 (a) What is the name given to the computer terminal at the checkout point of a supermarket? (1)

(b) What advantages does an itemised receipt have over conventional supermarket receipts? (1)

(c) What is the purpose of a bar code? (2)

(d) Why does a computerised checkout system result in fewer mistakes? (2)

(e) Write out the following list in the correct order of sequence of supermarket operations:
- Stock record updated
- Itemised receipt produced
- Bar code read by reader device
- Products taken off shelf by customer. (2)

(f) The above illustration shows a light pen being used to read a bar code. State one other method of reading a bar code. (2)

(g) Although point-of-sale terminals increase the efficiency of shops many do not have this facility. Give two possible reasons why some shops do not have them. (2)

(h) Briefly describe two jobs that supermarket personnel do not have to do if computers are used in the store. (4)

(i) Details of purchases can be input to the computer by *keyboard* or *a bar code reader*. Briefly compare these two methods. (4)

7 Refer to the article on the page opposite.

(a) Name the site of Argyll's latest distribution centre. (1)

(b) Draw a flow diagram to show the chain of distribution used by Presto's to get most of their grocery stock. (2)

(c) What are 'short life' products? Give examples. (2)

GIANT DEPOT NO 3 MAKES ITS DEBUT

JUST after *Argyll Express* went to press this month, Argyll's third new distribution centre opened, at Welwyn Garden City, Herts. Last year, depots at Bristol and Wakefield were completed and the new chain of three giant purpose-built distribution centres now forms a vital link with Argyll's existing centres at Felling, Abbotsinch and Portrack. The total depot network offers 1½ million square feet.

By March 1987, the new national network will be supplying 60 per cent of all Presto's grocery stock. The aim, by March, 1988, is to supply more than 70 per cent; eventually, 100 per cent of groceries, together with short-life products, will be delivered to the door by the company's own ordering and supply service.

The key advantage of an Argyll own-distribution system is control – over what needs to be delivered and when – to keep all the supermarkets well-stocked every day of the trading week.

Presto has had numerous food manufacturers supplying direct to its stores, a confusing and often 'clogged' system. Says Laurence Christensen, distribution director:

"Presto stores' hectic 300 deliveries a week should fall to around 25."

Double

While delivery numbers plummet, jobs opportunities rise. With between 300 and 400 new vacancies created in the three new centres, the employee figure for the whole division will double. Argyll has given backing of £21 million to distribution development, a hefty and determined commitment.

Wakefield, Bristol, Welwyn and a dedicated third party depot at Bathgate, due to come on-stream next January, will together provide 842,000 sq ft of space. Wakefield centre, which opened in July last year, houses 4,000 different product lines and can deliver a phenomenal 300,000 cases of goods every week. That's typical of the performance the company can expect from its modern, computerised network.

The system is already proving its worth. It is reliable and efficient, easing the pressures on store staff and pleasing customers, who will always return to shop again in a well-stocked and well-run store.

Source: Argyll Express, 1987

(d) What effect will the new distribution centres have on employment in the distribution sector of the economy in general? (3)

(e) Explain the advantages that having its own distribution has for:
- Presto's
- Presto's customers. (6)

(f) In the light of this type of distribution expansion what is the prospect of independent grocery retailers surviving? (6)

8

(a) Who do you think paid for this advertisement? (1)

(b) Who is the target audience for this advertisement? (2)

(c) What is the aim of the advertisement? (2)

(d) The advertisement says that 'Peterborough's overheads are amongst the lowest in the country'. What does this mean? (3)

(e) In what ways do you think that this could be said to be an example of informative advertising? (3)

(f) State four claims that the advertisement makes as benefits of moving to Peterborough. (4)

(g) This advertisement was produced by an agency called Deighton and Mullen. Briefly describe how this type of agency assists an advertiser. (5)

Part 3

MARKETING

1 Take any specific business in your area and assess the various ways it might increase its share of the market available.

2 Make a detailed price comparison of at least ten different products between shops in central sites and those on the outskirts of town. Include data to justify why the more expensively priced shops continue to exist.

3 To what extent are there regional differences between prices charged by shops of the same retail chain?

4 Choose one large and one small firm in your locality and comment on the different ways that their advertising policies will contrast due to the size of their business.

5 You have decided to purchase a hi-fi unit for which you could afford to pay a maximum of £250. Carry out detailed research to show:
   (a) how you will decide which make of hi-fi you will buy
   (b) which trader you will make your purchase through.

6 Make a survey of the various local outlets for the sale of a basic commodity (e.g. bread, milk etc.). Account for differences in prices and say why the outlets continue to exist in spite of price differences.

7 Carry out a survey to evaluate the effectiveness of a national advertising campaign by a major company on people locally. Include examination of 'target audience'.

8 Make a comparative study to illustrate the similar and the contrasting aims of the advertising policies of a commercial advertiser and that of the government. Use examples to illustrate your study.

9 Make a survey of the various retail outlets in your High Street and reasons why there are more of some than others.

10 Choose three well-known products manufactured by different firms and show how the chain of distribution differs between the products. (Choice of appropriate contrasting products is an important feature of this task.)

11 Take any local street market and explain the reasons why it is sited where it is. Assuming that there were plans to re-site the market, where would you consider an appropriate place to put it? Give reasons for your choice.

12 Visit your local shopping centre and make a comparative survey of:
   (a) types of products used by shops as 'loss leaders'.
   (b) techniques shops use to encourage 'impulse buying'.
   (c) different types of window display employed by various types of shop.

Part 4
COMMUNICATIONS

19 Communications in the business environment

What is communication?

Communication is a means of making contact. The contact may be between people, organisations or between places. It is the process by which the business passes knowledge, information and even items to others. In this respect communication may take written, oral, visual or physical form.

The post and telecommunication services and transport industries provide a communication system, and it is through the services provided by these that most external business communication is carried out. These aspects of communication are examined in detail in the following chapters. Advertising, which is another important method of communication, was examined earlier in Chapter 17.

The need to communicate

Communication is one of the most important activities of any organisation. It is used within the firm as a means of controlling its operations,

The transmitter   *The message*   *The medium*   *The receiver*

R.B. JACKSON

co-ordinating the activities of departments and employees and motivating personnel. Communication also provides important external links between the firm and its suppliers and customers.

There are four basic elements of all communication:

1 *The message* – the information or item that is to be communicated.
2 *The transmitter* – the sender, person or organisation that is the source of the message.
3 *The medium* – the method used, for example, memo, letter, telephone, telex, fax, vehicle, etc.
4 *The receiver* – the person or organisation where the communication terminates.

For communication to be effective all the four elements above must be clear and precise. If any of them are not clear some confusion is likely to occur. For example, imagine that a person giving some instructions to others cannot express themselves clearly, or that those receiving the instructions are not very attentive. Obviously the chances of the instructions being followed are limited. The ability to communicate well is an important aspect of 'leadership' (*see* Chapter 24).

Apart from the importance of the need for businesses to transmit messages accurately, communication is also important to businesses because it not only helps them to operate efficiently, but can play an important part in creating a good public image.

Communication can be an expensive part of a firm's operations, so it is important that the most appropriate methods are chosen, and then used efficiently and economically.

Internal communications

PURPOSE OF
INTERNAL
COMMUNICATIONS

Informing

The different parts of the firm must be kept informed of the activities of other sections so that they can ensure that their work fits into the overall pattern.

Organising

The various sections of the firm must be organised and co-ordinated so that they carry out the part they must play in the control and operation of the organisation's activities.

Directing

Circumstances on occasions require parts of the organisation to be directed in the specific tasks and duties they are expected to carry out in order to achieve the firm's aims.

Motivating

The various levels of management use communication to motivate departments and employees in order to gain maximum benefit from their efforts.

Negotiating

Policies have to be formulated and decisions have to be taken and communicated between members of the organisation. This may well require resolving of conflicts of interest. This may be achieved by informal discussions and interviews, although frequently through formal business meetings.

METHODS OF
INTERNAL
COMMUNICATION

Written

- *Letters* are not generally used as a means of internal communication except in the case of letters such as those related to employment, for example, appointments or promotion.
- *Memorandum* (memo) is the most frequent method of internal communication between members of the same firm. They tend to be brief and to the point, without formal opening or close.
- *Minutes* or summary of discussions that have taken place at a meeting.
- *Reports* may be received from committees, feedback from the sales-force or in the form of information supplied by specialist employees, for example, technical reports, financial reports, etc.
- *Notices* may be displayed to convey information to employees, for example, jobs being advertised internally, safety regulations, social/welfare information.

Oral

- *Spoken* communications are the most commonly used of all means of passing information. Within the organisation this will most

How many methods of internal communication in this illustration can you describe?

frequently be face-to-face contact, often in the form of instructions from superior to subordinate.

- *Telephone* and intercom usefully allow contact between sections of the organisation where face-to-face contact is not convenient.
- *Interviews* are a common means of selecting employees or considering a person for promotion, and for individual discussions.
- *Meetings* provide a convenient means of communication between several people where individual discussions are not convenient or practicable. Meetings are examined in greater detail in the next section of this chapter.

Visual

Pictures, diagrams, maps and plans, wallcharts, flowcharts, pictograms, pie charts and graphs are all ways in which visual communication is typically used within an organisation. They are used to make complicated ideas or information easier to understand. This is examined again later in this chapter, together with other applications of storage and retrieval of information.

Business meetings

Meetings are an important means of communication within organisations. They give the opportunity for exchange of ideas and collective efforts to solve problems and formulate policies. They also provide a convenient means of issuing instructions or information to many people at one time.

PRINCIPAL OFFICERS

The principal officers of a meeting are the chairman, secretary and treasurer:

- *The chairman* is responsible for the correct conduct of the meeting.
- *The secretary* sends out notices of the meeting and a copy of the agenda, records minutes and ensures meeting decisions are carried out.
- *The treasurer* is responsible for financial matters. Sometimes the job of secretary and treasurer are combined.

COMMITTEES

- *Standing* – permanent committees elected to carry out specific regular duties such as discussion of finance, overseas policy, etc.
- *Ad hoc* (or sub) – committee elected to deal with a particular matter over a short period of time, for example, organisation of a social event or to investigate a specific short-term problem.

TYPES OF MEETING

- *General* – open to all members of the organisation, these are held monthly, quarterly or annually (annual general meeting – AGM), and used for committee members to communicate with all members of the organisation. The AGM also serves as a useful time for re-election of principal officers.
- *Extra-ordinary* – additional general meeting called to discuss some special business or unexpected event.

- *Committee* – only attended by committee members, these deal with a specific aspect of the organisation's function. Committees report back to a full general meeting.

AGENDA

The agenda is a summary of the items of business to be discussed at a meeting. The agenda follows an accepted form of order in presentation as follows:

AGENDA

1 **Apologies** – received (usually in letter form) from those unable to be at the meeting.

2 **Minutes** – the minutes or notes made from the last meeting are read.

3 **Matters arising** (out of the minutes) – discussion and follow-up of matters or decisions taken at the last meeting.

4 **Correspondence** – discussion of important letters received since the last meeting.

5 **Reports** – may be made by people who have special information to give to the meeting, for example, reporting back from the work of a committee.

6 **Special matters** – here will be discussed the purpose of the present meeting; decisions which have to be made; proposals to be discussed and voted on; action to be followed before the next meeting.

7 **Next meeting** – date, time and place of next meeting.

8 **Any other business (AOB)** – at this point members bring up matters or questions not included in the agenda.

Minutes

The minutes are a record of what was decided at a meeting and they may include a 'verbatim report', which is a word-for-word record of a report verbally presented.

Voting

There are four basic ways of recording votes at a meeting.

1 *Secret ballot* – votes are marked on a slip of paper by the voters and then put into a ballot box for later counting.
2 *Show of hands* – hands are raised and counted for or against a motion.
3 *Standing* – at large meetings voters may be asked to 'stand and be counted'.
4 *Proxy* – members unable to attend meeting may vote by post or give permission for someone else to vote on their behalf.

External communications

External communications are the ways in which a firm makes contact with other organisations and people with which it is involved, for example, customers, suppliers and other sections of the organisation which are sited elsewhere. The effectiveness with which these communications are carried out can enhance or tarnish the firm's reputation, and help or hinder its efficiency.

The most basic way that a firm makes contact with others is through correspondence (letters). Although letters are slower than the telephone and other electronic means of communicating, they are relatively cheap. They are also in printed form which enables them to be stored in a

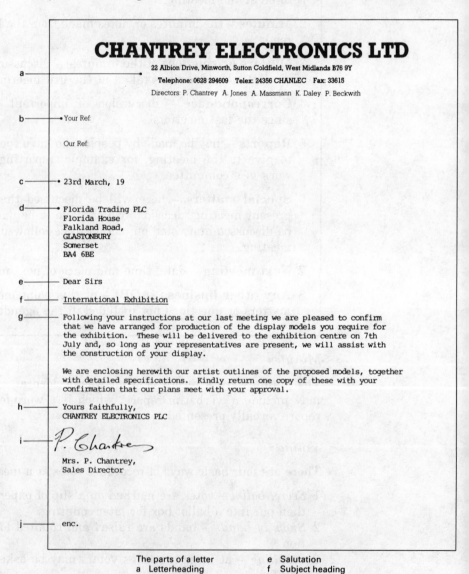

a

CHANTREY ELECTRONICS LTD

22 Albion Drive, Minworth, Sutton Coldfield, West Midlands B76 9Y

Telephone: 0628 294609   Telex: 24356 CHANLEC   Fax: 33615

Directors: P. Chantrey A. Jones A. Massmann K. Daley P. Beckwith

b   Your Ref:

         Our Ref:

c   23rd March, 19

d   Florida Trading PLC
         Florida House
         Falkland Road,
         GLASTONBURY
         Somerset
         BA4 6BE

e   Dear Sirs

f   International Exhibition

g   Following your instructions at our last meeting we are pleased to confirm
         that we have arranged for production of the display models you require for
         the exhibition. These will be delivered to the exhibition centre on 7th
         July and, so long as your representatives are present, we will assist with
         the construction of your display.

         We are enclosing herewith our artist outlines of the proposed models, together
         with detailed specifications. Kindly return one copy of these with your
         confirmation that our plans meet with your approval.

h   Yours faithfully,
         CHANTREY ELECTRONICS PLC

i   *P. Chantrey*

         Mrs. P. Chantrey,
         Sales Director

j   enc.

The parts of a letter
a Letterheading
b Reference number
c Date of letter
d Name and address of
   addressee

e Salutation
f Subject heading
g Body of letter
h Complimentary close
i Signature
j Enclosures

simple filing system, and to be read without the aid of 'reading' or trans-mission devices.

Most business letters have a printed letterheading. This shows the name of the firm, the address, and other information that is important to people the firm corresponds with. The letterheading also reflects the individuality of the firm, perhaps in the form of a logo, trade mark, or special form of lettering.

There is a basic format that most business letters tend to follow. Quite apart from the style of structure of the letter the wording is important, this needs to be clear and precise if the message it contains is to be conveyed accurately.

POSTAL COMMUNICATIONS	This type of communication is used in the form of letters, circulars and forms such as orders, invoices and other trading documents that were examined in Chapter 15. Postal services are dealt with later in Chapter 20.
TELECOMMUNI-CATIONS	They provide a wider and more speedy means of communication including telephone, telex, fascimile transmission, intercity conference links, data transmission services and other electronic communication systems that are examined in Chapter 20.
ADVERTISING	This was the topic of Chapter 17 and is also a means of external communication. It is through advertising that the firm makes potential customers aware of the goods and services it wishes to sell.
TRANSPORT	Transport provides a physical means of contact, particularly in respect of delivery of goods. This too is the subject of more detailed examination later, in Chapter 21.

Storage and retrieval of information

The use of modern technology for communication within organisations is increasingly evident today, particularly for storage and retrieval of information. Word processors and computers are playing a major part in this important aspect of business. The following are typical business applications of this technology.

- *Company registers* – of shareholders are constantly changing as company shares are bought and sold. A company can speedily update these records.
- *Stock records* – automatic updating of records as stocks are removed or added to store. Warnings are automatically given when stock level falls too low, and immediate stock valuation is available.
- *Payroll* (wages system) – maintenance of payroll and personal records for employees. Automatic calculation of wages, income tax, national insurance and issue of P60, etc.
- *Word processing* – copies of letters, invoices and statements of account can be typed into a computer and stored on magnetic disc or tape for later retrieval for review on visual display unit (VDU) or line

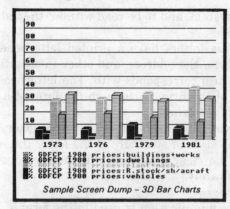

Sample Screen Dump – 3D Bar Charts

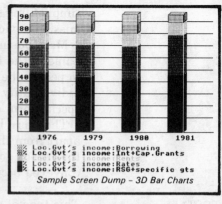

Sample Screen Dump – 3D Bar Charts

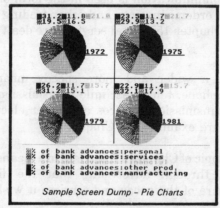

Sample Screen Dump – Pie Charts

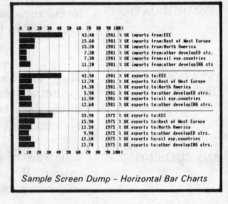

Sample Screen Dump – Horizontal Bar Charts

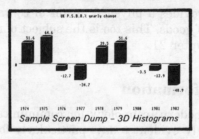

Sample Screen Dump – 3D Histograms

Today computers are playing a major part in communication and they can present data in a variety of stimulating and meaningful screen displays.

printer. Word processors are playing a major part in this kind of computer application. Standard letters can be stored on ' memory' for future recall and updating for reproduction, thus allowing much of the repetitive typing to be reduced.

- *Accounts* – issue of invoices, statements of account and maintaining records of customers' accounts.
- *Display* – of data in graphic form is particularly effective with a VDU. Graphs and charts can be displayed in a variety of forms and colours to give a simple representation of complicated data, making it easier to understand. For example, a comparison of the performance of different members of a sales team becomes immediately clear when displayed in the form of a bar chart or graph.

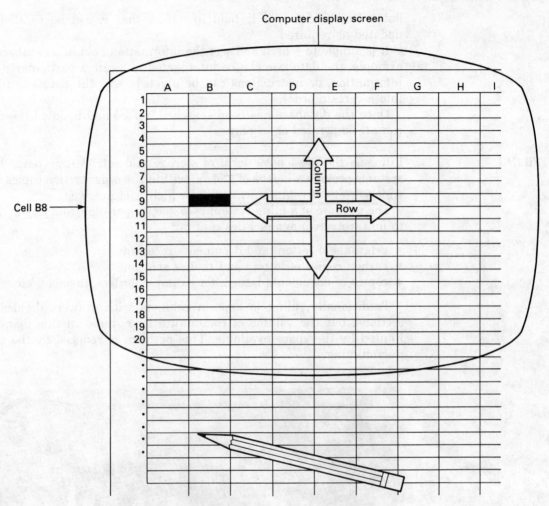

Spreadsheet worksheet

SPREADSHEETS AND DATABASES	Spreadsheets and databases are two important ways of using computers for storing and display of information.

Spreadsheets

A spreadsheet is a computer software package that allows the computer operator to enter and store data in columns and rows of figures, called *cells*, to be spread out on a VDU screen in 'grid' format. This data can be printed out as a whole or in part.

Spreadsheets are used particularly for financial planning, and preparation of management reports. They are also used to carry out 'experimental' work. For example, a spreadsheet can be used to assess what would happen to a set of figures if a particular factor were changed.

Databases

A database is a form of electronic filing. It is an organised collection of data. The information is held in a way that it can be recalled and updated as required.

It is simple to search and sort the information held in a database. For example, the database can be interogated to locate a particular item of information, or instructions can be given to sort the database records into a certain order.

Once the database has been searched, sorted and updated the record can all be printed or in part.

FILING

Filing is the most basic form of storage and retrieval systems. Filing systems provide a means of storing within the organisation copies of the wide variety of communications in which it is involved.

The purpose of a filing system is to keep papers safe and tidy and easy to find (retrieve) again. Files contain:

- originals of letters and documents received
- carbon copies of letters and replies sent out
- copies of documents issued, for example, orders, invoices, etc.

Traditionally, filing is kept in cabinets with drawers divided into sections, but the volume of communications stored in this manner is limited by the space available. This problem is reduced by the use of microfilming.

Microfiche reader

Microfilming consists of photographing documents and reducing them to a very small size. A single sheet of A4 information can be reduced to the size of a postage stamp or even smaller, and 8 000 'pictures' can be stored on a single spool of film. The film can be stored in a variety of convenient ways – reels, strips, aperture cards or microfiche. The documents stored in this way can be viewed by using a 'reader' or 'scanner' which magnifies the image and displays it on a viewer or VDU.

Advantages of microfilming

- Saves space and weight
- Convenient for posting
- More durable than paper.

Disadvantages of microfilming

- Requires special viewer
- Cannot update film: it must be replaced.

**MAKE A
NOTE
OF IT**

1 Why is communication important to a firm?
2 Name the four basic elements of communication.
3 What is the purpose of the internal communications of a firm?
4 List the main methods of internal communication available.
5 Give an example of the way in which graphs and charts might be used as a means of communication.
6 Name the two principal officers of a meeting.
7 What is the function of the chairman of a meeting?
8 Describe the purpose of three types of meeting.
9 What do the letters AGM stand for?
10 List in correct order six items shown on an agenda.
11 What do the letters AOB represent?
12 Explain the difference between the minutes and a 'verbatim report'.
13 Describe four methods of voting at meetings.
14 What is the purpose of external communications of a firm?
15 List the four main forms of external communication.
16 Name the two forms of modern technology that are now making a major contribution to storage and retrieval of information.
17 Briefly describe four applications of modern technology as a means of handling information.
18 What do the letters VDU stand for?
19 List the three categories of papers likely to be found in files.
20 What are the advantages of storing filing on microfilm?

20 Post and telecommunication

In the previous chapter we identified various methods of external communication used by firms. In this chapter we examine two of these methods in greater depth. Postal communications involving the letter and parcel services is the most traditional method. Telecommunication is the more recent of these methods of contact between firms, and it is rapidly changing in response to technological developments.

Postal communications

Businesses need to be able to communicate with each other in order to exchange the correspondence and documentation necessary for transactions to take place. The variety of postal services operated by the Post Office enable businesses to send and receive letters, parcels and payments. The existence of these services makes a considerable contribution to the effective operation of industry and commerce.

The Post Office is a public corporation and a detailed explanation of all postal services is contained in the *Post Office Guide*. *The Post Office User's National Council* exists to investigate complaints and enquiries related to the Post Office services.

Letter services

In the UK we say that we have a two-tier postal service. *First class mail* is faster and costs more than *second class mail*.

Today, in a move towards greater mechanisation of mail handling, the Post Office has identified standard sizes of envelopes (Post Office preferred – POP) which help mechanised handling of mail movement. In addition, postcodes have been issued to help the Post Office to sort mail automatically.

- Every street has a separate postcode.
- The postcode is shown as letters and numbers at the end of an address.

BUSINESS REPLY SERVICE

The trader provides potential customers with specially printed envelopes displaying a licence number and the class of postage. The trader pays postage on letters received, thus encouraging custom.

FREEPOST

This service also allows people to write to traders in reply to advertisements without paying postage, as long as the envelope is addressed in a special way.

- The address must include the word FREEPOST.
- Only second-class service is available.
- The trader is saved the expense of providing envelopes.

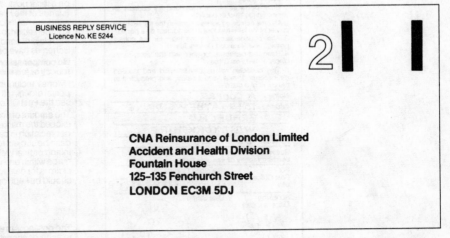

BUSINESS REPLY SERVICE
Licence No. KE 5244

CNA Reinsurance of London Limited
Accident and Health Division
Fountain House
125–135 Fenchurch Street
LONDON EC3M 5DJ

Business reply service envelope

REGISTERED POST

This service provides compensation to the sender for a lost postal packet. The compensation paid for a loss is proportionate to the value of the packet and the registration fee paid on posting. The letter or packet to be posted in this way must have a large blue cross on it. A certificate of posting is issued as proof of posting, and a signature is obtained on delivery. All valuable items should be sent using this service.

RECORDED DELIVERY

The recorded delivery service is cheaper than registered post, but in the case of a loss only a nominal compensation is paid. The service provides proof of posting and delivery and is suitable for important documents (e.g. a final demand for payment of a debt) but is not suitable for posting valuables.

SELECTAPOST

The Post Office will arrange for an addressee's mail to be subdivided (e.g. into departments) prior to delivery so long as some indication of the division required is shown in the address.

POSTE RESTANTE

Packets may be sent to a post office in a particular town 'to be called for'. The Post Office keeps the packet for up to two weeks and only releases it upon proof of identity. The service is particularly useful to sales representatives who are unsure where they will be residing during their sales tour.

CERTIFICATE OF POSTING

- The Post Office gives a receipt to confirm a package has been handed over the counter.

┌─────────────────────────────────────┐
│ **B 706105** Recorded   │
│   Delivery   │
│ - - - - - - - - - - - - - - - - - │
│   │
│ **Certificate of Posting**   │
│ **for Recorded Delivery**   │
│ **How to post**   │
│ 1 Enter below in ink the name and full address as │
│ written on the letter or packet.   │
│ 2 Affix the numbered adhesive label in the top left-hand │
│ corner of the letter (or close to the address on a packet) │
│ 3 Affix postage stamps to the letter for the correct │
│ postage and Recorded Delivery fee   │
│ 4 Hand this certificate, together with the letter, to an │
│ officer of The Post Office   │
│ 5 This certificate will be date-stamped and initialled │
│ as a receipt. Please keep it safely, and produce it in │
│ the event of a claim.   │
│   │
│ Name   A COOPER   │
│ Address 151 MATHEWS DRIVE   │
│   BRADFORD   │
│   WEST YORKSHIRE   │
│ Postcode BD3 7ZU   │
│ **Recorded Delivery should not be used for** │
│ **sending money or valuable items.** │
│ For   Recorded Delivery no │
│ Post Office   │
│ use   **B   706105**   │
│ Accepting   Date Stamp   │
│ Officer's initials   │
│   │
│ P2297 Nov 85   │
└─────────────────────────────────────┘

Recorded Delivery

Where a Recorded Delivery fee has been paid on a letter posted to an address in the United Kingdom, compensation for loss or damage in the post due to a wrongful act or neglect or default of The Post Office is payable if such conditions as are required by Post Office Schemes in relation to Recorded Delivery letters have been complied with.

Where a Recorded Delivery fee has been paid on a letter posted to an address in the Channel Islands or the Isle of Man, The Post Office, although not legally liable to do so, may pay compensation for loss or damage in the post if the relevant conditions required by Post Office Schemes have been complied with

No compensation will be paid in respect of money or jewellery sent by this service.

('Money' includes coin, paper money, stamps, postal orders, gift vouchers, etc). For full details see the Post Office Guide.

The amount of compensation paid will not exceed the market value in case of loss, or depreciation in case of damage, and will in any case be subject to the limit appropriate to the inland ordinary letter service. Claims should be made within one year of the date of posting. If a claim is for damage or loss of contents, the item should be kept for Post Office inspection

The posting is in all respects subject to and in accordance with the relevant statutory Scheme, and The Post Office assumes no contractual obligation.

For confirmation of delivery use the Advice of Delivery service. The fee for this service is lower at the time of posting than subsequently

Certificate of posting

- No charge is made for this receipt.
- Useful in establishing date of posting when there is a possibility of dispute.

Parcels and special services

PARCEL POST

Used for packages too large for letter post, and up to size and weight limits imposed by the Post Office. A 'postage forward' (postal charges to be paid by receiver) service is available using special labels and a licence allowing use of the service.

SWIFTAIR

This service is available for all letters to Europe and for airmail letters to countries outside Europe. Items are handed over a post office counter and an additional fee is paid. The packet receives accelerated treatment within this country, and within the country of destination.

EXPRESS POST

Letters and parcels up to a certain size and weight are accepted for delivery by special messenger. The word EXPRESS must be written clearly in the top left-hand corner of the package. Charges are based on distance as well as weight and, therefore, the service is only generally used for relatively short distances.

SPECIAL DELIVERY

Available as part of the first class service only, special delivery is carried out by messenger after the packet has arrived at the destination Post Office. It is suitable for use as a complementary service to the delivery of letters, parcels, recorded delivery and registered post. Packets must be marked 'special delivery'.

COMPENSATION FEE (CF) PARCELS

The Post Office will pay compensation for any parcel lost or damaged in the post if CF has been paid on posting. Amount of compensation is related to fee paid and a nominal maximum amount. Not suitable for very valuable items.

CASH ON DELIVERY (COD)

For a small charge the Post Office will collect a specified amount (not exceeding £100) before parting with a package and pass it to the person who sent the parcel. The money collected is known as a *trade charge*. All letters and packets sent COD must be registered.

DATAPOST

- Provides door-to-door overnight delivery service.
- Packets collected and can be returned at times pre-arranged with the Post Office.
- Particularly suitable for exchange of data such as computer material.
- International service also available.

datapost
A ROYAL MAIL SERVICE

Finance copy

Weight

Charge £   :

Initials of accepting officer   Time

Contract No **D/**   **/INT**

To   Date

This Datapost packet is posted in accordance with the Datapost service regulations and the terms of the contract number shown hereon.

I authorise the charges in respect of this packet to be charged to my/our account

Signature of sender

From

RED STAR

The Red Star service is operated by British Rail and not the Post Office, but it is sometimes used by businesses as an alternative to the Post Office parcels services.

Red Star is a strictly timetabled express service. Packages are handed in at railway stations and a number of different transit services are available; same day, overnight, station to station or delivered to the door – each with its own tariff.

RAILWAY LETTERS　Under an agreement with the Post Office some railway companies will accept first class letters at certain railway stations for transmission to another station on their own lines. The parcel may be collected at the railway station, or transferred to the post.

Franking machines

- Machines bought or hired from firms licensed by the Post Office.
- Hirer pays for units of postage value.
- Machine used to stamp letters and parcels with postage paid amount.
- A slogan can be printed at the same time as postage paid to advertise company's products.

A postal franking with a slogan

Telecommunications and technological change

Although the postal services described in the previous sections are varied and effective, they have one major limitation. Even the speediest of the postal services cannot compare with the instant delivery of messages possible through most telecommunications services.

The essence of speed has become an increasingly important aspect of business communication. Stockbrokers and other organisations in the financial markets need to know minute by minute changes in market prices; companies want to be able to contact their representatives in their cars at any time; contracts, plans, specifications and other important documents need to be transmitted around the world in seconds; access to a wide range of information from data banks must be at finger tip control. All of these facilities, and many more, are available through an ever increasing number of telecommunications services which have not been slow to exploit new advances in technology.

British Telecom is one of the major suppliers of telecommunications in the UK, although there are a considerable number of other companies such as Mercury Telecommunications Ltd competing with British Telecom. Until 1984 British Telecom was a public corporation. In that year the corporation was privatised (sold to private enterprise), but it still holds a monopolistic position for the supply of many telecommunication services. All of the following services, apart from Teletext, are operated by British Telecom, but you should remember that there are other firms competing in the telecommunications market.

Telephone

Advice of duration and charge (ADC)

Call connected and timed by operator. Caller is advised cost of call by operator when call is terminated.

Alarm call

Subscriber arranges for exchange to ring a specified telephone number at a particular time.

Transferred charge call (reversed charge call)

Operator connected call where the receiver of the call accepts the charge.

Personal call (person-to-person)

Telephone operator connects caller with a particular person. Charge does not begin until the requested person is obtained.

Telephone credit card

Allows holder to make operator connected calls and charge costs to their normal telephone bill.

Radiophone

Telephone contact to and from moving vehicles, e.g. Excel.

Freefone

Operator connected calls on a transferred charge basis. Used by businesses that wish to allow their customers or agents to make telephone calls to them without payment, thus encouraging custom.

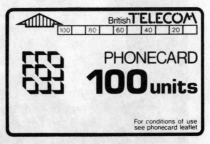

Call card

Call cards can be bought in the Post Office and some newsagents and used in special public call boxes. They are a useful alternative to coins.

TELEPHONE
DIRECTORIES

Issued free to subscribers together with dialling code booklets. Subscribers are listed alphabetically. Those who choose not to be listed are known as 'ex-directory'.

- *Classified Trades Directories* (Yellow Pages)
  Lists local businesses alphabetically by trade.
- *Green Pages*
  Special section of some telephone directories (or a separate booklet) giving details of a variety of services offered by British Telecom.
- *Dialling code booklets*
  Contains subscriber trunk dialling (STD) and international direct dialling (IDD) codes, and also codes for connection to various telephone information services such as correct time, test cricket score, weather, motoring information, etc.

Correspondence facilities

TELEMESSAGE

Messages are accepted by telephone or Telex at Royal Mail sorting centres for delivery with the next day's first class post.

FACSIMILE
TRANSMISSION
SERVICES (FAX)

This service provides facilities for transmission of black and white documents, letters, photos, etc. Customers can use machines:

- On their own sites.

Sending a document by fax

- Through British Telecom local centres.
- In association with services offered by organisations other than British Telecom.

The prepared A4 size document is fed into a machine and a copy of it is immediately transmitted to another machine sited elsewhere at home or abroad. The facilities can be used as an electronic mailing service, reducing the need to use conventional postal services.

TELEX

The main disadvantage of the use of the telephone in business is that the communications are not in printed form, and there are times when

```
87-11-20   10:03
67457
67457   BXNTER G
1792   87-11-20   10:03

ATTN:   DAVID EVANS
        PETER FOREMAN
        IRENE WALSH

PLEASE RELEASE:

273 08782 7   PARALLELISM IN PROD SYS
              12.95 H+E, CODE 01, U/C 1.600. ANS RPN NO DATE.
              CURRENT PRINTING DATE 20.11.87.

REGARDS,

SUSAN DRUMMOND   *
67457   BXNTER G
261367 PITMAN G
```

A modern Telex system

it is essential that a message is delivered immediately and also in printed form.

Subscribers to the Telex service rent a machine called a teleprinter and have their Telex call number listed in the *Telex Directory*. Subscribers can call up directly other subscribers at home and overseas.

Messages, which can be in code, are typed into the teleprinter and transmitted immediately to the receiving machine. The receiving terminal can be left unattended and will record messages twenty-four hours a day.

Charges for Telex calls are based on:

- Distance between Telex subscribers.
- Length of message.

TELETEX

Typed messages or letters can be prepared in the normal fashion on a special electronic typewriter terminal. The prepared text can be automatically transmitted in seconds, over ordinary telephone lines, to a receiving terminal where it is printed out or displayed on a screen in exactly the same format as the original.

(Do not confuse with Telex or Teletext.)

Conference facilities

CONFRAVISION

Attending conferences and meetings between executives is time-consuming and expensive. Those attending have to:

Modes of presentation

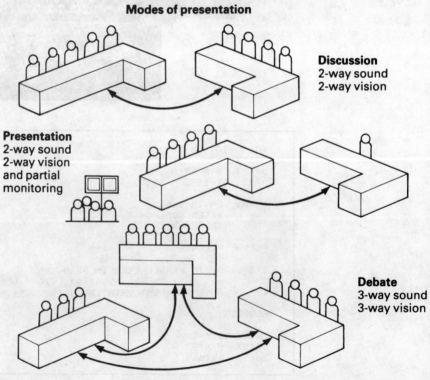

Discussion
2-way sound
2-way vision

Presentation
2-way sound
2-way vision
and partial
monitoring

Debate
3-way sound
3-way vision

Confravision

- Travel many miles to get to the meeting place.
- Face the hazards and delays likely to occur.
- Arrange overnight accommodation.

The Confravision service allows people to hold face-to-face discussions, but without the inconvenience of everyone travelling to the same meeting place. The Confravision service provides studios in cities throughout the UK, which link up by sound and vision, so that discussions can take place as if all those attending the meeting were present in the same room.

Data links

DATEL

A telecommunications system which allows a computer in a firm to communicate with computers on sites in other parts of the country, and in many overseas countries.

PRESTEL

Prestel is a two-way computerised information service. The service can be used by anyone who has a specially adapted television set and a telephone. The telephone connection is used to obtain up-to-the-minute news and information from an extensive data bank for display on the television screen. The Prestel service can respond to questions presented to it. For example, the data bank can be asked about road or weather conditions; availability of air or theatre tickets; and bookings can be placed and accepted through the system.

TELETEXT

CEEFAX and ORACLE services provided by the broadcasting authorities whereby people with suitable televisions can call on a wide variety of

Ceefax

Answering recording machine

Office switchboard system

information and news items from a central data bank. These are some-times referred to as view data systems because the information is viewed, but does not respond to inputs in the way that the Prestel system does.

Internal telecommunications

- *Intercom* – used for verbal communication between offices, departments or boss and secretary. Message relayed through small loud-speaker.
- *Telephone answering machine* – apparatus connected to telephone to record message when telephone is unattended.
- *Private manual branch exchange* (PMBX) – switchboard requiring telephone operator to connect all calls incoming, outgoing and between extensions.
- *Private automatic branch exchange* (PABX) – switchboard providing automatic transfer of internal calls and connection to outside line by dialling a special number (9).
- *Paging* – lightweight receiver carried on person which 'bleeps' when signal sent out to tell holder to telephone some central point.

> **MAKE A NOTE OF IT**

1 Why are postal services important to businesses?
2 Where are full details of all postal services to be found?
3 'The Post Office is a public corporation'. What does this mean?
4 What is the function of the Post Office User's National Council?
5 Why do we say we have a two-tier postal service in the UK?
6 What are POP envelopes?
7 What is the correct name for the letters and numbers at the end of an address?
8 Compare the business reply service with Freepost.
9 Describe the registered post and recorded delivery services giving appropriate examples when each would be used in preference to the other.
10 Name the postal service where mail is sub-divided prior to delivery. Give an example of how use of this service would help the firm that is receiving the letters.
11 Briefly describe the poste restante service and give an example of how it might be employed by a company engaged in sales.
12 What is the purpose of a certificate of posting?
13 Who would pay the postal charges for a package that is sent 'postage forward'?
14 The Swiftair and Red Star services both provide 'special' handling of packets. Explain what is special about these two services.
15 What is the basis of the charge to send a package by express post?
16 Briefly describe the special delivery service.
17 What do the letters CF stand for?
18 What do the letters COD stand for? Why is this service of particular use to a mail order company?
19 Briefly describe the Datapost service and give one example of how it might be used by a firm.

20 What is a franking machine? How can the use of such a machine help to increase efficiency in dealing with outgoing mail?

21 What is the main advantage that telecommunication has over postal communication?

22 Give three examples of circumstances in which businesses particularly need telecommunications facilities.

23 In 1984 British Telecom was privatised. What does this mean?

24 What is an ADC telephone call?

25 Who pays the cost of a transferred charge call?

26 Give an example of a situation where a business might decide to make a personal call.

27 What is the purpose of a telephone credit card? Give one example of how a firm might use this service.

28 Who pays the cost of freefone telephone calls? How might a company use this facility?

29 What kind of information is to be found in Classified Trades Directories?

30 With reference to telephone services, what do the letters STD and IDD stand for?

31 What is telemessage?

32 Briefly describe a facsimile transmission service.

33 What is Teletex?

34 Give a detailed description of the Telex service.

35 What is Confravision and how can this save time and expense for businesses?

36 Briefly explain Datel.

37 'Although Prestel and Teletex have some similarities, Prestel has a far wider application.' Explain this statement.

38 What is an intercom?

39 With a telephone answering machine you can be in when you are out. How could this machine be particularly useful to a small business person?

40 What is paging?

21 Transport

Importance of transport

Transport is a form of communication; a means of making contact between two distant points. It provides services that enable workers to go to and from work, raw materials to reach the producer and finished products to be distributed. An efficient transport system reduces the amount of capital needed to be tied up in stocks, because new supplies can be obtained quickly. It also makes international trade possible, which results in the many benefits discussed in Chapter 14.

Choice of transport

Each type of transport has its special uses. Some are more suitable for a particular task than others. Consequently, choosing an appropriate method of transport for particular circumstances is one of the skills

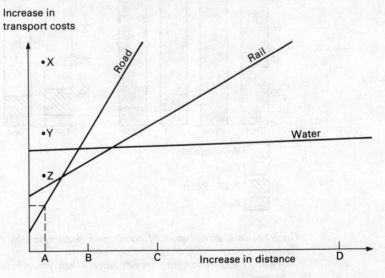

This graph shows the costs of various means of transport

(a) List the cheapest method of transport at each of the points shown as A, B, C and D

(b) Which of the points X, Y, and Z would you consider to be related to air transport? Give a brief explanation of your choice.

essential for business success. Transport users will take the following factors into account when choosing the form of transport to use:

- The nature of the goods.
- How urgently the consignment is needed.
- The value of each item.
- Cost of the transport.
- Distance the consignment must be transported.
- The size and weight of the load.
- Convenient position of terminals, e.g. station, docks and airport.
- Possibility of combining loads to reduce costs.
- The reputation of the carrier.

Road transport

Road transport carries 60 per cent of inland freight and 92 per cent of passenger traffic. There has been a steady growth in road traffic and this has called for the development of elaborate motorway systems to reduce congestion and maintain traffic flow.

All vehicles in Britain must be insured and those over three years old

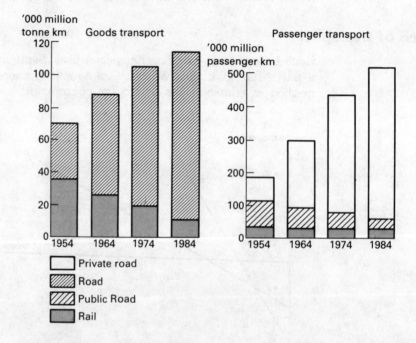

Changes in the transport of goods and passengers by road and rail in Great Britain.

1 What general changing trends have taken place between 1954 and 1984 with respect to

   (a) goods transport in total
   (b) goods transport by rail
   (c) passengers travelling privately by road

2 Give reasons for the trends you have identified

must pass a Ministry of Transport (MOT) test to show that they are fit for use on public roads.

ADVANTAGES OF
ROAD TRANSPORT

- Door-to-door service provides maximum flexibility.
- Fast over short distances of less than 200 miles.
- Risk of damage reduced by lack of need for trans-shipment.
- Can reach places inaccessible to other forms of transport.
- Motorway network speeds up movement and reduces congestion.
- Less tied to a rigid timetable than railways.
- Suitable for speedy direct delivery of perishable goods.
- Other forms of transport rely on road transport to connect with terminals such as airport, station, dock.

DISADVANTAGES
OF ROAD
TRANSPORT

- Expensive to operate in large congested cities.
- Subject to mechanical breakdowns.
- Affected by adverse weather conditions.
- Loads are limited in size and weight.
- Some roads unsuitable for very large vehicles.
- Slower than railways over long distances.
- Wastes resources if lorry returns empty.
- Tax on vehicles and fuel must be incorporated into costs.

Rail transport

The railways were nationalised (taken into state ownership) in 1947 and placed under the control of the British Railways Board. Control is delegated through five regions: Eastern, Southern, Midland, Western and Scottish. British Rail also operates some ferry services.

FREIGHTLINER
SERVICE

This is British Rail's high-speed container service which links up with special road and sea terminals.

Standard sizes (ISO) of containers are loaded direct from lorries on to special train bogies, and at their rail destination they are unloaded in a similar manner.

This simplified handling results in:

- Improved speed and handling economies.
- Simplified and more effective timetabling.
- Reduced losses from damage or theft.
- Direct links between terminals such as ports.

Freightliner service movements are carried out mainly at night when the lines are clear from other traffic.

ADVANTAGES OF
RAIL TRANSPORT

- Easier for passenger travel than road transport.
- Faster than road on distances in excess of 200 miles.
- Less labour intensive than road transport.
- Especially suited for container traffic.
- More economical in fuel use than road transport.

DISADVANTAGES
OF RAIL
TRANSPORT

- Routes determined by railway lines and stations.
- Equipment costs are very high.
- Relies on road transport for trans-shipment.
- Less economic than road movement for journeys of less than 200 miles.

Inland waterways (canals and rivers)

Despite the glorious past of the great canal era this form of transport has largely been replaced by road and rail transport. Its few advantages today are the smoothness of movement and the fact that it is the cheapest form of transport. But these advantages are generally outweighed by the main disadvantage which is slowness.

Sea transport

Shipping is particularly important to Britain as an island because it provides our main link to overseas markets. Transport is also one of Britain's invisible earners, contributing to the balance of payments (*see* Chapter 14).

There are four basic classes of ships: passenger liners, cargo liners, tramps and special freighters.

PASSENGER
LINERS

Passenger liners are built primarily for passenger (particularly cruising) travel. They carry some cargo, and as they follow fixed routes and keep to a regular timetable delivery dates can be guaranteed. However, high freight costs limit freight use to high value cargoes.

Sea transport

CARGO LINERS

This type of ship sometimes carries a few passengers, although their main purpose is to deliver cargo. They operate on fixed routes and to a regular timetable. The vessel will sail from a port on time, even if some of the scheduled cargo has not arrived.

TRAMP SHIPS

Tramps are ships that have no timetable or set route. They will carry any type of cargo to any port in the world. The vessels are chartered through a charter party agreement (*see* later).

SPECIAL
FREIGHTERS

For special cargoes there are a variety of purpose-built ships.

- *Container ships* – cellular. design vessels for fast load/unload.
- *Bulk carriers* – ore and grain.
- *Tankers* – oil and other bulk liquids.
- *Ferries* – roll-on/roll-off; hovercraft have proved particularly successful.

SEA PORT
REQUIREMENTS

Efficient sea transport operations require the provision of good terminal facilities which enable vessels to 'turn round' quickly. The following are the main requirements of a modern port.

- Clear access channel with deep water.
- Some protection from rough seas.
- Wharves with appropriate lifting gear and equipment such as that necessary for moving containers, etc.
- Warehouses, including specialist storage, such as refrigeration, bonded stores, hazardous cargo.
- Supplies of oil, water and other ship's requirements.
- Repair facilities such as dry dock.
- Customs and immigration facilities.
- Good links with road and rail network.
- Buildings for offices and commercial services such as banks, restaurants.

Air transport

This is the youngest but most highly technical form of transport. It is constantly expanding in the volume of both passenger and freight it handles. The major British airports are controlled by the British Airports Authority (BAA).

ADVANTAGES OF
AIR TRANSPORT

- It is the fastest form of transport.
- Operates to timetables, mostly on direct routes.
- Reduces risk of damage or pilferage.
- Shorter transit time reduces insurance costs.
- Packaging costs reduced.
- Particularly effective over long distances.
- Containers are now being used to speed up cargo loading and unloading facilities.

DISADVANTAGES
OF AIR TRANSPORT

- High operational costs result in high freight rates.
- Weight and size of cargo is limited.
- Sometimes affected by adverse weather conditions.
- Relies on other forms of transport to and from airport.
- Not suitable for short distances.
- Causes noise and pollution.
- Economic use is limited to certain cargoes, for example, light weight, high value, urgently required commodities such as drugs, mail or perishable goods.

AIRPORT
REQUIREMENTS

In a similar way that a sea port demands facilities that enable it to operate efficiently, an airport also has requirements that must be met if it is to fulfil its functions.

List the special facilities that are necessary to enable an airport to operate effectively.

Siting

The siting of an airport is very important. While it would be convenient to site an airport in a country area where land costs are cheaper than in cities, most air travellers are heading for one of the world's major cities where they can link up with other forms of transport. For this reason, an airport has to be sited as near as possible to a major city, but avoiding high rise buildings and causing as little noise and pollution as possible to local residents.

Road and rail links

Road and rail links play an important part in providing easy access to and departure of travellers and freight. If the road and rail links are speedy and efficient they can allow the airport to be sited further away from a city centre. The modern terminal also requires facilities for long- and short-term parking as well as freight storage areas such as a bonded warehouse.

Operational, repair and safety facilities

A wide range of equipment and repair services are necessary to keep aircraft flying. For example, sophisticated radio, radar, computer and other technical equipment and the people to operate them have become increasingly important at busy international airports. In addition, aircraft use vast quantities of highly inflammable fuel. This must be stored safely, and a fleet of tankers and other vehicles are needed to load fuel, luggage and freight on to aircraft. In addition, safety and medical services such as fire engines and ambulances must be permanently ready for action.

Customs and immigration officials

These are needed to regulate the import of goods on which duty must be paid, as well as to check for prohibited items such as drugs or fire arms. Immigration officials are also necessary to ensure that those who enter the country have the right to do so.

Terminal buildings and personnel

Terminal buildings containing baggage and freight handling equipment are required to ensure speedy movement of passengers and cargo. Within these buildings there may be incorporated hotel accommodation and commercial services such as banks, post office, duty free shop and bars and restaurants. Airports require a variety of personnel to operate the terminal buildings. Security staff have become increasingly important.

Pipelines

Pipelines allow the transport of commodities without using a vehicle. Examples are gas, oil and water.

Containerisation

A container is a large pressed steel box available in two International Standards Organisation (ISO) sizes (20 or 40 ft × 8 ft × 8 ft) capable of carrying twenty or thirty tonnes of cargo. The container is packed at the factory or inland pooling depot and delivered to the container terminal by rail (freightliner) or road and deposited in the container parking area in the dock container terminal.

The containers are moved around the terminal by straddle carriers. The container is loaded precisely into position in the ship's hold by special gantry cranes.

ADVANTAGES OF
CONTAINERISATION

- Reduced staffing requirements lowers transport costs.
- Damage and pilferage is reduced.
- Packaging and insurance costs are reduced.
- Ship 'turn round' is speeded up considerably.

Baltic Exchange

The Baltic Exchange is the centre for the following important markets:

- Freight market
- Air freight market
- Grain futures market
- Oil and oilseeds market.

FREIGHT MARKET

This market provides a market place for the sale of ships and the chartering of vessels or space on them. Dealing is carried on by three types of specialists.

- *Chartering agents* represent merchants who wish to charter vessels. The agreement is set out in a charter party. 'Voyage charters' cover the hire of a whole ship for a particular voyage. 'Time charters' give the charterer use of the complete vessel for a period of time.
- *Shipbrokers* are agents who represent shipowners and arrange charter party contracts between shipowners and charterers.
- *Independent brokers* act as intermediaries arranging ships for cargo and cargo for ships.

AIR FREIGHT
MARKET

This market operates similarly to the above freight market. It is here that arrangements are made for the charter of aircraft. These arrangements are carried out by classes of specialists with similar titles and functions to those of the sea freight market – charter agents and brokers.

GRAIN FUTURES
MARKET/OIL AND
OILSEEDS MARKET

These two markets provide facilities for the buyers and sellers of wheat and barley and primary commodities that are used to extract oils (fish, palm, sunflower, rape, linseed, etc.). The term 'futures' is used because these markets allow producers to sell their crop in advance of harvest, thus assuring the future price of their products.

TRANSPORT
TERMINOLOGY

- *Air waybill* – used in air transport as a receipt given to the consignor by the aircraft captain.
- *Bill of lading* – a document used in shipping and represents:
  (a) a description of the cargo and its destination;
  (b) title of ownership of goods in transit;
  (c) a receipt for goods aboard ship.
- *Charter party* – a contract made between a shipowner and a consignor for the transport of cargo.
- *Consignment note* – accompanies goods being transported by land and is signed by consignee on delivery.
- *Delivery terms*
  (a) *Carriage forward* – cost of transport to be paid by consignee.

CONTAINERISATION

Containers are packed at the factory by the manufacturer, or the packages are sent to a container pooling depot to be combined with other packages to make a worthwhile economic load.

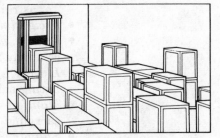

Containers can be taken to the port container terminal by road or rail freightliner.

Containers are moved around the port by straddle carriers and loaded precisely into the ship's hold by massive gantry cranes.

Hovercraft and roll on/roll off ferries are particularly suited for cross-channel movement of containers.

(b) *Carriage paid* – cost of transport is paid by consignor.
(c) *Cost insurance, freight* (CIF) – cost of goods includes freight and transit insurance.
(d) *Franco* – price of goods includes delivery to buyer.
(e) *Free alongside ship* (FAS) – cost of goods includes delivery to side of ship.

(f) *Free on board* (FOB) – cost includes freight as far as loading on to ship.

(g) *Free on rail* (FOR) – transport costs are paid by the seller as far as railway.

- *Freightliner* – a container-carrying train.
- *Freight note* – a bill presented to the consignor by the shipping company for shipping goods.
- *Lloyd's List* – a daily newspaper published by Lloyd's of London listing ship movements.
- *Manifest* – a summary of all the bills of lading and cargo a ship is carrying.
- *Shipping agent* (freight forwarding agent) – companies specialising in deciding the best form of transport and arranging necessary documentation.

MAKE A NOTE OF IT

1 Why can transport be looked on as a means of communication?
2 State one reason why transport is important to all countries.
3 List the factors that a business would take into account when deciding which form of transport to use.
4 Why are all vehicles over three years old required to pass a MOT test?
5 Give three advantages and three disadvantages of using road transport as part of the system of distribution of manufactured goods.
6 State one example where road transport would be preferable to rail transport for delivering goods.
7 Why is road transport important to both air and rail transport?
8 The railways were 'nationalised' in 1947. What does 'nationalised' mean?
9 What is the freightliner service?
10 List the advantages and disadvantages of the railways as a means of carrying freight.
11 State one circumstance where rail transport would be preferable to road transport for movement of freight.
12 Name the public corporation responsible for railways in the UK.
13 What is the main disadvantage of canal transport?
14 Why is sea transport particularly important to Britain?
15 Briefly describe the four basic classes of ships including mention of the circumstances or cargo for which each is particularly suited.
16 List the requirements of a modern port.
17 Name the organisation which controls the major British airports.
18 List the advantages and disadvantages of air transport as a means of carrying freight.
19 Give a detailed description of the facilities needed for an airport to function efficiently and safely.
20 List three examples of cargo for which you think air transport is particularly suited.
21 Name the method of transport that does not use a vehicle.
22 What is containerisation and what are the advantages of this system for freight handling?

23 Name the organisation in London which provides facilities for the chartering of vessels to carry cargo.

24 Describe the functions of the three main specialists who deal in the freight market.

25 Give a brief description of the air freight market.

26 What are 'futures'?

27 Explain the purpose of an air waybill and a bill of lading.

28 What is a charter party?

29 Explain the difference between carriage forward and carriage paid.

30 What do the following letters stand for: CIF, FAS, FOB and FOR?

DATA RESPONSE QUESTIONS

Part 4

COMMUNICATIONS

1 The following questions are all related to the Post Office Business Reply Service and you should consult the Post Office Guide for relevant information.

(a) Refer to the Post Office Guide and find out the following information related to the Business Reply Service.
- How much additional to the first or second class postage is payable by the addressee for each item received? (1)
- The additional fee charged is subject to various discounts depending upon the number of items received by the addressee per year. What would be the percentage discount for 100 000 items received during one year? (1)

(b) How does the Business Reply Service encourage potential customers to write to advertisers? (2)

(c) Briefly explain the purpose of the 'licence' necessary for a business to operate the Business Reply Service. (2)

(d) Summarise the regulations for use of pre-paid stationery for this service. (4)

(e) Compare the Business Reply Service and Freepost including examples of circumstances where a business might decide that one is preferable to another. (10)

2 Look at the advertisement on page 229.

(a) What is a credit reference agency? (2)

(b) What sort of information will a credit reference agency hold on a data bank? (2)

(c) Jenny Fox applied for a loan from a finance company. She was refused the loan because her name is included in a credit reference agency 'black list'.
- What is a 'black list'? (2)
- Assuming that the information held on computer file is incorrect, what action can Jenny take? (3)

(d) Where do credit reference agencies obtain the information contained in their computerised references? (3)

(e) How might a business legally use a credit reference agency to its advantage? (4)

(f) Examples of 'wise' use of personal computer data include the police and doctors. Briefly describe three other 'wise' examples and one 'unwise' example. (4)

Who's checking on the computers when the computers are checking on you?

Where would you expect to find the biggest list of people's names in the country? Perhaps your first thought would be the telephone directory.

If so, you would be wrong. Certainly there are over 23 million telephone subscribers in the UK and the gas and electricity boards and some government departments have similar sized information or data banks.

But even these do not match, for example, the 40 million separate records kept by the nation's leading credit reference agencies. And the Department of Health and Social Security has records on virtually everybody in the country.

The increasing use of computer technology allows such information to be compiled quickly and referred to almost instantaneously from anywhere in the country. So why should this concern you? Well, as someone who will have to face the challenge of leaving school and establishing a career, you may well find that you, yourself, are soon placed upon such a list – if you are not on one already!

In most cases, these lists, and the information they contain, are used wisely, as part of everyday life. For instance assisting police in their enquiries, government departments in deciding upon benefit entitlements, and many Doctors in providing health care.

These activities are sensible enough, assisting rather than hindering the normal processes of society. However, there can be problems, for if the information on the lists is incorrect, or if your details are mixed up with someone else's then things may go wrong. You may find your claim for benefit payment or credit being turned down, the mortgage for a house you want to buy refused, or even the police arresting you, all because of a simple mistake in the records.

Happily, this doesn't happen too often. But when it does, you will want to know how to identify – and to correct – that mistake.

The Data Protection Act is now here to help, giving us all new rights. Rights which enable us to inspect the information held about us on computer records, and to correct it if it is wrong. As importantly, the Act also allows us to claim compensation it we are damaged by any misuse of this information.

The Act is supervised by the Data Protection Registrar. He can follow up any complaints about the misuse of computer records, no matter how large or small the organisation concerned.

For more information on the Data Protection Act, please contact:-

*Information Services (BTA),
Office of the Data
Protection Registrar,
Springfield House,
Water Lane, Wilmslow,
Cheshire SK9 5AX.
Telephone: 0625 535777.*

THE DATA
PROTECTION
REGISTRAR

3

A question of communication

Dorothy Whitehead is the Managing Director (MD) of a medium-sized company in the North East. Her firm manufactures a range of cardboard boxes. In the years since the firm was established in 1980, Dorothy's company has steadily increased its sales until about six months ago. Then Dorothy noticed a distinct fall in orders received, even though the firm's prices still compared favourably with those of competitors.

One of the regular customers who had ceased to place orders was AJ Products of Redditch. Dorothy arranged to visit Mr Jones the MD of AJ Products, in an attempt to find out why his company had not placed an order with her firm for some time.

'Your sales staff could do with a bit of a shake up', said Mr Jones, 'Whenever my people 'phone your firm the person they want to speak to is never there, and it seems that the people in the office never know where they are or when they are likely to return. We have requested that someone 'phones us back, but this doesn't happen. And another thing, the people you have answering the 'phone are not particularly helpful, in fact some of them could be said to be downright rude. Quite frankly, until your staff learn to be a bit more helpful and efficient I can't see any immediate prospect of further trade between our companies'.

(a) What do the letters MD stand for? (1)

(b) What is the function of a MD? (2)

(c) In what ways can Dorothy's firm's problems be seen to be one of communication? (3)

(d) Imagine that you are Dorothy's Personal Assistant. Compose a brief memo to all senior staff requesting that they attend a meeting next Wednesday at 5.00 pm to discuss the problem. Include an indication of what the meeting will be about. (4)

(e) Dorothy has asked you to open the meeting by giving a brief summary of the reasons why the firm has been losing orders. Write out your notes for this introduction to the meeting. (4)

(f) Assuming that you were given sole charge of improving the company's image, explain the steps you would take in an attempt to solve the current problem. (6)

4 The following is an extract from *'The Post Office Guide'*.

Electronic Post

Electronic Post is the Post Office's laser printing service for business mailings, combining sophisticated technology with traditional delivery methods. All the customer needs to do is supply the Post Office with a computer tape containing a fully postcoded address list and details of the text to be mailed. The information on the tape is sorted and transmitted electronically to one of 6 regionally located Electronic Post Centres where it is printed in postcode order, enveloped and inserted with enclosures where appropriate, and placed in the mail stream for normal 1st Class delivery.

The service has the facility to incorporate the customer's own logos, letterheads, signatures and graphics. Textual personalisations can be inserted in every line and 24 different type faces are available to provide maximum variety.

Two service options are offered by Electronic Post; the Standard Service is available for mailings that can be organised in advance, ie the customer and the Post Office negotiate a drop date and time table the mailing accordingly. The Priority Service is designed to cope with those more time critical mailings – the customer submits his tape at a pretimed point during the day (the exact time will be determined by the size and geographical coverage of the mailing), the items are then processed and put into the 1st Class mail stream that night. Electronic Post is suitable for a wide variety of mailings; eg bills, dunning notices, statements, information updates, minutes of meetings, subscription reminders, advertisements, stop notices, etc. The service is completely secure, all mailings are processed in lockable rooms accessible to authorised personnel only and are identified by an individual code number visible through the envelope window to ensure that undelivered letters can be forwarded to the sender.

(a) Briefly describe the purpose of the Electronic Post service in your own words. (2)

(b) Why is the use of postcodes an important feature of the Electronic Post Service? (2)

(c) Why do the Post Office stress that 'the service is completely secure'? (4)

(d) Briefly describe circumstances when a business would use each of the two service options available. (4)

(e) Compare the Electronic Post service with two competing telecommunication services. (8)

5 Look at the article on page 232 and then answer these questions:

(a) How does a 'laptop' differ from a portable computer? (2)

(b) In what way can a laptop computer reduce time wastage for a busy executive? (2)

(c) State four items that a business person would be likely to produce using a laptop computer and while travelling. (2)

(d) What sort of information would a business executive be likely to want to receive from their base while travelling?   (4)

(e) Why has the development and wider use of portable telephones made the application of laptop computers more practicable?   (4)

(f) Why is the use of a laptop computer limited by its power, memory store and storage capacity?   (6)

Computing on the move

CAR

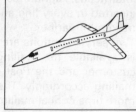

PLANE

TRAIN

Laptop computers provide tremendous benefits for those who need computing power while on the move. And when used in conjunction with the telephone network, laptops become the business traveller's lifeline for essential and complicated messages to and from base.

The computer industry differentiates between what it calls a portable and a laptop. Portables are full-sized mains-driven desktop micros that can be carried, e.g. to a car boot and then, set up at home.

Laptops are light, slim machines that can literally sit on your lap while you are in a car, train or aircraft seat. They are often battery-powered, and to minimise power loss the screens are usually liquid crystal displays (LCDs) – the same technology used in calculator screens. Depending on the machine's power, memory size and storage capacity, laptops can be used for all the jobs that are normally done on desktop micros, i.e. wordprocessing, communicating with electronic mail services, data storage, production of spreadsheets, keeping diaries, calculating figures, etc.

Both types are useful because they enable constructive use to be made of time often wasted while travelling or in hotel rooms. Memos, telexes, letters and reports can be written on the move and either printed on an office or portable printer, or sent to another computer over the telephone. Up-to-date price lists and quotations can be printed on demand for customers.

6 The following graph shows the cost per mile of transporting bulky and heavy loads for various journeys up to 350 miles.

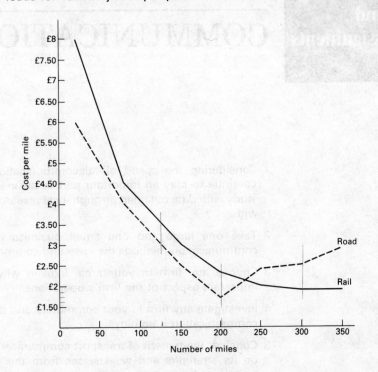

(a) (i) Which is the cheapest method of transport for a journey of 100 miles? (1)

(ii) Which is the cheapest method for journeys exceeding 300 miles? (1)

(iii) At what distance does it cost the same to transport goods by road as it does by rail? (1)

(b) Complete the following table which aims to show the difference in total cost between road and rail transport for various journeys.

Miles	Road	Rail
125		
200		
300		

(3)

(c) Why does road transport have an advantage over rail transport for shorter journeys, but is at a disadvantage for journeys exceeding 230 miles? (4)

(d) Why does rail transport depend heavily on road transport? (4)

(e) Other than distance, what other factors will influence a business's choice between road and rail transport for delivering goods? (6)

<table>
<tr><td>**Coursework and Assignments**</td><td>**Part 4**

COMMUNICATIONS</td></tr>
</table>

1 Considering the speed of telecommunications why do postal services continue to play an important part in business operations? Support your study with data obtained through local research, e.g. a firm you are familiar with.

2 Take one large and one small business in your area. Compare the communication methods they use and comment on any differences found.

3 Choose any firm in your area. Explain why telecommunications is an important aspect of the firm's operations.

4 Investigate any firm in your community and describe the forms of internal communication it employs.

5 Consider the pattern of transport communications in your town. Comment on its strengths and weaknesses from the point of view of both local traders and consumers.

6 Study any firm which you know sends its goods to a number of different markets. Comment on the various delivery methods the firm uses.

7 If a new factory were established in your locality producing household utensils for sale throughout the UK and overseas, what transport facilities would be likely to be used? Present evidence to support your research.

8 Carry out a minor research project to show how a *change* in some aspect of transport (e.g. road bypass, new bridge, Channel Tunnel, etc.) can create advantages for business but also perhaps disadvantages for other groups of people.

Part 5
PEOPLE IN BUSINESS

22 Recruitment, selection and training

Seeking employment

LOOKING FOR A JOB

Those seeking employment will want to investigate all available possibilities. The following are the main sources of information about job vacancies.

- Job centres run by the government's Training Agency.
- Employment agencies run by private firms.
- Local careers officers.
- Newspaper advertisements.
- Friends and relatives.

Advertisements are the most common way of publicising a job vacancy and inviting applications. Prospective applicants should read the advertisement carefully. Not only will it give important information about the job and the firm, but it may also offer clues of what should be included in the letter of application.

LETTERS OF APPLICATION

In some cases it may be acceptable to type a letter, in others the advertisement may state that the application should be in 'first hand', in

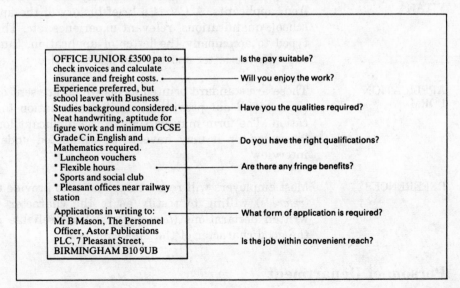

OFFICE JUNIOR £3500 pa to check invoices and calculate insurance and freight costs. Experience preferred, but school leaver with Business Studies background considered. Neat handwriting, aptitude for figure work and minimum GCSE Grade C in English and Mathematics required.
* Luncheon vouchers
* Flexible hours
* Sports and social club
* Pleasant offices near railway station

Applications in writing to: Mr B Mason, The Personnel Officer, Astor Publications PLC, 7 Pleasant Street, BIRMINGHAM B10 9UB

— Is the pay suitable?

— Will you enjoy the work?

— Have you the qualities required?

— Do you have the right qualifications?

— Are there any fringe benefits?

— What form of application is required?

— Is the job within convenient reach?

Job advertisement

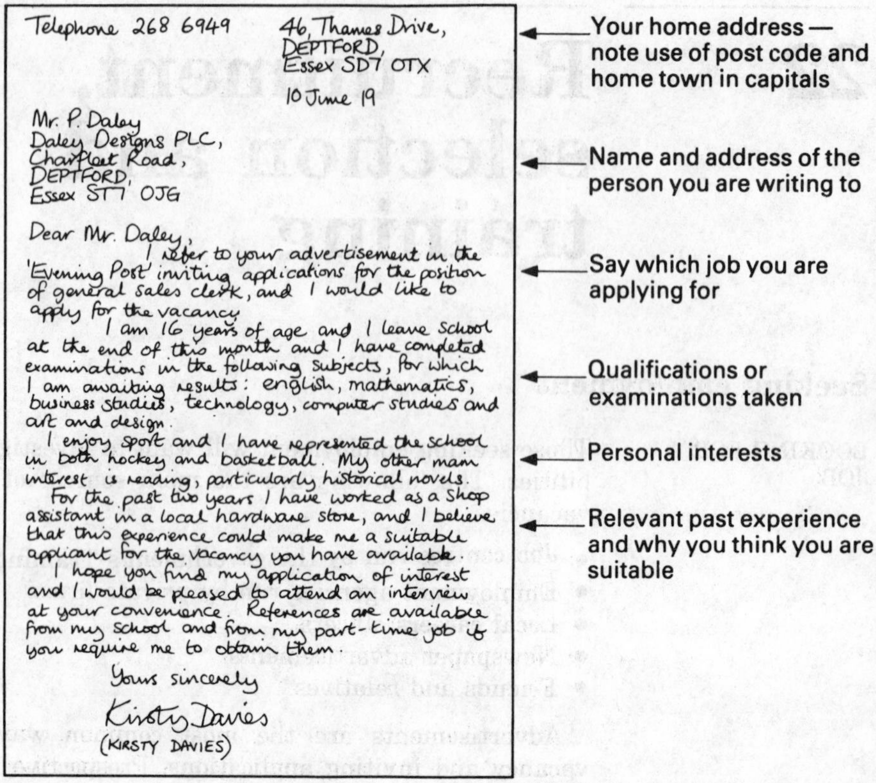

Telephone 268 6949 46, Thames Drive,
DEPTFORD,
Essex SD7 OTX

10 June 19

Mr. P. Daley
Daley Designs PLC,
Charlcot Road,
DEPTFORD,
Essex ST7 OJG

Dear Mr. Daley,
    I refer to your advertisement in the
'Evening Post' inviting applications for the position
of general sales clerk, and I would like to
apply for the vacancy
    I am 16 years of age and I leave school
at the end of this month and I have completed
examinations in the following subjects, for which
I am awaiting results: english, mathematics,
business studies, technology, computer studies and
art and design.
    I enjoy sport and I have represented the school
in both hockey and basketball. My other main
interest is reading, particularly historical novels.
    For the past two years I have worked as a shop
assistant in a local hardware store, and I believe
that this experience could make me a suitable
applicant for the vacancy you have available.
    I hope you find my application of interest
and I would be pleased to attend an interview
at your convenience. References are available
from my school and from my part-time job if
you require me to obtain them.
     Yours sincerely
     Kirsty Davies
     (KIRSTY DAVIES)

Annotations (right margin):

- Your home address — note use of post code and home town in capitals
- Name and address of the person you are writing to
- Say which job you are applying for
- Qualifications or examinations taken
- Personal interests
- Relevant past experience and why you think you are suitable

which case the letter should be handwritten, preferably on plain paper. It is sensible to make a rough draft of the proposed letter before writing it out in detail.

CURRICULUM VITAE

Job advertisements today frequently ask for a curriculum vitae (CV) from applicants. A CV is a brief history of the applicant, for example, school, qualifications, relevant experience, etc. This may be written or typed to accompany the letter of application, thus making it possible to make the letter shorter and more concise.

APPLICATION FORM

These are standard printed forms which are sent out by firms for applicants to fill out providing specific information to support their application. The form may be sent to the applicant for completion prior to interview, or it may have to be completed under supervision at the interview.

REFERENCES

Most employers will require applicants to provide the names of persons (*referees*) willing to testify as to the character of the candidate, or written declarations (*testimonials*) from reliable persons testifying to the good character of the applicant.

Personnel Department

The Personnel Department is concerned with finding the right person

```
CURRICULUM VITAE     SUNILA PATEL

ADDRESS              21 Courtfield Road
                     Nottingham

DATE OF BIRTH        12 October 1969

SEX                  Female

PLACE OF BIRTH       Nottingham

NATIONALITY          British

EDUCATION            St Martins School
                     Ladyfield Road
                     Nottingham

                     1981 to 1986

GCSE                 English language
                     Mathematics
                     French
                     Biology
                     History
                     Business studies

INTERESTS            Reading
                     Outdoor sports
                     Music

WORK EXPERIENCE      Saturday job in family general store
```

Example of a curriculum vitae

for vacant jobs, and if necessary giving them induction training. This department also deals with resignations, providing testimonials and dismissing unsuitable workers. It maintains personal records of all employees and is involved in the welfare and happiness of all personnel.

Applications for employment are received and considered by the Personnel Department which is headed by the personnel manager.

SHORT-LIST OF APPLICANTS

From the many applications received in response to the advertisement, the Personnel Department lists a few of the most promising applicants and invites them to attend an interview. For this reason, the written application is very important if the applicant is to reach the next stage in being successful in applying for the job.

INTERVIEWS

Short-listed applicants for employment are invariably interviewed (usually in the Personnel Department) before any job offer is made. The aim of the interview is not only to assess the suitability of the candidate for the vacant position, but also to give the applicant the opportunity to seek further information about the job. During the interview the applicant may be required to complete an aptitude test designed to assess their suitability for the job available.

The interview is crucial for the applicant because it is at this time that the interviewer assesses the candidate's appearance, ability to communicate and general manner. Consequently, it is important to be thoroughly prepared for the interview.

R.B. JACKSON

Preparation for the interview

- Do a little homework about the job for which you have applied.
- Use your common sense about your appearance.
- Remember the name of the person you have to see.
- Know exactly where the interview will take place.
- Plan the route to get there.
- Arrive promptly for the interview.

During the interview

- Only sit down when invited to.
- Do not smoke.
- Try to be relaxed and confident.
- Concentrate fully on the interviewer.
- Be prepared to answer questions.
- Try to ask some sensible questions when you are invited to do so.

At the interview

- Dress carefully.
- Take the letter inviting you for interview.
- Arrive promptly.
- Appear confident but not flippant.
- Do not be over-familiar.

Questions to be prepared for

- Why do you want the job?

- What qualities do you have to offer?
- What is your future ambition?
- What do you do in your spare time?
- What do you read?

Questions you could ask

- What does the job involve?
- What hours are involved?
- What is the salary?
- What are the opportunities for promotion?
- What are the holiday arrangements?

Staff training

All new members of staff need to be acquainted with other members of the firm, as well as becoming familiar with the organisation of the business. Many firms organise an induction programme to help new employees to become a useful part of the organisation, and to introduce them to their new job and work colleagues. The induction programme will often be managed by the Personnel Department.

Staff training does not only apply to new employees. Sometimes existing staff will be transferred to other departments or other jobs which may require training in new skills. A large firm may operate its own internal training school, or alternatively staff may be encouraged to attend college courses to learn new skills.

Welfare of employees

Welfare refers to the concern for the physical well-being of people. Social facilities, lighting and heating, hygiene and canteen services are all examples of things that contribute to the welfare of employees. These all come within the functions of the Personnel Department in a large firm.

The Personnel Department may be responsible for the operation of the company's sports and social club, organising activities and events which encourage employees to mix socially. A member of this department may also have the responsibility of visiting employees who are sick, or those who have retired.

The firm may have its own house newspaper or magazine which is used to keep the workers up-to-date with events in which the company is involved, as well as providing a means of general communication.

Most firms recognise that good working conditions not only keep the employees happy, but also help to make them more productive and efficient. For this reason, firms try to provide good working conditions, but there are five Acts which are particularly concerned with staff welfare. These are dealt with together with other aspects of working conditions in the next chapter.

1 Factories Act, 1961
2 Offices, Shops and Railway Premises Act, 1963

3 Contract of Employment Act, 1972
4 Health and Safety at Work Act, 1974
5 Employment Act, 1988.

Staff records

The letter of application for employment, the curriculum vitae or the completed application form, together with the results of any aptitude tests taken when the new employee joins the firm, form the basis of the record of the individual held by the employer.

Over the years of employment the file held is added to by progress reports from other more senior members of the firm. These reports and other records of progress will include reference to the following aspects of the employee:

- punctuality
- health
- academic progress
- promotions and salary increases
- suitability for further promotion
- misdemeanours.

From the foregoing it will be obvious that the contents of personnel records are highly confidential. For this reason, people who work in the Personnel Department are expected to be discreet. In addition, security of personnel records is of utmost importance.

Dismissal

In the following chapter reference is made to the Contract of Employment Act which requires all employees to be given details of the terms of their employment. The Contract of Employment includes the length of *notice* (length of time as notification of ceasing employment) to be given by the employer and the employee. When a worker wishes to take up new employment elsewhere they are required to give a period of 'notice' which allows the employer to look for a new employee. Similarly, if the employer wishes to dismiss the worker a period of notice is generally observed, although there are exceptions to this.

Today workers are protected against unfair dismissal by the Employment Protection Act which requires an employer to show that there are good reasons for terminating employment. An employee who feels that they have been unfairly dismissed can complain to an Industrial Tribunal. If the Tribunal finds that the employer has acted unfairly or unreasonably, it can order reinstatement of the employee. If this is not practicable, the Tribunal can award compensation against the employer.

Redundancy

This refers to a situation when an employee loses their job because it no longer exists. This may occur because the business has been forced to cease trading, or when the firm no longer has the capacity to employ the same number of workers.

When an employee loses their job as a result of redundancy they need financial help to enable them to make the transition to new employment.

The Redundancy Payments Act requires employees to make a lump sum payment to employees being made redundant (so long as they have served a minimum period of time). The amount of redundancy compensation depends upon the age, length of service, and pay of the employee.

MAKE A NOTE OF IT

1 List five sources of information about job vacancies.
2 Why is it important for prospective applicants to read job advertisements carefully?
3 List four specific pieces of information that the job applicant can obtain from the advertisement.
4 What does it mean when an advertisement states that applications must be in 'first hand'?
5 Make a list of six suggestions you would give someone to help them write a letter of application for a job.
6 What is a curriculum vitae? What information does it contain?
7 In what way does an application form differ from a CV?
8 What is the function of 'referees' and 'testimonials' in relation to applications for employment?
9 Give a brief summary of the main function of the Personnel Department of a firm?
10 What is a 'short-list'?
11 What is the main purpose of the interview?
12 Why might a job applicant be required to complete an aptitude test?
13 In what way can someone usefully prepare for a job interview?
14 List six points the candidate should observe during the interview.
15 Give four examples of questions that might be asked of an applicant at the interview.
16 Suggest four questions the job applicant could ask when invited to do so.
17 In what way might a firm show its care for the welfare of its employees?
18 Why would a firm be interested in the welfare of its employees?
19 How would the Personnel Department be involved in the welfare of employees?
20 Briefly describe the kind of information likely to be found in personnel records. Why is security and confidentiality important to personnel records?
21 What regulations exist to protect an employee from unfair dismissal?
22 Explain the purpose of redundancy payments.

23   Motivation

Job satisfaction

People spend a large percentage of their life at work. Therefore, it is important that they get some satisfaction from their job. Not all jobs can give satisfaction, and people have different ideas of what constitutes a good job. For some people pay is the most important factor, others will have some other priority. Often it is a combination of many factors which makes a job satisfying. The following are just some of these factors. What others would you include? What would be your order of priority?

- Pay and opportunity for wage increases.
- Promotion prospects.
- Working hours and times of attendance.
- Holiday arrangements.
- Job security.
- Friendship and relationship between employees.
- Conditions in which work is carried out.

Most jobs will include a combination of the above factors. Some are within the influence of the employee, but the employer has by far the greater effect on working conditions, however, there are laws which ensure that working conditions do not fall below an agreed minimum standard. Some of these laws are examined later in this chapter.

Wages

WAGE
DIFFERENTIALS

Wages are the reward paid for labour. Not surprisingly wages are considered more important to most people than many other things in life. This is because the level of earnings has such a considerable effect on the quality of life. The amount of income received influences the type of house and furnishings one can have, the quality of car owned and where and for how long holidays are taken. The poorly paid person cannot hope to compete with the highly paid person with regard to standard of living and leisure facilities. But for a variety of reasons some people are better paid than others, and it is important to understand why this is so.

The key to the reason for wage differentials is demand and supply. For the purpose of comparison we can take the wages of doctors and bus drivers as examples of where differences in wage levels exist. Both of these occupations are important to the community, but the doctor's wage is considerably higher than that of the bus driver. In other words, the cost of the doctor's services is far higher than the cost of the bus driver's services. Alternatively, we could say that the supply of doctors is smaller than the supply of bus drivers, forcing up the price of the doctor's services.

The following reasons that the supply of doctors is smaller than that of bus drivers can also be applied to many other examples of occupations where wage differences exist.

- The occupation requires a high degree of skill and academic ability.
- The training period is too long for many people.
- There is a degree of risk involved (e.g. infection).
- The work requires a special aptitude.

What other reasons can you think of for wage differentials?

RATES OF PAY

There are several ways that wages may be calculated, and sometimes a wage payment may combine more than one of these.

Flat rate

A set rate of pay per week or month based on a standard number of hours. Many workers are paid by this system but it does not always provide incentive to give extra time or effort.

Time rate

The worker is paid a set amount for each hour worked. The worker is paid 'overtime' at a higher rate of pay for additional hours worked.

Piece rate

This is not as common today as it has been in manufacturing in the past. A payment is made for each good quality item produced to encourage the production worker to give maximum effort.

Bonus

Paid to employees as a share of additional profits gained by the employer due to increased effort or efficiency of the work group.

Commission

A payment made additional to a flat or time rate as a percentage of the value of sales or business promoted.

DEDUCTIONS FROM PAY

Gross pay is the total amount earned by the employee before any deductions have been made.

Net pay is the amount received by the employee after any deductions have been taken away. This figure is particularly important because it represents the actual income the worker receives.

Statutory deductions

These are compulsory deductions enforced by law.

- *Income tax* – deducted from each wage payment through the PAYE (Pay As You Earn) system.
- *National insurance* – weekly contributions to the state welfare scheme (e.g. health services) taken from each payment of wages.

Voluntary deductions

- Union membership fees.
- Contribution to company social club.
- Payments to private pension schemes.
- Private medical schemes (e.g. BUPA) payments.
- Transfers to the state savings scheme (SAYE – Save As You Earn).

SAVE AS YOU EARN (SAYE)

The National Savings Bank SAYE service offers a form of regular saving that aims to not only give a return on the investment, but also to offset the effect of inflation and price rises by linking the interest paid to the retail price index. In other words, the interest paid is enhanced by any general increase in retail prices.

In this scheme the saver agrees to make monthly payments of a fixed amount (between £4 to £20) over a period of five years. At the end of the five-year contract period the saver can take repayment of his investment. At this time the investment is revalued to take into account any changes in the general index of retail prices between the time of the initial investment and the month of repayment.

Alternatively, at the end of the five-year contract period, the saver has the option to leave his savings invested for a further two years without making any further payments. At the end of this additional two-year period, the value of the investment is again revalued to take into account changes in the prices index at the time of the repayment. In addition, a bonus, equal to the monthly payments, is also paid.

SAYE contracts can be made in three ways:

1 Through a post office by monthly cash payments or by National Girobank standing order.
2 Through a commercial bank by standing order.
3 Through an employer who participates in the SAYE scheme and deducts monthly payments from the employee's salary.

PAYMENT OF WAGES

A wages department is responsible for the payment of wages. People employed in this department need an aptitude for work with figures and are often required to be familiar with the use of a computer.

When an employee is paid at a time rate, they will have a time card (clock card) which is kept in a rack near a time clock. As the employee arrives and leaves work they 'clock' on and off by inserting their card into the time clock. The times printed on to the time card are used by the Wages Department to establish how much the employee should be paid.

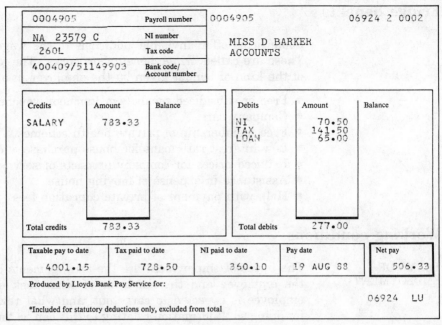

	Payroll number	0004905			06924 2 0002
0004905					
NA 23579 C	NI number				
260L	Tax code	MISS D BARKER			
400409/51149903	Bank code/ Account number	ACCOUNTS			

Credits	Amount	Balance	Debits	Amount	Balance
SALARY	783.33		NI	70.50	
			TAX	141.50	
			LOAN	65.00	
Total credits	783.33		Total debits	277.00	

Taxable pay to date	Tax paid to date	NI paid to date	Pay date	Net pay
4001.15	728.50	360.10	19 AUG 88	506.33

Produced by Lloyds Bank Pay Service for:

06924 LU

*Included for statutory deductions only, excluded from total

Pay advice

Whether payment of wages is made by cash, cheque or credit transfer, the employee receives a pay advice. This is usually a slip of paper which is filled in by the Wages Department, often by computer, so that the employees can see how their net pay has been reached. The pay advice will contain the following information.

- Employee's name and work number.
- Tax code.
- National insurance number.
- Gross pay.
- Bonus, commission, overtime.
- Compulsory deductions.
- Voluntary deductions.
- Net pay.

Much of the Wages Department work of calculating wages and producing pay advices can be assigned to computers. When the worker 'clocks' in and out the time data can be recorded on the time card by punch holes or magnetic ink characters. The data can be 'read' by computer and used to automatically:

- Calculate gross and net pay.
- Print out pay advice.
- Maintain cumulative records for the production of:

Form P45 – statement provided to an employee changing jobs to inform the new employer of the amount of income tax paid to date.
Form P60 – annual certificate or statement notifying employee of gross wages, gross tax, and net wages paid for the whole year.

Fringe benefits

Some firms offer 'invisible' additions to the wages of their employees. These are called 'fringe benefits' or 'perks'. The following are examples of the kind of benefit given by the employer in addition to wages.

- Free or subsidised meals (e.g. luncheon vouchers – LVs).
- Company car.
- Free membership of private health schemes.
- Low interest rate loans for house purchase, etc.
- Reduced prices for company products or services.
- Assistance in expense of moving house.
- Help with payment of private education fees.

Working conditions

TERMS OF
EMPLOYMENT

The terms of employment are the arrangements or agreement between the employee and the employer of what task or responsibilities the employee is expected to carry out, and what reward they will receive for doing so. Information relating to this can be found in the job description, the job specification and the contract of employment.

Job description

This is a broad general statement which may include:

- Job title
- Details of duties and responsibilities
- Place or department where work is to be carried out
- Special features or skills/qualifications related to the job
- Supervision and assessment arrangements.

Job specification

This is a detailed statement drawn up from the job description and it contains references to the qualities required of candidates for the job. This will include:

- Responsibilities involved
- Qualifications and past experience needed
- Skills of initiative or judgment necessary
- Physical fitness required
- Personal characteristics considered important.

Contract of Employment Act, 1972

This Act requires employers to give employees particulars of their terms of employment. This contract must either be given to the employee or kept where they have access to it. The contract includes:

- Job title
- Hours of work
- Holiday arrangements

- Rate of pay and how frequently paid
- Period of notice to be given by either side
- Person to contact in event of a grievance
- Legal rights such as belonging (or not belonging) to a union.

HOURS OF
EMPLOYMENT

One of the most important terms of employment is the hours of work. This refers not only to the total number of hours to be worked, but also what times of the day or night the hours have to be worked.

Although some people work shift work, most people work fixed hours. Consequently, most people are travelling to and from work at similar times. This results in traffic jams and congestion on public transport, and discomfort for travellers. It also means that public transport is not being used economically.

Not everyone finds it convenient to work the same hours as others. Workers sometimes need periods of time when they are not required to be at work. In addition, many businesses have periods of the day when not all members of staff are required to be present. At other busy 'core' times, everyone is needed at the same time.

Flexible Working Time (FWT)

Flexitime, FWT or flexible working time is a system of arranging working hours so that at 'peak' or 'core' times all members of staff are at work. Outside core time employees are allowed to choose the hours they work, so long as they complete the required number of overall hours in the week.

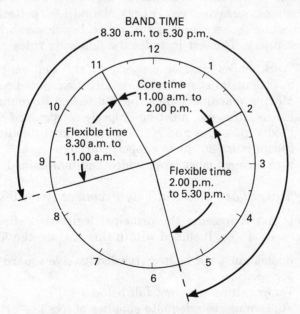

Total hours to be worked by employee = 35 hours

Flexible working time

The working day of the firm is defined in three ways:

1 *Band time* – this is the total period of time the business operates, for example, 8.00 am to 6.00 pm.
2 *Core time* – this is the period of time when all members of the firm are expected to be at work.
3 *Flexible time* – this is the period outside the core time when employees can choose whether they work or not, so long as they complete the total number of weekly hours they are paid for.

To choose their working hours employees first calculate core time. Core time in the above example is 5 days × 3 hours (11.00 am to 2.00 pm) = 15 hours. This leaves 20 hours (35 − 15 = 20) of working which can be chosen from FWT. Before choosing the hours of flexitime, employees will have to take into account the time they wish to use for lunch breaks. Most firms will insist that the employee takes at least a 30 minute lunch break.

HEALTH AND SAFETY

The health and safety of employees is a major aspect of working conditions. The duty of employers to provide safe working conditions is often backed up by statutory requirements. The three main Acts which relate to health and safety are the Factories Act, 1961, the Offices, Shops and Railway Premises Act, 1963 and the Health and Safety at Work Act, 1974.

Factories Act, 1961

The Act in fact covers more than factories in the normal sense of the word. It includes brickworks, cement works, construction sites, dry cleaners, garages, gas works, laundries, potteries, printing works, slaughter houses and many other businesses which use mechanical machinery. The Act includes the following rules:

- Work places must be properly lit and well ventilated.
- Sufficient toilet and washing facilities must be provided.
- Moving machinery must have a fenced surround.
- Hoists, lifts, etc. must be properly constructed and maintained.
- Floors, passages and stairs must be kept unobstructed.
- Floors must not have slippery surfaces.
- Fire escapes must be provided and maintained.

Offices, Shops and Railway Premises Act, 1963

This Act represents the principal legislation affecting working conditions in offices. Included within this Act are the following provisions:

- Rooms must not be overcrowded (twelve square metres of floor space per person).
- Temperature must not fall below 16°C.
- There must be adequate supplies of fresh or artificially purified air.
- Suitable natural or artificial lighting.
- Suitable and sufficient sanitary conveniences must be conveniently accessible, clean and properly maintained.

- Accessible washing facilities with running hot and cold water, soap and clean towels.

Health and Safety at Work Act, 1974 (HASAWA)

This Act sets out the duties of both the employer and the employee relating to health and safety.

- The employer's duty can be summed up as the responsibility to provide a safe workplace, including arrangements for hazards such as fire, and the maintenance and safety of machinery and equipment.
- Employees also have the duty to take reasonable care for the safety of themselves and other working colleagues at all times, and to cooperate with the employer on all matters of safety.

MAKE A NOTE OF IT

1 Why is it important that people gain satisfaction from their jobs? List six factors that you think make a job satisfying.
2 Why are wage differentials often the source of envy and discontent between workers?
3 List five factors which influence the supply of people suitable for a particular form of employment.
4 Briefly describe each of the following ways of calculating wages: flat rate; time rate; piece rate; bonus; commission.
5 Explain the differences between gross pay and net pay.
6 If you have earned a gross wage of £110.28 and must pay deductions totalling £27.36, what will be your net pay?
7 Give examples and explain the difference between statutory deductions and voluntary deductions.
8 Cash is one way of paying wages. Name two others.
9 What is the purpose of a time card system? How can this system be of help to the Wages Department of a firm?
10 List at least six items of information likely to be found on a pay advice.
11 Briefly describe the way that a computer could be employed in the Wages Department.
12 Explain the purpose of forms P45 and P60.
13 What are fringe benefits? Give six examples.
14 List the kind of information that is contained in the contract of employment.
15 How does a job description differ from a job specification?
16 Why are hours of employment important to the working conditions of an employee?
17 What is flexible working time? Why is it possible to operate this system for people working in a restaurant, but very difficult to adopt for a school?
18 'The Factories Act, 1961, the Offices, Shops and Railway Premises Act, 1963, and the Health and Safety at Work Act, 1974, all aim to protect working conditions, but they each have differences in their application.' Explain this statement.

24 Management

Responsibilities of management

Everyone in an organisation has some responsibility, even if it is only to have regard for their own safety and that of their work colleagues. But the higher in the hierarchy a person is, the greater will be their responsibility. Consequently, the greater degree of responsibility lies with the managers of an organisation, whether they are the managing director or a department manager. Managers in this respect are those who have the responsibility to direct, control and co-ordinate others.

The management of an organisation are responsible to the firm's:

1 *Owners* to achieve the best possible return on the capital invested and to reinvest capital wisely in order to secure sound future growth and development of the business.
2 *Clients* to provide goods or services, of the specified quality, within the agreed time period and at a fair and economic price.
3 *Employees* to provide the safest and most comfortable working conditions possible, to pay a fair wage and to secure future employment as far as possible.

In order to meet the above responsibilities the manager must organise the work of others, and in this respect the manager will from time to time be required to do the following:

- Appoint and train new staff.
- Communicate company policy.
- Give instructions and set tasks.
- Assess performance.
- Discipline and dismiss staff.

Superiors are expected to be responsible for the actions of their subordinates. Although they can delegate the power or authority to carry out tasks to subordinates, the responsibility for actions cannot be delegated and ultimate responsibility always remains with the manager.

Management functions

The functions of management can be grouped into four areas:

1 *Planning* – making decisions and policy formation on the intentions

and objectives of the organisation, and the methods to be used to achieve the objectives.

2 *Co-ordinating* – directing and integrating the activities of the team under their direct supervision. And contributing to the overall co-ordination of the activities within the organisation in order to form a united strategy of operations to achieve the organisation's objectives.

3 *Motivating* – encouraging other members of the organisation to carry out their tasks properly and effectively. The ability to motivate others is very much dependent upon leadership qualities which are discussed later.

4 *Controlling* – supervising and checking the activities and performance of subordinates to ensure that instructions are being carried out properly and plans and methods are being followed.

Span of control

Sometimes referred to as 'span of management', span of control refers to the number of subordinates a manager supervises, or the effective limit to the number of others that a manager can supervise efficiently. A number of factors govern the span of control and they include the following:

- *The complexity of the work* – some work is easy to check while other work demands closer supervision by the manager.
- *Self-discipline of workers* – where workers are motivated and professional a greater number can be supervised.
- *Method of communication* – some methods of communication (e.g. face to face) are more demanding than others (e.g. electronic methods).
- *Frequency of supervision* – how often the manager needs to see subordinates.
- *Capability of the manager* – some managers have more ability to lead and motivate than others.

Leadership

It is important that people who are in a supervisory position in business have some understanding of group dynamics, that is, the way that people interact in a group situation. The extent to which people work effectively (or not) together affects the overall success of the firm's operations. In the business sense there are four basic elements of group behaviour.

THE GROUP

Informal groups have usually come together voluntarily (e.g. a music group), and the purpose of the group is not too rigidly defined. There are no set rules (although an informal group may have an objective, e.g. to entertain friends), and the leader will be decided by the members of the group.

Formal groups are usually created for a specific purpose, such as a department in a firm. This type of group has a formal structure, a specific objective, and an appointed leader. In fact the leader may be the one who chooses the members of the group, and consequently enjoys the power of authority. People in businesses and factories work in formal groups, with expected standards of production and behaviour.

AN OBJECTIVE

Most groups in business are formal ones. As such they require a clear objective, e.g. to produce a certain quantity of high quality products. Unless the objectives are clearly defined (i.e. by the leader) the group will lose direction; the objectives will be liable to be misinterpreted.

THE INDIVIDUAL

Even though they are part of a group each person still has to work as an individual in order to make their contribution to the group objective. This can result in a problem if the individual's views, attitude or behaviour are not in harmony with the rest of the group. Under such circumstances the importance of the objective may itself solve the conflict, alternatively it may be the skill of the group leader that will be the deciding factor.

THE LEADER

Whereas the leader of an informal group may be chosen by the group members, with formal groups the leader is often appointed, e.g. managers, chairperson etc. In this position the leader may have the power to regulate the group behaviour, but to use their authority in this way may affect the group morale and attitudes. For this reason the leader will try to identify parameters within which the group can operate, often delegating some responsibility to members of the group.

We saw earlier in this chapter that motivating is a major function of management. Wages are often assumed to be a major motivating factor, but an unlimited resource of wages can never be guaranteed, and wages alone are limited in the extent to which they can be relied on to encourage people to work hard and effectively.

The success of management, and the ability to motivate others, is very much dependent upon the ability to lead. But leadership qualities are difficult to identify and to define. First, because they depend on the manager's own attitude towards the responsibilities delegated to him and his subordinates. Second, the ability to lead is considerably influenced by the attitude of the manager towards the problems of his subordinates. Third, some of the qualities required to lead others differ from one occupation to another.

To be able to inspire others managers must also be inspired. They need to be committed to their organisation and must have interest and pride in the products or services which they produce or sell. Leadership qualities are particularly revealed by the willingness of superiors to listen to, and understand, problems from their subordinates' point of view.

Communication

Earlier, in Chapters 19 to 21, we examined in detail the various forms of communication used by businesses. Here we are concerned specifically with the methods of communication used by management to pass information to employees.

The success of any organisation is greatly influenced by the participation of all members in its activities. We have seen earlier in this chapter that managers have an important part to play in co-ordinating and motivating all workers to achieve a common goal. But for all members of the organisation to make a worthwhile contribution, they need to know what goals they are expected to achieve. And experience has shown that people are more committed to involvement in an organisation when they are well informed of policies, and even more so when they have participated in making decisions.

Communication is a valuable tool for involving all members of an organisation in its activities. Effective management communications require a two-way flow of information – downwards from management and upwards from the employees.

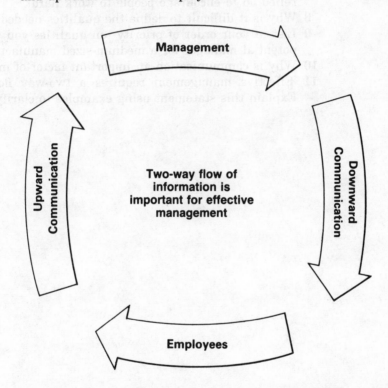

| DOWNWARD COMMUNICATION | Downward communication is initiated by management and is used to inform employees of company policies, proposals, decisions and progress. There are two main methods used in downward communication: |

- *Oral* – direct command, meetings, loudspeakers, intercom, closed circuit television, telephone.
- *Written* – memoranda, notice boards, reports, company journal, employee handbooks, letters.

| UPWARD COMMUNICATION | Upward communication may be initiated by employees but is frequently 'collected' by management. It feeds back to management the views, |

suggestions, proposals, reactions and difficulties of employees. Upward communication can be 'collected' by direct and indirect methods:

- *Direct* – managers talking to employees and elected representatives.
- *Indirect* – suggestion schemes, attitude surveys.

MAKE A NOTE OF IT

1 Why is management an important aspect of the firm?
2 Briefly describe the responsibilities of management.
3 List the tasks that a manager may be required to carry out in order to meet his responsibilities.
4 'The ultimate responsibility for an employee's actions lies with management.' Explain this statement.
5 Describe the main functions of management.
6 Why are there so many variations of span of control?
7 Why is it that wages are limited in the extent to which they can be relied on to encourage people to work hard?
8 Why is it difficult to define the qualities needed to lead others?
9 List in your order of priority ten qualities you would look for in a potential manager for a medium-sized manufacturing company.
10 Why is communication an important factor of management?
11 'Effective management requires a two-way flow of information.' Explain this statement using examples to clarify your explanation.

25 Industrial relations

People are not only the most important resource of an organisation, they are also the most costly resource. It might, therefore, be considered almost impossible to avoid at least some conflict between the employer and the employee. The employees will want to achieve the highest pay they can, while the employer will want to minimise the firm's wage costs. The term 'industrial relations' is generally used when statements are made which refer to the extent to which conflict or peace exists in industry, or between employers and employees.

Trade unions

Trade unions are associations of people who join together in their common interest to regulate the relations between employees and employers.

Unions are important from the point of view of workers because they enable them to pay a small subscription each, which the union then uses to employ skilled officials to act on the workers' behalf. Unions are also important to employers because they enable them to have discussions and negotiations with a small number of people rather than many.

TRADE UNION AIMS

Trade unions aim to secure for workers:

1 Improved wages and reduced working hours.
2 Improved working conditions.
3 Full employment and national prosperity.
4 Job security.
5 Benefits for members who are sick, retired or on strike.
6 Improved social security schemes such as unemployment, sickness benefit and pensions.
7 A say in government.
8 Participation in company decision processes.
9 A reasonable share in the wealth of the country.
10 Improved public and social services.

TRADES UNION CONGRESS (TUC)

The TUC is the central body of the trade union movement. It is the representative voice of the many member trade unions, and consequently the government often discusses industrial policies with the TUC and attempts to obtain its co-operation. The TUC tries to promote the aims of the unions and to encourage support for them.

Although the TUC is an important part of the industrial scene, people often overestimate its powers. The TUC's powers are in fact very limited. The real power in the TUC lies with the member unions and a democratic process which produces overall union views and policies.

Most of the main unions are associate members of the TUC, and the amount of power each union has within the organisation is determined by the size of its membership.

At the TUC Annual Congress, which usually takes place for one week in September, the General Council is elected to carry out TUC policies and work throughout the year. It is responsible for most of the main decisions and actions, whilst taking into account the wishes of the associated unions.

Each member union can send a member of delegates with voting power to the Annual Congress. The number of delegates is related to the size of the union's membership. The Annual Congress provides an important public platform for the unions to discuss important issues affecting the economy.

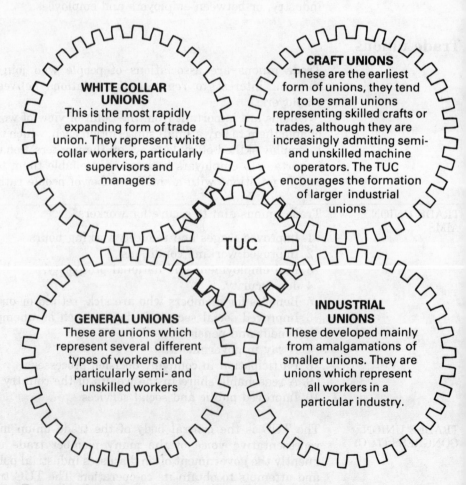

WHITE COLLAR UNIONS
This is the most rapidly expanding form of trade union. They represent white collar workers, particularly supervisors and managers

CRAFT UNIONS
These are the earliest form of unions, they tend to be small unions representing skilled crafts or trades, although they are increasingly admitting semi- and unskilled machine operators. The TUC encourages the formation of larger industrial unions

TUC

GENERAL UNIONS
These are unions which represent several different types of workers and particularly semi- and unskilled workers

INDUSTRIAL UNIONS
These developed mainly from amalgamations of smaller unions. They are unions which represent all workers in a particular industry.

Types of trade union

CRITICISMS OF TRADE UNIONS
: One of the main criticisms of trade unions is that the typical member does not actively participate in its activities until there is some crisis or conflict which affects them personally. During the absence of active interest by the majority of the union's members, those with more positive and sometimes extremist political views can move into positions of influence and control in the unions. In such circumstances, the union could be open to abuse by persons using conflict situations for their own political ends.

COLLECTIVE BARGAINING
: The main function of trade unions is to obtain improved wages and working conditions for their members. Sometimes the employer reaches a satisfactory wage agreement with individual employees, but wage settlements are often the result of collective bargaining.

  The union represents a group of workers and negotiates a settlement on their behalf with an employer or a group of employers. It is just as much in the interest of the unions as it is in the employers to reach a speedy settlement, because both sides can only benefit if there is continuity in working. However, where negotiations are not successful there are other possibilities to solve the deadlock.

CONCILIATION
: Conciliation is where a third party is appointed (sometimes by the government) to try and help find a solution acceptable to both sides. The Advisory Conciliation and Arbitration Service (ACAS) is particularly used to attempt to bring the two sides of a dispute nearer together. The work of ACAS is examined in more detail later.

ARBITRATION
: This is where both sides of a dispute request that the dispute goes before an arbiter. Both sides agree to accept the verdict of the arbiter.

Restrictive practices

Restrictive practices are the methods or weapons used by the unions in an industrial dispute. The following are some of the most used methods.

STRIKE
: - *Official* – on advice, in consultation or with union approval and backing, workers cease work (withdraw their labour). Under these circumstances the union may provide strike pay from the funds contributed by members.
  - *Unofficial* – sometimes called a 'wildcat' strike, the workers cease work without union backing.

DEMARCATION DISPUTE
: A demarcation dispute is one where 'who does what' is in question, and is often a dispute between unions. This is a situation where one group of workers objects to another group doing particular work. Often this sort of dispute is the result of differences in rates of pay between one group of workers and another. It may be that one group of workers is doing work thought to 'belong' to another group, and for a lower rate of pay.

OVERTIME BAN
: Overtime provides a convenient way for employers to obtain extra

working hours without taking on additional employees. When an overtime ban is in force the workers refuse to work additional hours.

WORK TO RULE

Workers follow the rules and regulations of the company exactly. By adhering strictly to the rules in this way work is slowed down and productivity is reduced.

GO SLOW

This is similar to a work to rule. The workers do their work thoroughly, but at a slower pace than normal, causing a fall in output.

CLOSED SHOP

A closed shop means that all workers in a firm belong to one union and they refuse to work with anyone not a member of that union.

PICKETING

In order to maximise the effect of their industrial action, a group of striking workers may stand outside the firm's entrance and try to persuade other workers not to 'cross the picket line', i.e. not enter the premises.

SIT-IN

Workers occupy the premises ensuring that no goods enter or leave, and preventing the operation of the firm. Sometimes, such as when a factory is threatened with closure, the sit-in becomes a 'work-in'. Workers occupy the factory and keep it in operation without the presence of the management.

BLACKING

Union members may refuse to work on or move certain machines or equipment, or refuse to work with other people or groups.

Employers' organisations

From the foregoing description of the ways in which trade unions organise their activities, it can be seen that a large and powerful union could easily put a small firm at a disadvantage. For this reason firms also need to get together and form associations to protect and promote their interests. By combining in this way the employers are able to match the power of the trade unions. In addition, employers' associations can act as a single voice for many employers. They also provide a means of industrial research and the communication of ideas and information.

CONFEDERATION
OF BRITISH
INDUSTRIES (CBI)

The CBI is the major employers' association in Great Britain and it is the opposite number of the TUC. The CBI represents employers in a similar manner to that in which the TUC represents the trade unions.

Although they disagree on many issues, the CBI and the TUC are frequently in consultation with each other and their combined co-operation on many matters related to industry results in useful contributions to industrial policies and plans.

Like the TUC, the CBI has some permanent staff led by its Director General. Also similar to the TUC, the real power of the CBI lies with its members and this is also focused at the Annual Conference.

ADVISORY,
CONCILIATION
AND ARBITRATION
SERVICES (ACAS)

ACAS is a body available for use by both the employers and employees. The function of ACAS is to conciliate (pacify) and arbitrate (mediate) on matters related to industrial relations. It is managed by a council of nine members, three of whom are independent of it, three are appointed in consultation with the CBI and three are appointed in consultation with the TUC.

Where the parties to a dispute are in a 'deadlock' position, some progress may be made with the help and consultation of a third 'outside' party such as ACAS. In such circumstances an officer of ACAS examines the issues involved and tries to conciliate the parties.

Another avenue that can be explored through ACAS is to seek arbitration, that is to allow a third party to act as a kind of referee. ACAS will provide arbitration facilities, but only if both parties to the dispute agree to go to arbitration, and both also agree to accept the conclusions reached.

THE EMPLOYMENT
ACT 1988

The Employment Act 1988 gives union members rights which they can use to prevent abuses of union power against them. Members of some unions already had similar rights in their union's rules, but this law now guarantees all union members the same rights.

- Union members can restrain their union from calling them to take industrial action without support for the action from a properly conducted secret ballot;
- Union members have the right not to be unjustifiably disciplined by their union, e.g. for deciding to honour their employment contract and go to work or cross a picket line rather than take part in industrial action;
- Industrial action to enforce or maintain any kind of closed shop is unlawful and dismissal from employment for not being a member of a union is not acceptable.
- Postal voting subject to independent scrutiny is required for many of the situations where union members are required to make decisions.

Role of the government

The activities of the government obviously affect the lives of workers in a variety of ways. Not only through their success or otherwise in managing the economy, but also through the laws which are brought into being. Some of these laws may be seen by trade unionists as being against the interest of their members, especially those laws which aim to place restrictions on what a union can do. Consequently, the unions see part of their responsibilities as to try to prevent such laws from coming into existence. This of course brings the union movement into direct conflict with the government and can contribute to a deterioration in industrial relations.

Traditionally, the trade union movement has always supported the Labour Party and, generally speaking, the movement has always been suspicious of the Conservative Party. Although there do appear to be more conflicts between trade unions and Conservative governments, this is not always the case, and there have been occasions when Labour governments have not been able to rely on the full backing of the trade unionists.

While we have acknowledged in this chapter that trade unions aim to improve conditions of work for their members, unions cannot do this without taking into account government policy. Workers can only hope to achieve full employment and choice of occupation and place of work, if the government is able to plan the economy. For this reason, governments have an important role to play in industrial relations by producing imaginative ideas, and communicating them in a way that is open, honest and clear.

Enlisting the co-operation of the unions in implementing government policies has become an important feature of modern society. This entails involving the trade union movement in matters of economic policy formation, primarily through consultation. It is in this aspect of government that the roles of the CBI and the TUC can prove valuable.

These protest notices are all related to general issues pressure groups might wish to influence. Design some notices that might be used to influence businesses.

Pressure groups

Pressure groups are voluntary organisations which seek to encourage the government, council, or some other organisation to recognise their views and respond to them. They try to influence the decision-making process by demonstrating the strength of their feelings.

Perhaps one of the most well-known pressure groups in Britain are trade unions. The TUC acts on their behalf to influence the government's thinking on issues that concern trade unions (particularly those connected with pay and working conditions). The TUC also acts in a similar way as a pressure group on employers. The CBI acts on behalf of employers and tries to influence the government from their point of view.

Pressure groups are not all formal ones such as those examined so far. Sometimes an informal group will form spontaneously, perhaps due to a passing situation, e.g. a no waiting system in the local town.

Although pressure groups are often portrayed in the media as trying to influence local or central government, they do at times try to influence business also. Apart from workers trying to influence pay awards, the general public may try to put pressure on businesses to protest about issues such as advertising techniques, building expansion, or use of certain raw materials.

Governments and businesses are subjected to pressure from groups of people or organisations who are trying to influence policies to be adopted. Sometimes continual pressure is put on the government, industry or specific businesses to acknowledge or make concessions to the views of the pressure groups. The pressure may be exerted through the press or TV propaganda, or it may be less formally organised.

Firms face pressure from groups both internally and externally. Internal pressure sometimes comes from groups of shareholders trying to influence company policy. However, the main pressure on firms tends to be external – that is consumer pressure.

The most basic form of consumer pressure is the opportunity customers have to take their custom elsewhere, although where the firm is in a monopolistic position (e.g. supply of electricity or gas) this possibility may be limited.

The Consumers' Association plays an important role as a pressure group. The group obtains funds from members who buy the magazine called *Which*? The funds are used to test a variety of products and to publish comparative reports in the magazine. These reports are frequently quoted in the press and TV and radio and consequently they influence producers and traders. The Association also publishes books of consumer-related interest.

Some television and radio programmes also act as watchdogs to expose firms who are guilty of malpractice. Many newspapers and magazines also publish details of investigations carried out by their 'Consumer Watchdogs'.

Many of the national organisations providing domestic supplies and services who are in a largely monopolistic position are subject to the scrutiny of consumer councils. For example, the Post Office Users' National Council investigates complaints about the postal service, and there are similar councils for other large domestic suppliers and state-owned industries.

Trade unions and the CBI also act as pressure groups. They not only represent the interests of their members, but they also put forward views on a wide range of issues such as trade, education and consumer affairs. Other organisations such as the AA and the RAC represent the interests of motorists.

There are also environmental pressure groups who represent those who are particularly concerned about the environment. Currently the organisation called Greenpeace is gaining a lot of attention worldwide in its attempts to get government and industry to recognise the need to protect the environment.

**MAKE A
NOTE
OF IT**

1 What do you understand by the term 'industrial relations'?
2 To what extent would you say that it is inevitable that employers and employees will come into conflict?
3 What is a trade union?
4 List the aims of trade unions. What part does the TUC play in putting across the aims of the unions to others?
5 What is the Trades Union Congress? Why do you think that the government often discusses industrial policies with the TUC?
6 Describe the organisation and functions of the TUC.
7 Give a brief description of the four main types of trade union in the United Kingdom.
8 What are the main criticisms of trade unions?
9 What is the main function of trade unions?
10 Say what you understand by the terms 'collective bargaining', 'conciliation' and 'arbitration'? What is the relationship between these terms?
11 What are restrictive practices? Why are they adopted?
12 Explain the difference between an official and an unofficial strike.
13 Shop stewards are ordinary full-time workers who are elected by a group of union members to represent them to the union and also to the management. Bearing this in mind, why do you think that it is often shop stewards who call a 'wildcat' or unofficial strike?
14 What is a demarcation dispute?
15 Trade unions use a variety of methods to try and persuade employers to agree to wage claims. Explain how the following methods operate:
   (a) overtime ban
   (b) work to rule
   (c) go slow
   (d) sit-in
   (e) blacking.
16 Two controversial aspects of trade union activity are:
   (a) picketing, and
   (b) the closed shop.
      Describe these two forms of action. Why do you think they are controversial? Do you think they should be allowed? Give reasons for your answer.
17 Why do employers need representatives just as much as employees?
18 Describe the functions of the Confederation of British Industry. Explain the relationship and similarities between the CBI and the TUC.
19 What is the function of the Advisory, Conciliation and Arbitration Service (ACAS)?
20 Explain the role of the government in industrial relations.
21 What is a pressure group?
22 Why are pressure groups important to consumers?

DATA RESPONSE QUESTIONS

Part 5

PEOPLE IN BUSINESS

1 The following questions are all related to this application for employment.

(a) Name the person who is applying for employment. (1)

(b) How important is it to the employer to know about details of the applicant's previous employment when it was only done on a part-time basis? (2)

(c) Why is the employer interested in the applicant's 'hobbies and interests' even though they may have no relevance to the vacant position? (2)

(d) What is the purpose of 'referees' and why are two requested? (4)

(e) Briefly state the purpose of each of the small sections within the part of the form marked 'office use only'. (5)

(f) What is a 'short-list' and what factors might an employer take into account in deciding whether this particular applicant should be short-listed? (6)

APPLICATION

Surname ..... Mc.Meakin.. (Mr/Mrs/Ms)
Forename(s) ..Richard..David.................................
Address ...10,.Juniper.Close., CATERHAM, Surrey..CR3.6SZ........
Nationality .British.................... Date of birth 24/12/69

EDUCATION

School or college	Dates	Examinations taken
King Edward Caterham Surrey	1982 – 1987	GCSE: English, Maths, Science, Art, Business Studies, Geography

PREVIOUS EMPLOYMENT

Name of employer	Dates	Position held
The Bargain Shop High Road Caterham	1985 to present	Part-time shop assistant, some experience on cash till

Other relevant experience: Two weeks of work experience arranged by my school in a local estate agents. I answered the telephone, did some duplicating, and prepared mail for the post. Sometimes I went out with one of the agents visiting properties.

Hobbies and other interests: I belong to a local drama group presenting small shows for charity

Referees

Name   Dr. K. Beasely   Name   Mrs. B. Rose
Position Headmaster   Position Manager
Address King Edward School   Address The Bargain Shop
         Southwick Road CATERHAM   High Road CATERHAM

Signature R. Mc. Meakin .... Date ....

OFFICE USE ONLY

Medical Report		References Received	
Date appointed	Department		Position

2

What is ACAS?

ACAS – the Advisory, Conciliation and Arbitration Service – is an independent body charged with the duty of promoting the improvement of industrial relations. It seeks to discharge this responsibility through the voluntary co-operation of employers, employees and their representatives and it has no powers of compulsion. Its approach is impartial and confidential. The service it provides is free. ACAS is run by a Council nominated by the Secretary of State for Employment consisting of a Chairman and nine members – three nominated by the CBI (Confederation of British Industry), three by the TUC (Trades Union Congress), and three independent members. It is staffed by people with special experience of industrial relations.

What does ACAS do?

ACAS provides advisory and information services

Advice and practical assistance is available to everyone concerned with employment – employers, workers and their representatives – in organisations of all sizes in every sector of commerce and industry on matters such as:

- negotiating machinery; local collective bargaining arrangements
- consultative and participative arrangements
- communications and disclosure of information
- personnel policies and organisation
- labour turnover, absenteeism and manpower planning
- payment systems including productivity schemes and job evaluation
- effective use of manpower through productivity improvement
- industrial relations and employment legislation
- procedures for settling disputes and grievances
- disciplinary, dismissal and redundancy procedures
- trade union recognition
- recruitment, selection and induction
- equal pay and anti-discrimination legislation
- hours of work and other conditions of employment
- training in industrial relations

The ACAS Work Research Unit (WRU) provides employers, employees and their representatives with information, advice and practical assistance on issues concerning job design, work organisation and related matters like ergonomics, motivation, management of change, job satisfaction and stress at work.

ACAS provides conciliation in trade disputes

Conciliation is voluntary. The eventual level of settlement will be the joint decision of both parties. The conciliator cannot decide or even recommend what that settlement should be.

ACAS provides arbitration services if requested

Arbitration is also voluntary. An arbitrator or board of arbitration examines the case for each side and makes an award. Arbitration awards are not legally binding but since arbitration is chosen by both parties as a means of settlement such awards are morally binding. Before seeking arbitration, efforts should be made to settle a dispute by conciliation.

ACAS provides mediation

Sometimes the parties to a dispute may ask for the help of an independent third party to mediate and make recommendations for a settlement or to suggest a basis for further discussion. If so ACAS may appoint a mediator.

Source: Executive Post

(a) What do the letters ACAS stand for? (1)

(b) How much does ACAS charge for the services it provides? (1)

(c) How is the membership of ACAS made up? (2)

(d) Who are the services of ACAS aimed at? (2)

(e) What is meant by the words 'collective bargaining' used in the data? (3)

(f) What do you understand by the term 'industrial relations' and why is this important to both employees and employers? (3)

(g) Briefly explain the words conciliation and arbitration in the context of the information given. (4)

(h) Why is it possible that ACAS could help to solve an industrial dispute when other attempts have failed? (4)

3 Refer to the following newspaper article related to a sales career and answer the following questions.

(a) What work do you think a careers' counsellor does? (1)

(b) Why is it in the interest of both the employer and the employee that the salesperson is successful? (2)

(c) What do you understand by the word 'extrovert' in the context that it is used in this article? (3)

(d) Why does age and previous job experience affect a person's chance of success in a sales career? (6)

(e) The article states that the type of person most suited to sales work is determined by the type of business or product involved. Take two contrasting types of business and explain why they require a different type of sales person. (8)

4

Discover if you've got what it takes for a sales career

By ROGER LAY

THE EXPERIENCE of careers' counsellors is that very few people have in mind a sales career as their first choice.

But the sales team is an essential element of any commercial enterprise. Quite a lot of people therefore, find themselves in selling roles.

Clearly, if you are faced with the prospect of a sales career, it is in both your interests and that of your future employers that your chances of success be as high as possible. How can you tell if you are likely to make a successful salesperson?

The popular image of the successful salesperson is of someone who is highly extroverted or outgoing, socially confident and who tends to be fairly aggressive in their approach to people.

Although there would appear to be an element of truth in this, research into the question reveals a far more complicated picture.

Some of the factors which determine the type of person most suited to sales work are;
- The type of business or product involved.
- The selling techniques used (telephone sales, face-to-face contacts, cold calling, maintenance of major accounts etc.).
- The extent to which technical product knowledge is required.

Age and previous job experience also effect a person's chance of success in a sales career.

Although the factors which determine success in sales are complex, it is clear that personality type is important.

The difficulty in predicting what type of person is likely to be successful, is that even where the type of business and selling techniques are known, there are still quite wide variations in personality type. Nevertheless, there are some common factors:
- Social confidence or social sophistication, and the ability to relate easily to others.
- Organisational effectiveness and independence, and the ability to formulate and carry out a plan of action without close supervision.

- Emotional resilience, and the ability to keep going even when the customer says 'no.'
- Energy, enthusiasm and competitiveness, and the ability to go out looking for a sale rather than waiting for the telephone to ring.
- Persuasiveness, and the ability to change a person's inclinations, opinions or decisions.
- Lack of modesty also appears to be a characteristic of some successful salespeople.

It is perhaps worth noting that there is little support for the idea that successful salespeople need to be outgoing in nature and aggressive in their approach (although some people with these characteristics do in fact succeed in sales work).

Most recruiters who are looking for salespeople refer to the importance of motivation — by this they usually mean the motivation induced by monetary rewards.

However, research evidence suggests that financial motivation is only significant where a commission pay system operates.

As far as abilities are concerned, successful salespeople tend to be above average in intelligence. More specific aptitudes which are relevant include the ability to understand and manipulate numerical data (eg: price lists, numerical tables) and to be able to read and understand product information.

Where the product or service being sold is highly technical in nature, a salesperson is likely to be more effective if they have a good familiarity and understanding of technical aspects.

A number of special psychological tests have recently been developed to assess sales potential. These tests typically concentrate on evaluating personality factors relevant to selling.

Age is another factor related to sales success — sales effectiveness tends to increase up to the age of about forty and to decline in later years.

A final observation — although as observed earlier, quite a wide range of personalities can be successful in selling roles, sales managers (having almost always been successful salespeople themselves) usually believe that only people in their own image will be successful and recruit accordingly.

Source: Executive Post

The following questions are all related to the 'sales career' article above.

(a) Why do sales people need to be able to 'understand and manipulate numerical data and to be able to read and understand product information'? (2)

(b) The article says that 'sales effectiveness tends to increase up to the age of about forty and to decline in later years'.

   (i) Give two reasons that support this statement. (2)

   (ii) Give one example of type of sales where this statement may not apply, giving reasons for your choice. (3)

(c) 'Most recruiters who are looking for sales people refer to the importance of motivation – by this they usually mean the motivation induced by monetary rewards'. Briefly explain how most firms motivate their sales people. (3)

(d) Sales people need to be able to work on their own initiative. What does this mean? Quote from the article to support your answer. (4)

(e) If you refer to the list of common factors identified as likely to influence a person's success as a sales person, some of these tend to contradict the later statement – 'there is little support for the idea that successful sales people need to be outgoing in nature and aggressive in their approach'. Discuss this observation. (6)

5 The following newspaper article is related particularly to 'personnel professionals'. These are people who work in the Personnel Department of a company.

Personnel stress

THE MOST stressful activity for personnel professionals is the closure of a plant or the announcement of a redundancy programme. The second most stressful situation is the firing of a senior executive.

This is in contrast to the threat of industrial action, which rates only as a 'fairly stressful' situation. These are the findings of a recent survey in Personnel Today.

The survey asked the heads of personnel departments in some of Britain's largest companies to name the areas of their work which they found most stressful. A second survey, also looked at the new responsibilities which personnel departments are facing.

The responsibilities identified reflect the profession's increasing involvement in corporate activities, with 58% of those questioned noting their increased involvement in business strategy.

In the traditional area of trade union negotiations, however, 24% felt that they are now much less involved.

New responsibilities have included the use of computers and the administration of company pension schemes. The latter has become especially complex following changes in legislation.

Another major area has been the introduction of new staff evaluation and grading schemes, and employee share or profit-related pay. The introduction of such schemes now involves 59% of those asked.

"The findings of this latest survey reflect the changing business environment in which the personnel professional is working," explains Helena Sturridge, editor of Personnel Today.

"Their growing responsibilities have brought with them the need to cope with a number of stressful situations, and to manage a workforce in a far more sophisticated nature than ever before."

Source: Executive Post

(a) What do you understand by the term 'stress' in relation to working? (1)

(b) Why have the new responsibilities of personnel professionals contributed to their stress? (2)

(c) What do you understand by the term 'redundancy programme'? (2)

(d) Why would a redundancy programme result in stress for 'personnel professionals'? (3)

(e) Briefly describe two forms that industrial action could take and say why such action would contribute to the stress of workers in a Personnel Department. (4)

(f) What is a 'staff evaluation and grading scheme' and why can this contribute to stress levels for personnel professionals in particular? (4)

(g) One way that a Personnel Department might be involved in business strategy is through public relations work. What does this involve? (4)

6 Look at the following 'Situations Vacant' advertisement and answer the questions that follow.

SITUATIONS VACANT

PERSONNEL ASSISTANT
AGE 17+ £7500 pa
Excellent benefits

Additional team member to join this busy personnel environment. Sense of humour, bags of stamina, good typing/administrative skills essential. Good telephone manner. Ref 134

SALES OFFICE CLERK
We are an extrovert team working in a busy sales office and we need help! If you enjoy dealing with people, have legible handwriting, numeracy skills and a good telephone manner – contact us now. Salary negotiable. Ref 207

RECEPTIONIST
TO £6000 pa Age 16/18
Young, bubbly, well presented young lady required for superb reception area. Excellent benefits to include gym, subsidised restaurant. Typing an advantage, pleasant personality essential, willingness to learn PABX switchboard as relief operator. Ref 166

ACCOUNTS CLERK
LV's, pension scheme ideal opportunity for a person with all-round knowledge of accounts and experience of computerised systems. Immediate interviews. Salary £6250. Any age. Ref 222

TELEPHONIST/TYPIST
We require a Telephonist Typist for our large car showrooms. Will train on switchboard but accurate typing is essential – 40 wpm. Some clerical work involved. Good salary and some perks. Ref 281

AUDIO TYPIST
£6000 Age 16+
Busy office needs extra pair of hands typing correspondence, reports, etc. Duties will include client/telephone liaison. Solicitors. Good salary offered, increments for RSA/LCCI qualifications at higher levels. Apply in writing in first instance. Ref 285

SHORTHAND SECRETARY
£9000. Good s/h skills/audio. Working on a one-to-one basis for partner. Lots of variety. 5 weeks' holiday. Early finish Friday (4.30). Ref. 294

WP SECRETARY – LOCAL £8000
Lovely position for a confident secretary with a flair for admin. Meeting and greeting clients, cross-train on our WP system and Telex. Never a dull moment! Qualifications required in word processing. Ref 298

All applications quoting reference number to:
Topline Employment Agency
17 Primrose Park
UXBRIDGE
Middx
UB10 9TZ

(a) Considering that a typed application is easier to read, and a telephone application quicker to deal with, why do many job advertisements ask for applications in writing? (2)

(b) Why do all the jobs here quote reference numbers and no individual addresses? (2)

(c) What is meant by 'a good telephone manner' and why is this important to both a firm and its clients? (3)

(d) One of the advertisements shown states 'good salary and perks'. What are perks? Give some examples. (3)

(e) These jobs are all advertised through an employment agency. What services would such a business provide to help a firm to obtain appropriate new employees? (4)

(f) Applicants for jobs would be 'short listed' by the firm looking for new staff. What is a 'short list' and what factors might the employer take into account when deciding who to include in the list? (6)

7 The following questions are also related to the job advertisements on page 271.

(a) What is meant by the wording apply 'in the first instance'? (2)

(b) Take any two *contrasting* job advertisements shown here and briefly explain the work involved. (2)

(c) Choose any one of the jobs advertised and draft a letter of application for yourself. (6)

(d) All of the following terms have been used in the job advertisements shown here. Briefly explain each one.

£6000 pa	PABX
Salary negotiable	LVs
S/h skills	increments
WP system	Subsidised
one-to-one	40 wpm

(10)

8 Refer to the newspaper article on page 273 and answer the following questions.

(a) Why would a management consultant be particularly useful to a small firm? (1)

(b) What service would a management consultancy give its clients? (2)

(c) Briefly say what an executive is and give two contrasting examples. (3)

(d) What is executive leasing and how does it differ from management consultancy? (3)

(e) Executive leasing is often used for handling 'one-off' assignments. Give three examples of 'one-off' assignments where an executive might be leased. (3)

(f) Why does executive leasing demand people with 'proven experience at middle or senior management level'? (4)

(g) State one advantage of executive leasing from the point of view of the executive. (4)

Dramatic Leap in Executive Leasing Now Seen as a Credible Professional Career

There has been a dramatic recent increase in the number of firms offering management consultancy services. These services are particularly useful for smaller firms with insufficient funds to employ suitable management executives.

This trend has been accompanied by the development of executive leasing: the engagement of an executive for a limited period to fill a particular short-term gap; for example, handling a 'one-off' assignment, or bridging a gap between one senior executive leaving and a successor starting.

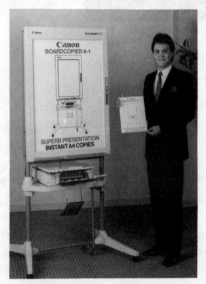

Executive leasing offers one of the best ways of handling specific but short-term problems.

Executive leasing is now increasingly seen as a credible professional career, but success requires the executive to have had proven successful experience at middle to senior management level.

Part 5

PEOPLE IN BUSINESS

1 How do local employers attract staff?

2 Design an induction programme to introduce pupils new to your school, or those joining a business with which you are familiar.

3 Make a study of the induction programme of a firm with which you are familiar and suggest ways that it might be improved.

4 Select four contrasting advertisements for business jobs and describe how you would ensure that you accept the most appropriate applicant for the vacancies.

5 Use personal interviews with workers in a variety of occupations to examine to what extent job satisfaction is important.

6 Make a comparative study of wages for different occupations in the same industry giving reasons for differences that exist.

7 Make a comparative study of wages for the same occupation in different industries giving reasons for differences that exist.

8 What evidence can you find that indicates the effectiveness of legislation on equal pay for women in your locality?

9 Interview a cross-section of office workers and people involved in some form of production. Find out how informed they are about the aims of their employers. Comment on your findings.

10 In many organisations there are often people who are keen to be promoted, and there are others who are not interested in advancement. Interview a cross-section of people in employment with the aim of establishing why these attitudes exist.

11 While you are out on work experience make a comparative study of your job and another within the same organisation.

12 Visit your local Job Centre. Identify at least three contrasting job vacancies which illustrate wage differentials. Give a detailed explanation of the reasons for the different wage levels.

13 Obtain an example of a completed P45, P60 and P2 and clearly explain the function of each, identifying the purpose of particular data on each form.

14 Make a survey of job vacancies at your local Job Centre and find out from the Centre how many local people are unemployed. Give suggestions why such jobs remain unfilled while there are people unemployed.

Part 6
SOCIAL ACCOUNTING

26 National accounts

National income

Economic growth refers to an increase in the output of all things we consume, use, invest in or otherwise produce. Economic growth is important because it usually means that the country is increasing its wealth, and probably improving its living standards. One way to assess economic growth is through measurement of the national income.

WHAT IS
NATIONAL
INCOME?

Imagine you were asked to calculate the total income of your family for the year, how would you go about doing so? You would probably add together the total yearly income of each member of the household, including any return received from savings or investments. But there are other ways of reaching the same figure. For example, it can also be obtained by adding together the total amount spent, and the total amount saved by each member of the family in the year. You should

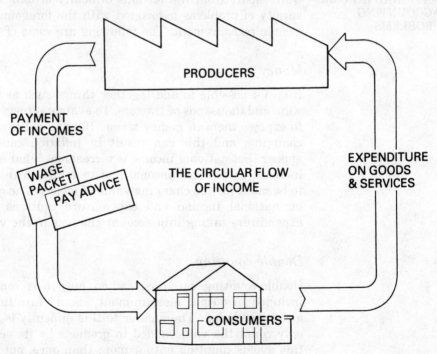

Circular flow of income

understand that both methods reach the same answer because both look at the same amount of money, but in a different way. The national income of a country can also be assessed in a similar way.

If you were asked to assess your income you would refer to wages and other returns which add to your wealth. You would not count money you invested in the building society last year, but you would include the interest you received this year. Income is a *flow*, and not a stock of money or equipment. National income is concerned with new additions to the wealth of the country.

There are three approaches that can be used to measure the national income, and all the methods should reach the same answer because in a way they are all measuring the same thing.

1 *Income method* – the aggregate value of all forms of income, including personal incomes, profits of firms, rents, etc.
2 *Output method* – the total net output of every form of production taking care not to count any output twice. 'Net' in this case means including an allowance for capital consumption (depreciation – fall in value due to wear and tear) on all buildings and machinery.
3 *Expenditure method* – the total value of all expenditure by consumers, firms and the government.

Measurement of all of the foregoing three ways of looking at national income are made annually by the British government and are published in the Blue Book on national income and expenditure.

NATIONAL INCOME ACCOUNTING PROBLEMS

Quite apart from the obvious difficulty of data collection there are a variety of problems associated with the foregoing methods of national income measurement. The following are some of these problems.

Money terms

It is not possible to add together things such as tons of fish, bottles of wine and thousands of tractors. To evaluate items such as these we have to express them in money terms. But the value of money is constantly changing, and this can result in inflation causing it incorrectly to appear that national income is increasing. What is important is the *real* increase in national income and to establish this requires allowances to be made for the changing value of money. The government Blue Book on national income and expenditure contains tables of consumers' expenditure taking into account changes in the value of money.

Double-counting

Double-counting can occur when output is considered. If timber is included in output measurement, should furniture made from timber also be included? The answer to this difficulty is that each firm should only count the value added to products by its activities. Theoretically this avoids counting output more than once, but in effect the result is still not a very precise measurement.

The 'black' economy

Babysitting, bartending, taxi driving and car repairs are typical examples of jobs that are sometimes being done 'on the side', that is, without the Inland Revenue knowing about them because the income is not declared for tax purposes. The work is usually done for cash rather than cheque payment, and for a charge lower than for 'official' work. Activities such as these are sometimes called the 'hidden' economy, but most commonly they are referred to as part of the 'black' economy.

Probably every developed country has its own 'black' economy, and in some countries it is so substantial that it props up the official economy. It has been estimated that the 'black' economy adds almost a third to the gross national product.

The 'black' economy is to be condemned because tax evasion by some in this way increases the tax burden of others. However, more important here is the fact that the 'black' economy creates a problem for recording domestic statistics. The main source of information for the income method is the Inland Revenue, but we have seen that the 'black' economy shows that a large proportion of income is not recorded.

USES OF NATIONAL INCOME STATISTICS

The final national income figure is only an estimate because of the foregoing and other accounting difficulties which result in discrepancies. However, in spite of all the difficulties of measuring National Income the figure has several uses.

1 *Changes in living standards* – Most governments use national income statistics to indicate changes in living standards.
2 *Comparisons with other countries* – it enables comparisons to be made between one country and another.
3 *Economic growth* – A comparison can be made between one year and another in respect of economic growth.
4 *Instrument of economic planning* – It provides the government with information which can be used to assess the effectiveness or otherwise of its past policies. This information can then be used in the planning of the economy, and implementation or redistribution of wealth.

NATIONAL INCOME AND STANDARD OF LIVING

While national income is of vital importance in determining our standard of living, a high national income does not necessarily mean a high standard of living exists generally.

To illustrate this point, let us imagine that there is a Middle East country called Hullabahoo, and that country had made dramatic economic growth because of the discovery of vast deposits of oil five years ago. If Sheik Shinpad, ruler of the state of Hullabahoo, receives the vast majority of the national income, the country may be earning more, but its people will see little improvement in their living standards. Therefore, the way that the wealth is distributed is just as important to the population as the national income.

Gross national product (GNP)

When we looked at the output method of measuring national income earlier we said that an allowance was made for 'capital consumption' or loss in value (depreciation), of buildings and machinery. In other words, in the case of national income measurement we only know the total production output after taking away that allowance. But in national accounting it is useful to be able to measure the total value of all things actually produced in a country, that is, a figure which does not include a reduction for capital consumption.

In Britain, the principle measure of the total output of the country is called gross national product (GNP). The word 'gross' indicates that no deduction has been made for capital consumption.

The word 'national' in this instance does not imply that GNP is the total output produced within the borders of the UK. The GNP measure includes some output taking place and produced by resources owned by people from other countries. Clearly, this outflow cannot be counted as part of our national income. At the same time, some sources of output are situated in other countries but owned by UK citizens. Therefore, the GNP can be defined as the total output of all the resources owned by residents of this country, wherever the resources themselves are situated.

Measure of the total output actually produced within the borders of the UK is called the gross domestic product (GDP). In this respect GDP can be defined as the output of all resources located within the UK, wherever the owners of the resources happen to live. In a similar manner to GNP, the GDP becomes net domestic product when an allowance for depreciation is deducted from it. In many ways GDP is the more important measure.

National Income of Noland

Simple imaginary analysis by expenditure method

	£ billions
Consumer expenditure	168.2
Public authorities expenditure	60.1
Gross domestic fixed capital investment	43.5
Value of physical increase in stocks	2.1
Exports of goods and services	73.3
Total final expenditure	347.2
less imports of goods and services	− 67.1
less taxes	− 38.3
plus subsidies	+ 4.1
Gross domestic product	245.9
Net property income from abroad	+ 2.2
Gross national product	248.1
less capital consumption	− 36.9
National income	211.2

THE NATIONAL CAKE

The amount of wealth or gross national product the country is generating each year is sometimes referred to as the 'national cake'. The national wealth 'cake' is made up of contributions from various parts of the economy and commercial activities such as services, distributive trades and transport make the largest contribution, followed by a smaller contribution by industrial production and a yet smaller contribution by agriculture, forestry and fishing. This illustrates the importance of commercial activities to the economy.

Wealth in this sense is more than a stock of money and possessions. Wealth is the total of what the economy produces each year in the form of goods such as clothing and food, or services such as those of doctors or teachers. We normally find it convenient to measure wealth in money terms, but this can create problems because not all wealth can be counted in money terms. For example, how do we put a precise value on the quality of education, medical care or environment? And yet sometimes the effect of things such as these can be greater and more important than the production of goods to which we normally attribute wealth.

The well-known saying 'you cannot have your cake and eat it', is undoubtedly true, and yet many people want to do just this. As a country we cannot have what we have not earned; we cannot eat more cake than we have. Consequently, the bigger slice of the cake one person or group takes, the less there is left to distribute to others. Clearly, we must make a bigger cake before we can distribute bigger slices from it. This is often the source of a continual wrangle between governments, employers and workers over demands for wage increases.

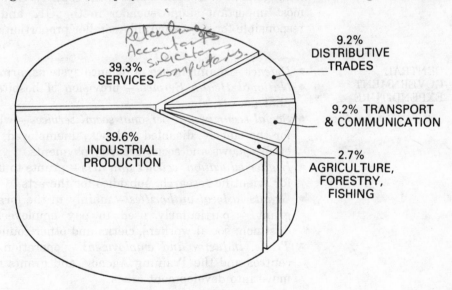

Where the national wealth comes from

National expenditure

While the gross national product tells us what was produced in a country, national expenditure tells us who bought what was produced. In this respect we can say that national expenditure is the sum of:

1 *Private expenditure* – this includes every kind of consumption spending by the population, from food and clothing to cars and entertainment (but excluding the purchase of homes).

2 *Public expenditure* – central and local government spending on goods and services, for example, salaries of teachers and soldiers, provision of pensions and family benefits, etc. (but excluding capital expenditure on durable assets such as buildings).

3 *Gross domestic capital formation (GDCF)* – this refers to the total investment by business firms, public enterprises and public authorities in new fixed capital such as new plant and equipment, buildings, ships and other durable means of production. The purchase of new dwelling houses is also included in GDCF.

4 *Overseas trading* – the effect of the net difference between the value of UK exports and imports of goods and services (balance of payments).

From the foregoing it can be seen that national expenditure is necessarily identical in value with the national product because it is merely another way of classifying the same information.

PUBLIC
EXPENDITURE

This term refers to government spending. In the UK there are two types of government, central and local government. Central government governs the whole country, whereas local government is concerned with management of a smaller part of the country. Central government is the most important single spender in the UK, and local government is responsible for a considerably smaller proportion of public expenditure.

CENTRAL
GOVERNMENT
EXPENDITURE

- *Defence* – maintenance of defence systems, army, navy and airforce.
- *National Health Service* – provision of hospitals, doctors, dentists, pharmacists, etc.
- *Social security and personal social services* – which includes benefits for the elderly, disabled and sick, unemployed, family (child benefit, etc.), widows and social security payments.
- *Higher education, science and arts* – grants to universities, subsidies for scientific research, subsidies for the arts.
- *Grants to local authorities* – mainly in the form of the rate support grant – particularly used to pay employees such as teachers, dustmen, social workers, clerks and other council employees.
- *Trade, industry and employment* – operation of job centres, skill centres and the Training Agency, and grants to encourage firms to move into development areas.
- *Overseas aid* – money lent to poorer countries.
- *Agriculture, fisheries, food and forestry* – grants for research, land reclamation and subsidies to farmers, etc.
- *Finance for nationalised industries* – loans to public corporations for new investment, etc.
- *Environmental services* – water, sewage disposal.
- *Roads and transport* – money for trunk roads and motorways, and subsidies for various forms of state run transport such as railways.
- *Debt interest* – when the government spends more than it obtains in revenue it has to borrow. The total amount owed is known as the national debt. The government has to pay interest on this debt.

LOCAL GOVERNMENT EXPENDITURE

- *Education* – the provision of nursery, primary, secondary and further education is the single most important item of local authority expenditure.
- *Law, order and protective services* – the police and fire services are the major items of this aspect of local government expenditure.
- *Roads and transport* – local authorities are responsible for minor local roads. They may also subsidise local bus and rail services.
- *Housing* – provision of council houses and sheltered accommodation.
- *Environmental services* – refuse collection, parks and cemeteries, etc.
- *Social services* – old people's welfare, and facilities for other people who need help, for example, 'battered' wives and children or poor families. Also libraries, museums, sports facilities, magistrates, ambulances and probation services.
- *Debt interest* – like central government, local councils also borrow money and have to pay interest on it.

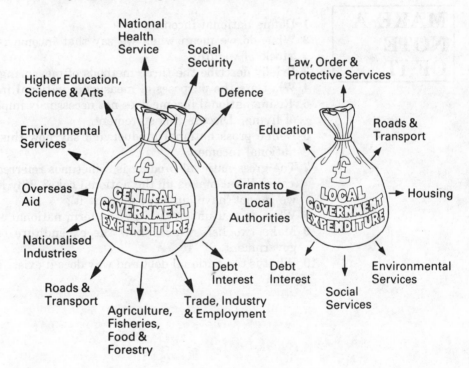

National debt

If you spend more than you earn you will end up in debt. There are two ways you can put the matter right. You can earn more or you can borrow to pay off the debt. In the latter case you are creating another debt, but delaying ultimate payment. The government faces a similar problem.

Each year the Chancellor of the Exchequer prepares the Budget in which he plans the next year's government revenue and expenditure. If expenditure equals revenue the budget is in *balance*. When income exceeds expenditure a *surplus* has been created, and a *deficit* results when expenditure exceeds income.

Public sector borrowing requirement (PSBR) indicates the extent to which the public sector borrows from other sectors of the economy and overseas to balance its deficit on the expenditure and revenue accounts. The public sector includes central government, local authorities and public corporations. PSBR is an important indicator of how the government's policies are affecting the economy.

The national debt is the total amount owed by central government to people both in Britain and abroad. The national debt has accumulated over many years and today the total is so huge it is no longer possible for it to be repaid, although it is still important to restrict growth of the debt as far as possible. Wherever there is a budget deficit, PSBR bridges the gap and results in an increase in the national debt. Most of the national debt is owed to British residents who hold government stocks or money invested in the various forms of national savings which were described earlier in Chapters 5 and 7.

MAKE A NOTE OF IT

1 Define national income.
2 What do we mean when we say that income is a 'flow' and not a 'stock' of wealth?
3 Briefly describe the three methods of measuring national income.
4 What are the purposes of measuring national income?
5 'Rising national income does not necessarily imply a rising standard of living.' Discuss this statement.
6 Define gross national product and say how this figure differs from national income.
7 The gross national product is sometimes referred to as the national 'cake'. What makes up the national cake? Why is it true to say that we cannot 'have our cake and eat it'?
8 What do you understand by the term national expenditure?
9 Make two lists which show the expenditure of central and local government.
10 What is the national debt and why does it exist? To whom is the debt owed?

27 Taxation

Everyone pays tax in some form, either directly or indirectly. The government does not just take money from us without reason. The money taken is used to control and direct the economy as well as to fund government expenditure.

Principles of taxation

The following four 'rules' of taxation were stated by Adam Smith over 200 years ago, but they are still sound guides that apply today also.

1 *Equality* – taxes should be based on the ability to pay. Those with higher incomes should pay a higher proportion of their income in tax than those with low incomes. Thus, people bear an equal burden rather than all paying the same amount.

2 *Economic* – taxes should be collected as economically as possible because there is little to be gained if the cost of collection is more than the money received.

3 *Certainty* – the easier it is to understand a tax system the less incentive there is to evade paying the amount levied. The form and manner of payment, and the quantity to be paid should be clear and unambiguous to the contributor and everyone else. In other words, the tax system should be clear enough so that those liable know what is expected of them.

4 *Convenience* – a tax should be convenient to collect. The Pay As You Earn (PAYE) method of collecting income tax is convenient because it is collected by the employer before the employees receive their pay. PAYE is also a convenient system because it fits in with the normal activity of regular payment of wages.

Functions of taxation

TO RAISE
REVENUE

The primary function of taxation is to raise revenue to pay for those goods and services supplied by the state and which private enterprise is unable or unwilling to produce at prices that the majority of the population are generally able to pay. Defence, medicine and education are examples where the cost of provision is largely met through taxation.

TO INFLUENCE EXPENDITURE

Taxation can be used to influence the level of total expenditure. The higher the level of taxation the lower the level of real expenditure is likely to be and vice versa. This principle can be used to deflate or reflate the economy.

TO REDISTRIBUTE INCOME

Taxation can effectively redistribute income and capital ownership in the community, by taxing some members of the community higher than others, for example, redistribution in favour of poorer members of the community. Redistribution of income will, in the long term, influence the distribution of wealth.

TO SATISFY SPECIFIC OBJECTIVES

Taxation can be used to achieve specific objectives such as discouraging habits like smoking, drinking and gambling or encouraging other activities, for example, movement of industry into depressed areas.

Types of taxation

PROGRESSIVE, PROPORTIONAL AND REGRESSIVE TAXES

These ways of looking at the different forms of taxes compare the amount of tax paid to the income of a person.

- *Progressive tax.* The proportion taken in tax rises as income rises; it takes a larger proportion of income from higher income groups. Income tax is a progressive tax.
- *Proportional tax.* A change in a person's income does not on average affect the proportion of their income that they pay in tax. National insurance is an example of a proportional tax.
- *Regressive tax* is where the proportion of income taken in tax falls as income rises. Value added tax (VAT) is regressive because it is charged at a uniform rate irrespective of the purchaser's income.

DIRECT TAXATION

A direct tax is one which is paid directly to the tax authority by the person against whom the tax is levied. Income tax, corporation tax, capital gains tax, capital transfer tax and North Sea oil tax are examples of direct taxes.

INCOME TAX

Income tax is both a direct tax and a progressive tax. It is a tax on personal earned income. Wage earners are allowed a certain amount in tax-free allowances and the rest of their income is taxed. The proportion of tax paid increases as taxable income increases.

CORPORATION TAX

Corporation tax is a tax on the profits of companies. Similar to individuals and income tax, companies are allowed to deduct certain expenditure as tax-free allowances from their gross profit. The remaining net profit is liable for tax.

CAPITAL GAINS TAX

When individuals sell assets such as shares, land, property and works of art, any profit or gain above a certain 'threshold' is liable for capital gains tax. Certain personal assets such as a person's home are exempt from this tax.

CAPITAL
TRANSFER TAX
(GIFTS TAX)

Capital transfer tax is a tax on gifts or gratuitous transfers of personal wealth from one person to another, whether they take place during a person's lifetime, or on their death. The rate of tax varies according to the sum transferred. There are various exemptions available to certain forms of enterprise such as farming and small businesses, and transfers to and from a husband or wife. There is also a 'threshold' below which transfers are tax free.

INDIRECT
TAXATION

An indirect tax is paid by the taxpayer indirectly to the tax authority, i.e. levied on one person but is collected and ultimately paid by somone else such as a retailer, for example, value added tax.

Value added tax (VAT)

VAT is the most important indirect tax in Britain, because it is the main general expenditure tax levied by central government. It is a tax imposed on the value added to goods and services at every stage of production.

When several traders are involved in the movement of goods from the producer to the consumer, each will charge VAT to the person to whom they sell. Each trader, however, only pays to Customs and Excise the amount of VAT they have charged their customers less the amount of tax paid to their suppliers. In this way we can see that each trader pays VAT on the difference between what he has sold the product for and what he paid for it. This difference is called 'value added'. Therefore, tax is paid on the value that has been added to the product, and this is how this tax gets its name.

The rate of VAT to be charged is announced by the Chancellor of the Exchequer in the Budget, and the rate is varied from time to time. Some goods and services are not liable for VAT because they are zero rated or exempt.

Where VAT is applicable, it is charged on the net value of the goods or services, in other words, the value of the invoice after taking into account trade or cash discounts (even if the buyer does not take advantage of them).

Example 1	£	*Example 2*	£
Gross invoice value	10 000	Gross invoice value	40 000
less 20% trade discount	2 000	*less* 25% quantity discount	10 000
	8 000		30 000
plus 15% VAT	1 200	*plus* 15% VAT	4 500
Invoice total	£ 9 200	Invoice total	£34 500

PROTECTIVE
(CUSTOMS) AND
EXCISE DUTIES

These taxes are collected by HM Customs and Excise Department and are charged in addition to VAT on a variety of important goods such as alcohol and tobacco products. Prior to Britain's entry to the EEC, customs duties were taxes levied on imported goods, and excise duties were taxes placed on certain home-produced goods. Since Britain became a member of the EEC the terminology has changed.

All revenue duties are now termed as excise, which is payable on both imported and home-produced goods. Protective duties refers to customs duties on non-EEC goods, used to put into effect the common external tariff policy of EEC member countries which was examined earlier in Chapter 14. The purpose of protective duties is to raise the final market price of cheaper foreign products to a level with which home producers can compete.

OTHER FORMS OF TAXATION

National Insurance (NI)

NI is a form of direct taxation where contributions are made by both employers and employees. The money raised by this tax is used specifically for the National Insurance Fund, the National Health Service, and the Redundancy Fund.

Employers have to pay contributions for every person they employ, and in fact they pay over 50 per cent of NI contributions. Not surprisingly this tax has been called a 'tax on jobs', because every new person employed is an additional financial burden for the employer.

Motor vehicle duty

Sometimes referred to as 'road tax' or 'car tax'. The owners of motor vehicles must pay a tax for each vehicle used on public highways.

Local authority rates

About one-half of local authority income comes from central government, and this income is supplemented from local rates.Unlike most other taxes, rates are not levied by the Inland Revenue but are raised by local authorites. Rates are a tax based on the rateable value of properties.

The community charge (poll tax)

The poll tax, or to give it its correct name, the community charge, is a new system of paying for local government services. It will be introduced into Scotland in 1989 and to England and Wales in 1990. It will be phased in over a four-year period and will replace the rates system.

Unlike the rates system, which is a tax on property paid by some 18 million householders, it will be paid by all 35 million adults. In other words, it is a tax on people as opposed to a tax on property. The tax will be paid by all those entitled to vote – hence the term 'poll tax'.

Each local authority will decide its own level of community charge, and every adult in the area will be charged the same amount. Businesses, however will be treated differently. They will still pay money to the local community under the existing rating system but the 'rate poundage' will be set by the Government whereas in the past it has been set by the local authority.

Inflation

Inflation describes a situation when prices are persistently rising and the real value of money is declining, which means that the cost of living has increased. If people's incomes do not improve, then their income purchases less. Under such circumstances we say that real income has fallen, and this leads to a fall in the standard of living unless some factor changes.

Inflation is the result of many factors but two broad types of inflation can be distinguished; 'cost-push' inflation and 'demand-pull' inflation.

DEMAND-PULL INFLATION

This type of inflation involves 'too much money chasing too few goods', that is, an excessive supply of money relative to the goods and services available for purchase. Upward movement of wages can be an explanation of this, but 'too much money' usually refers to excessive credit expansion, for example, easier bank loans and hire purchase, etc., which encourages people to spend money that they do not immediately have available.

COST-PUSH INFLATION

This form of inflation is caused by rises in the cost of factors of production such as raw materials or labour, for example, oil prices or wages. For example, wage increases may not be matched by increased productivity. When such increased costs are passed on to the consumer in the form of increased prices this results in cost-push inflation. The resultant increase in the cost of living encourages workers to press for further wage increases causing a continuing inflationary spiral with rising wages chased by rising prices, or vice versa.

CONTROLLING INFLATION

If the government believes that demand-pull is the cause of inflation it can put a number of measures into effect. The government can:

- Reduce its own demand for goods and services.
- Try to reduce demand by consumers and producers.
- Take more in taxes than the government spends.
- Make credit more expensive and more difficult to obtain.

Where cost-push inflation is thought to be the cause the remedies are more complex, and often open to political argument. For example, the price of imported goods and raw materials is outside the control of the UK government. However, some control can be exercised over wage increases and the cost of home produced goods through a firm prices and incomes policy, although the desirability of this is subject to political debate and there is no clear evidence that such a policy works.

MAKE A NOTE OF IT

1 Briefly explain each of the four principles of taxation.
2 What are the functions of taxation?
3 Explain the differences between progressive, proportional and regressive taxes.
4 Distinguish carefully between direct and indirect taxation. Include a description of at least two of each form of taxation to illustrate your answer.

5 How does the tax VAT get its name?
6 Calculate the missing figures in the following table.

	(a)	(b)	(c)	(d)
Gross invoice value	240	1200	800	?
less 20% trade discount	?	?	?	100
Total goods	?	?	?	400
plus 15% VAT	?	?	?	?
	£?	£?	£?	£?

7 Explain the difference between protective duties and excise duties.
8 What is National Insurance and why is it sometimes referred to as a 'tax on jobs'?
9 How do local authority rates differ from other forms of taxation?
10 What is inflation? Explain the difference between demand-pull inflation and cost-push inflation.
11 Describe some of the methods the government might use to fight inflation.

28 Population

Importance of population

Consider making a list of every single item that you have consumed during the last three days. Assuming that you can remember every item, the list that you will end up with will be surprisingly long. But you will no doubt be well aware that there are people throughout the world who are suffering from malnutrition. In fact, two thirds of the world's population is in this position. The source of this problem can be found in our inability to grow enough food to feed an increasing world population. The shortage of resources required by the world population is not restricted to food alone, many other material shortages also exist such as housing, education, medical care, etc.

Obviously many of the existing shortages would be easier to resolve if there were fewer people in the world, yet some countries are actually trying to persuade their inhabitants to have more children to increase the size of their population. But serious consideration of the problem will lead you to realise that it is not just the size of population, but also the structure of it that is important. For this reason demographic (population) studies are important to economic planning. It must also be remembered that population not only provides the labour to produce goods and services, but it is also a source of demand for the goods and services which the labour produces. Population studies are also important because changes that occur require changes in planning strategies to ensure that resources are used efficiently. For example, a straightforward increase in population will require increased resources devoted to education, welfare services and medical care.

Factors influencing population size

Before 1801, when the first official census (official counting of the inhabitants of a country) was held, there was little information on the size of Britain's population although it has been estimated to have been about 5½ million in 1688. In 1801, and periodically ever since, the government ordered the first official census of the UK.

You can see from the diagram below that the population of the United Kingdom has steadily increased since 1801, with some levelling off in recent times.

There are three factors which influence the size of population – migration, births and deaths.

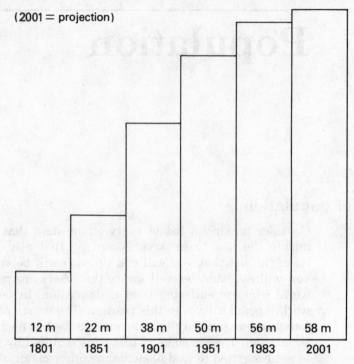

(2001 = projection)

| 12 m | 22 m | 38 m | 50 m | 56 m | 58 m |
| 1801 | 1851 | 1901 | 1951 | 1983 | 2001 |

UK population growth (millions)

MIGRATION

Migration refers to the movement of people from one country to another to live. More people may come into a country to live (immigration), and people may leave their home country to go and live abroad (emigration). Depending whether immigration exceeds emigration, or vice versa, the population increases or decreases.

Migration is influenced by economic conditions and official policies and controls. Poor economic conditions in one country and brighter prospects in another country encourage migration. But some countries may enforce controls which limit immigration or emigration, and this can influence population size.

BIRTH RATE

The birth rate can be expressed as a percentage or as a figure representing the number of births per thousand of the population. From the diagram below it can be seen that the trend in the UK is one of a steadily decreasing birth rate since 1801. The birth rate is affected by a number of factors:

- *Standard of living* – where a standard of living is high, the birth rate tends to be low. When the standard of living is low, the birth rate tends to be high.
- *Attitudes, customs and beliefs* – religious beliefs (e.g. Catholicism) and attitudes to contraception influence the birth rate. A reduction in prejudice to women working, coupled with a desire for a better standard of living that can be achieved by both partners of a marriage working, affects the willingness of women to have children.

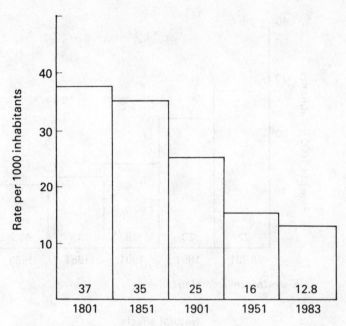

UK birth rate from 1801

- *Women of child-bearing age* – assuming that the average number of children born to women remains unchanged, then the greater the proportion of women of child-bearing age, the higher will be the birth rate.
- *Government policies* – the birth rate is influenced by the level of welfare benefits, child benefit and rate of taxation, all of which are directly controlled by the government. The government also influences the provision of facilities which provide advice on contraception and family planning (e.g. through the education system), which also affects the birth rate as do laws and attitudes to abortion.

DEATH RATE

The death rate is the number of deaths per thousand of population per year. It can also be expressed as a percentage figure. Obviously, if people begin to live longer this contributes to an increase in the size of the population. This is the case in the UK. It can be seen from the diagram below that there has been an almost continuous decline in the death rate since 1801, although the trend has evened out in recent times. The reasons for the fall in death rate are clearer than those influencing the fall in the birth rate.

- *Standard of living* – improved living standards such as better housing, clothing and diet contribute to better health and reduce mortality.
- *Medical knowledge* – advances in medical knowledge, new discoveries, drugs and inventions have all contributed to a significant reduction in the death rate.
- *Public health measures* – many basic services provided by local authorities have improved considerably and have contributed to a

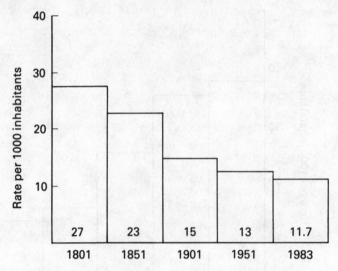

UK death rate from 1801

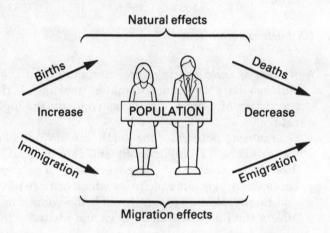

reduction in illness and disease. For example, improvements in services such as refuse collection, water purification and sewage disposal have contributed to a reduction in death from infectious disease.

Optimum population size

OVERPOPULATION   This creates many problems, whether it occurs in a single country or worldwide. Poverty, food shortages and a low rate of investment are all features of overpopulation. It is a familiar feature of an agriculture-based society which experiences difficulty in accumulating sufficient capital necessary to industrialise the economy. The difficulty in accumulating capital for industrial development occurs because a large percentage of all available resources is needed to keep the population alive.

DECLINING
POPULATION

This also creates problems. A falling population implies that the average age of the population is increasing. This reduces the mobility and the quality of the labour force. It also makes demands for higher welfare benefits and a higher taxation on the younger sections of the working population. There is a greater need for hospitals, old people's homes and related services. On the other hand, there could be a reduced need for schools and teachers.

If the population is declining, a smaller domestic market exists – there are fewer customers for the goods and services produced. This can reduce the opportunities for large-scale production and the economies of scale associated with it. It may also result in reduced enthusiasm and initiative in the workforce.

OPTIMUM
POPULATION

The optimum, or most beneficial, population is one which makes maximum effective use of the resources (land, labour and capital) available. Optimum population is that which gives the highest output per head of population.

- If the average output per head is rising as population increases, then the country is underpopulated.
- If the average output falls as population increases then the country is overpopulated.

Distribution of population

AGE DISTRIBUTION

Age distribution refers to the numbers of the population in the different age groups. Age distribution is important because it is directly related to the proportion of producers to consumers. It is influenced by both past and present birth and death rates.

When looking at the age distribution of the population it is usual to classify the population into three groups.

1 Those below school leaving age.
2 Those of working age.
3 Those above retirement age.

Obviously, those of working age are required to support people within the other two categories.

Working population

All these people are at work or available for work. The size of the work force will be influenced by:

- Total population size
- School leaving age
- Retirement age
- Percentage of non-workers in the working age group
- People working who are beyond retirement age
- Age distribution of population
- Sex distribution of population.

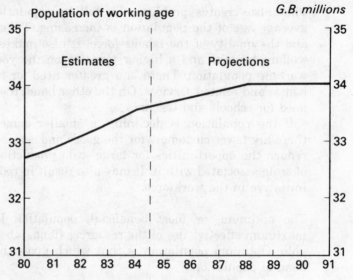

Source: *Economic Progress Report* (HMSO)

In the UK we say that the population has 'aged' during the twentieth century. In other words, there has been a tendency for an increase in the proportion of those above retirement age; those leaving the work-force to retire are exceeding those entering employment. This trend has its origins in past and present birth and death rates, but it has also been influenced by an increasing number of young people entering full-time education and other 'non-employment' schemes beyond school leaving age, and a tendency for people to retire earlier than they used to.

Dependency ratio

The dependency ratio is the proportion of the working population to the non-working (dependent) population.

$$\frac{\text{Number of workers}}{\text{Number of dependents}} = \text{Dependency ratio}$$

Economic effects of an ageing population

1 *Changes in spending patterns* – As the population ages spending patterns change; there is an increased demand for goods related to the older population, and reduced demand for goods for the young.
2 *Increased dependence on working population* – As the proportion of non-working population increases there is an increase in the number of those dependent on the output of the current working population (increased dependency ratio).
3 *Less adaptive workforce* – There is a reduced mobility and adapta-bility of the labour force because an older population tends to be less energetic and enterprising than a younger population. Alternatively, we could say that there is a need for the younger proportion of the population to be more mobile, adaptive, energetic and enterprising.

SEX DISTRIBUTION

As long as the proportion of males to females is similar, sex distribution is of less significance to population than age distribution.

In the UK more males are born than females and men outnumber women of all age groups up to 44 years of age. But in the older age groups there are a greater number of women than men. Whilst this may at first sight seem a contradiction, the reason for the differences is quite simple; more women survive beyond the age of 45. Three factors explain this:

1 *Work pressure* – physical and mental pressure of work affects men more than women.
2 *Emigration* – more men leave the UK than women.
3 *Wars* – affect the male population more than the female population.

GEOGRAPHICAL DISTRIBUTION

Geographical distribution refers to the distribution of the population in different regions at various dates. We can usually see a direct relationship between location or relocation of industry and geographical distribution of the population.

In the UK we have seen that as the location of industries has changed, so has the geographical distribution of the population. Prior to the Industrial Revolution, the population was located mainly in rural areas, and concentrated in areas where the farming land is good (particularly in the south-east). Following the Industrial Revolution there was a movement from the countryside into towns, and particularly into the northern parts of Britain where the major impact of the development of coal, steel, cotton and shipbuilding was taking effect. As these industries declined between the wars and after 1945, newer industries in light engineering located in the midlands and the south attracted labour away from the north.

Years of age	Further expectation of life		
NOW	MALE	FEMALE	
20	54.6	58.3	
25	49.9	53.6	
30	44.9	48.8	
35	40.1	44.0	
40	35.3	39.1	
45	30.6	34.3	
50	26.1	29.7	
55	21.9	25.3	

Expectation of life table

OCCUPATIONAL DISTRIBUTION

Occupational distribution statistics show the numbers of people employed in various occupations. Job distribution depends on a country's stage of development. Underdeveloped countries tend to have a large proportion (75 per cent) of their workforce employed in the agricultural sector, while developed countries have 10 per cent or less in this section of the economy.

By examining such statistics over a period of time we can see changes that have taken place. For example, prior to the Industrial Revolution Britain's workforce was largely involved in agriculture. The Industrial Revolution necessitated movement from agriculture into manufacturing and construction industries. This trend has continued and it has also contributed to increased employment in the tertiary sector. The table below shows the movement away from the primary industries such as farming, forestry, fishing and mining. However, the percentage of the total workforce employed in manufacturing has changed little.

	1841		1901		1981	
	'000s	%	'000s	%	'000s	%
Agriculture, forestry, fishing	1639	22.30	2243	11.8	360	1.7
Mining, quarrying	225	3.20	944	5.0	337	1.6
Manufacturing	2452	35.50	7000	36.9	6038	28.1
Construction	377	5.50	1336	7.0	1132	5.3
Transport/communications	200	2.90	1497	7.9	1429	6.6
Others	2014	30.60	5954	31.4	12229	56.7
Total	6907	100.00	18974	100.0	21525	100.0

Mobility of labour

Mobility in this respect is the movement between occupations. The efficient working of any economy depends not only on the size and structure of the workforce but also how mobile it is, so that maximum use is made of it. Mobility of labour can be viewed in two ways.

1 *Geographic (lateral) mobility*
 The ability to move from one area to another.
2 *Occupational (vertical) mobility*
 The ability to change one's job, profession or industry.

OBSTACLES TO
MOBILITY OF
LABOUR

Look at the following list of factors that inhibit labour mobility. Which ones can you identify that can be clearly associated with geographic mobility and which are related only to occupational mobility?

- *Inertia* – the desire to remain in one place.
- *Family* and friendship ties have to be broken.
- *Education* of children may be disrupted.
- *Re-housing* involves costs and inconvenience.
- *Prejudice* – people may dislike particular jobs or areas.
- *Knowledge* of alternative jobs is not always readily available.
- *Wages* of alternative occupation may be unattractive.
- *Retraining* costs may be too high.
- *Skills* to do alternative employment may be lacking.
- *Trade* unions may resist occupation movement.

MAKE A NOTE OF IT

1 What do you understand by the word demography?
2 Give four reasons why population studies are important.
3 What is a 'census'?
4 What has been happening to the size of the UK population since 1801?
5 Explain the meaning of the word 'migration' and show its relevance to population.
6 Define birth rate and list the factors which affect its growth or decline.
7 What trend can be seen in the UK birth rate over the last 150 years?
8 What factors influence the death rate and why is this figure important to population?
9 Why are overpopulation and declining population problems?
10 What do you understand by optimum population?
11 'The age distribution of the UK population has increased during the twentieth century.' Explain this statement.
12 What is the dependency ratio?
13 Explain the term 'sex distribution of population'.
14 Give a brief description of the geographical distribution of the UK population since the Industrial Revolution.
15 What does examination of statistics related to UK occupational distribution show us?
16 What is mobility of labour and what factors influence it?

DATA RESPONSE QUESTIONS

Part 6

SOCIAL ACCOUNTING

1

(a) Give the alternative name for the community charge tax. (1)

(b) What is the name of the system of taxation that the community charge replaced? (1)

(c) Who is liable to pay the community charge? (1)

(d) What does it mean in this newspaper article when it says that the community charge is a tax on the person instead of a tax on property? (2)

(e) Why is it that in some towns twice as many individuals will be paying the community charge as those that used to pay rates? (3)

(f) State two ways in which the community charge differs from the business rate. (4)

(g) What happens to money collected by councils through forms of local taxation? (8)

2

(a) What do the letters NNDR stand for in relation to local taxation? (1)

(b) Why does local government charge both rates and community charge? (3)

(c) How does the fact that the Government decides the level of rates paid by businesses affect firms? (3)

(d) Name three major services provided by your County Council. (3)

(e) The community charge tax and the business rate are just two sources of income for local government. Briefly describe two other sources of income used to provide local services. (4)

(f) Drawing on the information given about the Carter, Monk and Davis families, discuss the reasons why there is such a wide difference in the amount of community charge paid by each of the households. (6)

THE COMMUNITY CHARGE

THE COMMUNITY CHARGE, also known as the poll tax, is a relatively new way of paying for local services provided by councils. It replaced the system of rates in April 1990.

The poll tax is a tax on the person instead of the previous system of a tax on property. Rather than charge householders an amount based on the rateable value of their home, the Government decided to spread the charge over virtually all adults aged over 18, with some exceptions and reduced charges for some groups on low incomes.

In some towns, this means that twice as many individuals are paying than the number of householders in the previous system.

There are three types of charge, the main one being the charge on all adults. The level of this is decided by the local council and varies from one area to another. There is also a standard charge for people with second or unoccupied properties, and a collective charge affecting landlords with frequent changes of occupancy.

Everyone liable receives a personalised bill and is responsible for paying it themselves. Exceptions to this are married couples and those living together as husband and wife. In these cases one partner can be held responsible for the other's charge. So, if one partner has no personal income the other partner will have to pay on his or her behalf.

Businesses still pay rates in a manner similar to the previous system. The difference in the new rating system for businesses is that the amount businesses pay is set by the Government and not by the local council. This means that all businesses throughout the country pay at the same rate in the pound.

This charge is called the National Non-Domestic Rate (NNDR), although it is sometimes called the 'business rate'. The district councils collect NNDR on behalf of the Government, who then redistribute the income back to local councils.

1 **Carter family**
   Alan Carter: age 47 – Bank
                 Clerk
   Lisa Carter: age 44 – Nurse
   Yearly total income £22 000
   Community Charge £5000

2 **Monk family**
   William Monk: age 70 –
                  Retired
   Lillian   Monk: age 66 –
                    Retired
   Yearly total income £5800
   Community Charge £400

3 **Davis family**
   Peter Davis: age 50 – Baker
   Kathy Davis: age 48 –
                 Machinist
   Adam Davis: age 22 –
               Carpenter
   Olive Davis: age 20 – Clerk
   David Davis: age 18 – Cleaner
   Yearly total income £52 000
   Community Charge £1250

2 Two-tier system brings big gains for the highest-paid, but low earners lose out as their outgoings increase

'Champagne budget' slashes top rate and cuts basic payments to 25 per cent

Tax rates and allowances

Before the budget

Taxable income (£)	Rate (%)	Cumul-ative tax (£)
0–17,900	**27**	4,833
17,901–20,400	**40**	5,833
20,401–25,400	**45**	8,083
25,401–33,300	**50**	12,033
33,301–41,200	**55**	16,378
Over 41,200	**60**	

After the budget

Taxable income (£)	Rate (%)	Cumul-ative tax (£)
0–19,300	**25**	4,825
Over 19,300	**40**	

Personal allowances	**Old**	**New**
Allowances for people under 65		
Single person and wife's earnings	2,425	2,605
Married man	3,795	4,095
Age allowance for people aged 65–79		
Single person	2,960	3,180
Married man	4,675	5,035
Age allowance for people aged 80 and over		
Single person	3,070	3,310
Married man	4,845	5,205
Income limit for age allowance	9,800	10,600
Additional relief for single parent	1,370	1,490
Widow's bereavement	1,370	1,490

Source: The Guardian March 16th 1988

(a) What was the highest rate of Income Tax
   (i) before the Budget?   (1)
   (ii) after the Budget?   (1)

(b) Calculate the increase in the single person's allowance given in the budget.   (1)

(c) State 2 possible reasons why the Government was able to reduce income tax rates. (2)

(d) Calculate the tax bill of a married man earning £12 095 a year. (3)

(e) Did the budget make Income Tax more or less progressive? Explain your answer fully. (6)

(f) How might the changes affect:
   (i) workers
   (ii) unemployment
   (iii) overall spending in the economy? (6)

3

Changing age structure of UK population 1901–84

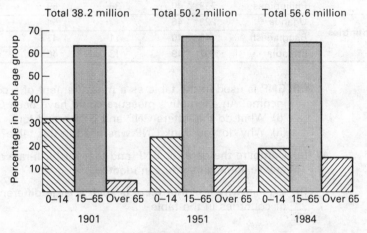

Total 38.2 million Total 50.2 million Total 56.6 million

Source: Annual Abstract of Statistics (HMSO)

(a) What was the population of the UK in 1951? (1)

(b) What has happened to the percentage of the 0–14 year-olds in the population since 1901? (2)

(c) Calculate the number of 0–14 year-olds in the UK for 1984. (3)

(d) Why is the age distribution of the UK often shown using the categories that have been used in the data? (2)

(e) (i) What evidence is there in the data that the UK has an ageing population? (2)
   (ii) What factors have contributed to the ageing of the UK population? (4)
   (iii) What are the economic implications for a country of having an ageing population? (6)

4

The following table shows a variety of comparative data related to a number of countries. Answer the questions that follow.

(a) Which country has the hightest GNP and which has the lowest? (1)

(b) Why is the GNP measured in US Dollars for all countries in the table? (2)

(c) State four differences between countries with a high GNP and those with a low GNP. (2)

	Country	GNP $US	Birth rate per 1000	% Urban dwellers	Life expectancy	Calories per day	% in agriculture
Market (capitalist) economies	Sweden	14 881	11	83	75	2 849	6
	USA	11 363	16	76	74	3 580	4
	Japan	9 352	16	76	76	2 552	10
	UK	8 873	12	76	73	3 340	3
Centrally planned (socialist) economies	USSR	2 086	18	65	70	3 460	17
	Poland	1 876	21	62	70	2 880	44
High income (oil producing) countries	Kuwait	18 086	36	58	69	2 728	17
	Libya	7 289	50	41	56	2 690	21
Middle income (developing) countries	Costa Rica	1 860	31	43	70	2 329	38
	Bolivia	757	47	33	51	1 970	65
	Philippines	733	40	36	59	2 241	69
Low income (developing) countries	Uganda	222	46	17	54	2 146	68
	Bangladesh	145	40	11	47	2 113	71
	Ethiopia	97	49	13	40	1 826	76

(d) GNP is used in the table as a measurement of a country's national income. An alternative measure could have been GDP.

   (i) What do the letters GNP and GDP stand for? (2)

   (ii) Why do you think GNP was used in this table? (3)

(e) Compare the data for GNP and that for birth-rate and comment on any relationships you can identify. (4)

(f) Explain why it is that there is such a large difference between GNP of countries in the table. (6)

5

Poll tax will rocket prices – Expert claims

The poll tax due to be introduced in 1990 could put house prices in the south east up by 35 per cent, according to a well-known economist.

Mr Alan Jones claims that home prices will zoom even higher in London – 50 per cent – and 35 per cent in the rest of the country outside of the south east.

He argues that certain categories of people – couples in larger houses in particular – will have reduced bills from local authorities, and they will be tempted to move into bigger houses, thereby causing greater demand. If you pay the same tax on a small house as you do if you live in a mansion, it is argued that you might as well move to a larger property.

The resulting rise in house prices, argues Jones, will be in addition to the expected rise in prices through the inflation in house sales.

Our property correspondent comments: 'Jones' speculation is interesting but following the enormous increases in prices in recent years, prices will ultimately depend on people's ability to pay and many experts in the field say that this saturation point has nearly been reached.'

'Also many people will be paying more with the poll tax than under the old system leaving them with less money rather than more to fuel inflation.'

The best advice according to one major estate agent is to get on the property ladder as soon as possible.

(a) In which part of the country does the article predict that house prices will rise the most? (1)

(b) What does the article say is likely to happen to house prices in the south east? (2)

(c) What is the 'poll tax'? (2)

(d) How does the 'poll tax' differ from the rates system? (3)

(e) Why is it predicted that demand for houses will rise from 1990? (3)

(f) What is meant by the advice 'get on the property ladder as soon as possible'? (3)

(g) Explain with the use of simple diagrams, why house prices may rise after the introduction of the poll tax. (6)

Coursework and Assignments

Part 6

SOCIAL ACCOUNTING

1 To what extent is your local population economically mobile?

2 What effect has the national fall in the birth rate had in your local area?

3 Investigate the following question over a 6 month period. Is your family's personal rate of inflation the same as the official Government rate?

4 Should the Government levy a 'health tax' on alcoholic drink to partly fund the National Health Service? Include a survey of local views.

5 Which of the following countries would you advise a refugee from the Third World to go and live in: France, Italy, Spain?

6 By examination of your household or a local firm, show that National Income can be measured in terms of output, income or expenditure.

Index

Soletraders

Benetton

Mrs Mare Hosson

68 Culmore Point

owner